TAIL OF THE TIGRESS

VIEWS ON THE ROAD TO GENDER EQUALITY

TAIL OF THE TIGRESS

VIEWS ON THE ROAD TO GENDER EQUALITY

DAVID deVIRE

backdaw
publishing

Paperback edition first published in Great Britain in 2016 by backdaw publishing

Cover and interior design © Rachel Lawston at Lawston Design, www.lawstondesign.com

ISBN 978-0-9954576-0-7

CONTENTS

With particular thanks to

All those kind individuals who have divulged their personal
perspectives and life-experiences for the benefit of others

Helen Baggott
www.helenbaggott.co.uk

Deborah Elliott
www.cameronpm.co.uk

Lindsey Harris
www.m35design.co.uk

Rachel Lawston
www.lawstondesign.com

INTRODUCTION

Premature girls are almost twice more likely to survive than premature boys. It's a statistic. Nice and clean and unemotional.

Now let's put this statistic more graphically: imagine a hospital with a Premature Baby Unit with two identical wards. Each ward has one hundred premature babies in it.

In one ward all the babies are girls; in the other ward all the babies are boys.

In the ward where you have the cohort of one hundred premature baby girls let's envisage that they miraculously all survive and go home to bring everlasting joy to their parents and their families.

In the ward where you have the cohort of one hundred premature baby boys, only fifty will miraculously survive and go home to bring everlasting joy to their parents and their families.

Fifty baby boys will die; fifty sets of parents and their families will take home a lifeless body, will have to arrange a funeral; fifty sets of families will have everlasting pain and anguish.

That is the reality of a statistic. I use quite a few statistics. Like it or not, we are all a statistic – recorded by someone, somewhere. I will not let you forget that statistics mean people; people with feelings, people whose value is equal to each and every other person. People like you and me and our families and our friends.

As you read this book your views will, at some level, be changed. In all our lives, truths and propaganda have been intertwined; our perspectives are intentionally distorted. I will try to enhance your understanding of the immense and ongoing influence of both our history and everyday acts and facts, ones we have all grown accustomed to and continue to live with, whose potential for social change may either empower you or scare the hell out of you. If my premise is true, then it follows that any conclusions you draw from it must also be true.

Every era, in every civilization, has had its own comprehensive value system; a set of beliefs which that social grouping has relied upon as undeniable facts and which were backed up by what they considered substantial and irrefutable evidential proof. These truths, for each generation, formed the basis of both the legal system and their social mores. For these societies any practical change would be subject to a long, considered and incremental process; any sort of social restructuring was glacially slow. Subsequent generations may gradually learn new ways and eventually readjust values which had once been accepted; these erstwhile 'truths' would then become dis- approved of, if not actually disproved. This model of slow incremental development had always sustained the needs of traditional societies.

As a consequence of the Second World War our technological ability – and thereby, people's expectations – has increased. From the 1960s, the pace of development has been progressing at an expo- nential rate, hurtling us into the 21st century. Most of us stumble along behind – with our new gadget in one hand, an instruction manual in the other and an uncomprehending expression on our face – unable to keep up with anything more than the most basic of technological developments.

A fairly new but now well recognised phenomena that we are going to have to find a way of coping with is the 'half-life of truth'. Harvard scholar Samuel Arbesman, has postulated that scientifically based theories, facts which were once proven to be true, are, because of rapidly advancing science and technology, quickly becoming obsolete. It is a corollary of the decay of radiation – whose potency halves over a given period. In a recent study only half of the technical information and scientific data from fifty years ago, was found to still be true today. And this does not only apply to all of the 'hard' sciences, it applies to the social sciences too. It is not that things are necessarily changing 'of themselves'; rather, it is our ability to be able to see and understand things which is changing. We have to accept that we are now playing a game where the goal posts are continually moving. Potentially, 50 per cent of the facts we learned when we were at school will no longer be true for our grandchildren.

There is a new class of technocrats able to create and manipulate this technology and engineer solutions to our every need. Now they are using their technological expertise to devise solutions for problems we were not even aware that we had. We are in danger of becoming overwhelmed by the consequences of this potentially uncontrollable technological tidal wave. As the Internet gobbles up snippets of information, automatically cross-references them and then regurgitates the results around the world, it has revealed technology's potential to evolve into an almost self-perpetuating monster – capable of becoming the master rather than being the servant.

Communications technology, primarily through television, radio and films, has had an interesting and unintentional effect. It has not just reflected differing aspects of society, it has begun recreating 'norms'. For the millennia before such technology existed, the only 'norms' were within one's own family, village or town. What happened there, in that small and isolated world, was normal. The way people behaved and dressed and lived their lives was how it was, how it should be, the only way it could be; there was no alternative. The only truth was what you saw with your own eyes. Everything else was just stories. Now, with the advent of technology, we can see live pictures and news from every region of our own country, from all over the world. We can see the portrayal of other people's ideas; often illustrated with the benefits of CGI. We can see wild creatures on the land, in the air and under the sea; we can even look out into space and look back at Earth from space. All this whilst sat in the comfort of our own home. And that has happened in the span of one person's lifetime.

After millennia of technological invention and discovery, at a level of complexity and speed of development capable of comprehension by most men, an elite few technocrats have become adept at creating miracles or mayhem. Traditionally we have, for instance, watched the components of a working steam engine and have had some chance of understanding it; and, more importantly, how to keep it in good working order and how to repair it when it breaks down – which it will. And now, the mobile phone in your pocket...

There is also a very realistic fear of what is being called the Digital Dark Ages; where, as technology advances at an exponential rate, systems become outmoded. There is a potential that we could lose the ability to read archived electronic files which are only a few decades old because they are stored using now obsolete formats which we have lost the ability to interpret. Digital information stored less than a generation ago could become as obscure to us as Sanskrit.

One of the early benefits of technology to emerge – since the Industrial Revolution – is the reduction in the need for so much hard manual labour and with it, the ability for dangerous procedures to be made safer. War has also, as a result, become less dependent on physical prowess, less personal and much more destructive. The strength of men and animals has been substituted by increasingly more powerful and sophisticated machines.

It is these changes in technology which have devalued the traditional strength advantage which men had over women. This has allowed women to advance their cause of equality. It has increased the credence of their rationale; because men's strength advantage is less frequently a positive attribute, equality should become more achievable. But, it's not the physical jobs that the feminists have in their sights...

So, through the chapters of this book I will try to look at every facet of humankind in relation to gender differences, how and why such disparities have evolved, their effects on society and society's effects on them, facts which may be pertinent, some diverse and often overlooked snippets of information, at those 'curved balls' and urban myths. We will also look at those gender biased, pointed and often offensive cameos, the caricatures of both males and females which engender ridicule and which we feel both amused by and are uncomfortable with at the same time. Let's get it all out in the open and decide what is relevant and needs to be taken into account, at both a positive or a negative level, and which are just amusing, or not so amusing, observations, diversions from the serious issue in hand. Become well informed, be amused, be annoyed but do not be dismissive without investigation. All these facts, the anecdotal misinformation, the painful sleights, they all exist; avoiding the ones which do not support your standpoint will not obliterate them, it will only confer unworthy power to them; acknowledging their existence and then dismissing them as an irrelevance is what will deny them credence.

I have begun this book with a wide and far-reaching, yet hopefully concise, historical perspective of male and female roles in traditional society, their juxtaposition and their interdependence. I then look at some of the individuals and groups who have challenged the structure and hierarchy of traditional society, particularly with respect to its gender roles, and the subsequent effects of their dissension. I look at the results of modern medical research, created using the latest technological methods of investigation, in determining the interrelationship between the physical and physiological in explaining some of the differences between males and females. Next, how our parenting, educational and social systems influence the way children grow up and their developing relationship with the society they find themselves part of. How society uses and abuses the strengths and weaknesses of men and women to better its own ends and how individuals and groups thrive or strive within those constraints – sometimes for recognition, sometimes for equality, sometimes for dominance. I provide factual information and the results of varied and various research. I paint cameos and reveal vistas. I suggest what the views might be from different perspectives. Much can be revealed by investigating everyday behaviour, rites of passage, social mores; information readily available from books and other media and, of course, from the Internet.

By linking together widespread and seemingly disjointed pearls of information, which have hitherto lain scattered across our world of information I have, hopefully, and without undue bias, shown these differences between the genders to have traditionally been both unerringly interrelated and totally interdependent.

But now, there is the potential for change. If those who advocate a restructuring of society chose to rally their followers behind their

5

flag, to train them to be technocrats able to manipulate technology for the benefit of their cause, to be social and educational reformers, to be political activists and business magnates – at the same time as disempowering their erstwhile subjugators – society could be virtually unrecognisable within a generation or two. And who are these would-be reformers? Well, just 52 per cent of the population – that's who!

Approximately 52 per cent of the UK population are female (just under 50 per cent worldwide). They nurtured all of us – as our mothers, grandmothers and school teachers. And now they nurture the will to become equal with men. In the far less egalitarian times of the Second World War they kept things going and produced our armaments, whilst the men were off fighting, and would have done more given the chance. When they first begun this gargantuan effort, many were not sure they would be capable of doing much of their men's work; they soon adapted, found their strength of will, of character. Since then, technology has replaced almost all of the need for manual strength with machines and women have become educated to levels in excess of their male counterparts. Women now have the skill – but do they have the will?

To get a clear picture yourself I suggest that you will need to try to take a dispassionate, detached view; and, to control the urge to react to or to be swayed or blinkered by, upbringing, class, gender or expectation.

What I will not do is to define one absolute conclusion. It is for each of you to identify your own perspective; to make up your own mind as to where you stand. Might you choose to strive to protect the status quo from external influence and thus any subsequent change? Are you going to passively watch a slowly changing world go by, a passenger, observing in its passing one group's manipulation by another; or, perhaps, you will decide to actively participate in creating a radical new world?

CHAPTER 1
A CONFLICT OF INTERESTS

Global religions have some degree of unanimity in the belief that God created humans to populate and be masters of the world. The Hindu religion has, apparently, been in existence since the dawn of time, long before the ancestors of humankind could leave any form of record or a traceable imprint; but, there were legends and myths. There is evidence of burial sites from 100,000 years ago and of rituals including sacrifices which tend to support the existence of belief in some form of super-human creator, of gods, and therefore of religions paying homage to these deities. The Aborigines originate from around 50,000 years ago and tell of 'Dreamtime' – when the gods created man and everything else on Earth; their records too have been handed down verbally. Indeed the true origin of all of our history has at its source the unwritten stories, songs and poetry of our yesterdays.

Looking back at a very approximate timeline, the first texts seem to be those written in Sumerian of Gilgamesh from Babylon in about 2500 BCE; this was around the same sort of period as the Egyptian hieroglyphs and the early pyramids in Egypt. In around 2000 BCE tales of Abraham begin; he was the patriarch at the root of Judaism, Christianity and Islam. The first writings of the Jewish Torah or the Christian Old Testament of the Bible, founded on the words of Moses, originate from 1500 BCE. It was 1,000 years later that Buddhism began in Asia and that the Greeks feted their numerous gods. Two thousand years ago saw the birth of Christianity and 1500 years ago was the origin of Islam.

It is the trio of Abrahamic religions who seem to be the first to have created a history of divergence and dislocation between men and women. This is the focal point where the temptation of mankind, the origins of our undoing, began. Genesis and the Quran tell us of the hierarchy of God who created the first man, Adam, in his image, of Eve, the first woman, being made from man himself for his command, support and pleasure, and of all the animals created for the benefit of mankind. And, of our inherent goodness continually under threat of being subverted by all the myriad incarnations of the Devil. In the Garden of Eden it was the Serpent who was to tempt us away from our innocence; the Quran attributes no blame specifically to Eve but according to Genesis, the Serpent chose the woman as the most easily corruptible of the couple; her duplicity was there to be exploited. And, all women are the daughters of Eve. The further inference being that men were incorruptible then, too strong a foe even for the Devil himself, both physically and morally. The serpent represents all things immoral, malevolent; the Devil incarnate. It was Eve who plucked the apple from the Tree of Knowledge and it was Eve who then tempted Adam to eat from it. It is, perhaps, surprising that the humble apple is still such a popular fruit worldwide.

For all those people who have been, from their earliest childhood, directly or indirectly influenced by any or all of the teachings of these religions, Man has been depicted as the more important figure with Woman merely created from part of him. God told Man that he was to rule over Woman. It was her actions which were the cause of them being sent from heaven to live on Earth. And, she was the one who caused the corruption of all humankind as a result of her avarice and thereby imposing on all humans a life of misery culminating in their death and, on all women, the penalty of pain in childbirth. Like some form of subliminal indoctrination, throughout history, most of our lives have been drip-fed this story of the origin of the difference between men and women. Most persons of influence in most religions are men; cause or effect?

This view of the relationship between Man and Woman has apparently been imposed by the actions of Eve; and humankind must eternally pay the price. These religions have their origins in patriarchy; a system which implicitly values Men whilst, at the same time, deliberately undervaluing Women. Given the enduring global influence of these three major religions it has never been an easy social or religious position to challenge without offending someone, somewhere.

The sponsoring, writing and nature of most forms of literature has, historically, always been dominated by men. Aristotle, from his observations of mankind and of animals thought men to be active whilst women were passive, that it was the man who gave the child its soul. Sophocles told the story of Oedipus, then Shakespeare in *Hamlet* of Gertrude and later, another Gertrude in D.H. Lawrence's *Sons and Lovers*. All stories related to uncomfortable family relationships across genders and generations. The common theme, a woman's existence being the root of a man's destruction. Sigmund Freud spoke of boys being lured into a sexual love with their mothers and therefore of being in a bizarre, and potentially lethal, form of competition with their own fathers. Ergo, the Oedipus complex. And, if this perspective is true then so is a reverse-gender perspective also potentially true.

Historically, a man was seen as the authoritative head of the household and all females within that family as his property. A good wife or daughter was to be acknowledged as a reflection of a good man being at the head of the household; a bad woman or a mismanaged household was therefore seen as a poor reflection on his status as the patriarch. Boys are just men in training. In children's literature, boys were always the heroes (although Hero from Greek mythology was actually a girl!). Males 'do things'; females service the needs of the males in their lives. Men were able to oppress and dominate women whilst women tried, at best, to control the excesses of their menfolk.

A woman's status, and therefore her value, had a direct correlation with her sexuality. To be alluring and capable of satisfying a man was the raison d'être of a female from puberty until the onset of the menopause. Girls were taught, by women, how to use their attractiveness and the lure of sex as a currency. Thus, during her lifetime, a woman had a fluctuating value proportionate to the potency of her sexuality. Most began their sexual lives with their value well in credit due to the rarity value of virginity and through canny exploitation of their youthful bodies quickly learned to amass a considerable cache of credits. But, as the years passed by and motherhood beckoned, a woman's appeal and thus her reserves of sexual credit, became depleted at an ever increasing pace until as middle age approached, sexual poverty grew. With an eroded sexual value in comparison with younger women and girls, sexual bankruptcy became the unavoidable finale. An older woman behaving in a sensual manner was often seen by a younger generation as her making a desperate last bid to try to retain her sexual appeal as it was slipping away, like sand, through her ever tightening fingers. This was graphically depicted in Hamlet's words to his mother who had swiftly married her late husband's brother only a few weeks after Hamlet's father's death. The whole of his speech is a venomous attack on all women of her age and their right to feel rejuvenated and to enjoy their own sexuality and ends with his words 'Frailty, thy name is woman'.

Whilst the erect penis and its phallic representations have traditionally denoted absolute male power and domination it is an irony that the weakness of man is that he must seek out a woman to quench his fiery lust. And, in so doing, it is she who devours his manhood as her body sucks out the venom from within him, absorbing and transforming his energies, and in the process bonding with him, calming, yet empowering his very being. From before the onset of puberty, boys train themselves to emulate this rite of passage into manhood. Does, therefore, the female's lack of a penis infer the lack of power and status? Such an irrational perspective would surely represent a triumph of an impulsive bodily function over intellect.

One perspective of an ideal eternal relationship between men and women has been described thus: just as light is to dark, where neither can exist without the other nor is more important than the other, so women and men should define each other. The interrelationship between them should be one of eternal interdependence, like ying and yang, as interlocking parts which together create the whole.

The vast majority of men are, in truth, absolutely nothing even vaguely like women haters. It cannot be denied that a few men do show overt and abhorrent violence towards women but whether the true root cause of their behaviour can be directly attributed to an actual hatred of women is open to debate. Men, in general, may well under-appreciate women but not as a part of some subversive gender-biased plot. Men are, as a direct result of their upbringing by women, covertly fearful of a woman's potential, of women's almost incomprehensible power over men. Men are mystified by women, scared of women, turned on by women, in awe of women, in need of women's emotional and practical attributes, in need of women's caring. Male humans can see female humans as mystical, almost mythical creatures, desirable yet illusive beings. Men deprived of female company eventually become hollow, fragile vessels.

Men do not hate women; they are not misogynists. Men do not hate themselves; they are not misandrists. Men really cannot be bothered to be either; why would they? Men happen to have grown up in a world where they are members of the gender which has always been dominant in the majority of socially significant situations. They know no other way.

Many women are exasperated by men and their seemingly incomprehensible ways. A small but vociferous group of media savvy women may well be overt misandrists. There is, however, a large group of misogynists, strong, blatant, almost venomous, haters of women. It is women who appear to hate women most. Women accusing men of being the misogynists deflects the attention away from those who are truly dissatisfied with women. Women hate themselves for what they perceive to be so many of their own personal, physical, emotional and social traits. Most women are brought up to see themselves as not good enough and spend their lives berating themselves for their own perceived inadequacies. For not being pretty enough, slim enough, tall enough; for the size of their bum or their thighs, the shape of their nose or chin; the list is endless. It is just the ranking on the list – of each blemish, of each of their misconceptions, which changes throughout a woman's life. The ignominy of spots on the chin of an adolescent girl will eventually be replaced by the appearance of hairs on her chin as a more mature woman. There will always be a reason for a woman to feel that she is flawed, inadequate, unlovable.

And, the nearer any woman is thought to be to perfection by her peers the more she is both admired and hated by them. That small voice inside the mind of a jealous onlooker asking why she too cannot be as beautiful. Dr Dale Archer, in his article 'The Psychology of Beauty' for *Psychology Today*, outlines the various lines of research which map the advantages of being beautiful. In women's magazines, indeed, in all forms of female-centred media, there are articles which, unintentionally, reinforce these negative thoughts; they even print surveys which confirm the female tendency to undervalue themselves. In a wholesale betrayal of their gender, women spend much money on clothes and beauty products, they endure painful treatments and even surgery just to make them feel better about themselves. All in the name of self-esteem, to make them feel more alluring, more loveable. And women, they say, know women.

Men carry power well; like wearing an expensive tailored suit, everyone can see it, it is an overtly displayed air of superiority. Power and status were once based on physical strength and prowess in aggressive and defensive behaviour. Now, whilst there may still be some level of empowerment in these attributes, the real power comes from financial status and the elevated social position which this confers. Men command undue respect for this social status.

Women carry power less well; society sees powerful women as misfits, intruders into an alien male-dominated society. To some, their achievements are to be lauded and to others, denigrated. They may display the overtly superior behaviour of successful males but, somehow, they usually look as though they are wearing someone else's ill-fitting clothes. Society has determined these attitudes. The traditional female strengths of cooperation, nurturing and compassion hold little value in the world of high achievers; a successful woman is not necessarily a feminist. Women covet equal social status and respect. Women do not, by nature, command.

The reason things are like this is fairly simple – social constructs. These are the values which society has put on things; they are relative to each other – some things have a high value others have a low value. The importance or significance of certain attributes within society – certain gender roles, certain ethnicities, certain religious beliefs, certain ages, certain dress codes, whether you are fat or thin or tall or short – will each raise or lower your level of status within that society. In our modern world they are all totally artificial values.

Once upon a time, physical strength was an essential attribute for defence and for hunting; a different type of strength was needed for raising and nurturing a family. Then, of necessity, the former role was performed by the male and the latter by the female. Nowadays, these once very pertinent constrictions on lifestyle choices are, theoretically, virtually irrelevant. Except for two things; firstly, because humans have performed these gender specific roles for so long they have become hard-wired into the human brain; secondly, because of this hard-wiring society has created certain restrictive constructs for both males and females. These social constructs have formed the norms for each gender. As long as the majority of people do not dispute the relevance of maintaining this social hierarchy it will remain.

If we want to change the way society is structured, to change its value systems, we first need to acknowledge and examine the ways in which we act and interact within our existing society; we then need to be able to highlight certain of these gender based differences and their potential effects on our behaviour as a society. If we try to take a dispassionate, value-neutral view we will see how our perspective, as both an individual and as a member of one gender, has been formed and reformed; we must be able to accept that both genders have positive attributes and behaviours and also that we both have negative attributes and behaviours. We must be open to a critical self-examination of our own gender, at both individual and group levels, and thereby be able to acknowledge its strengths and weaknesses; we must also be able to make a comparative evaluation of our opposite gender. The stereotypical behaviours which are so readily the subject of comedy sketches are, in fact, based on truths, albeit grossly distorted caricatures of these truths; we really do behave in ways which can be seen as amusing or which can also engender pathos. We must acknowledge these differences and, when appropriate, be able to laugh at them; determine which are of real value and which are nothing more than amusing distractions.

Not being able to look at society's use of humour in this way would make it the 'elephant in the room', a potentially morale devouring omission. Laughing, like crying, can be a release mechanism for relieving tension.

Then, from an informed and dispassionate position decide if we, as an individual, believe there is a need for a radical change in the structure of society and, if our beliefs are purely personal or are reflected more generally in society as a whole. Just like a political election campaign the only way you will get change is by all of the 'electorate' being well-informed, for them to know all the positive arguments and all the negative and destructive counter-arguments, for them to have a free vote and for the system to be equitable. But, in the case of this type of radical social change, it certainly isn't going to be brought about by any form of election. An enduring change to the structure of society of such magnitude can only be brought about by either a relatively slow evolutionary process or by a revolution. Women are the seekers of this change; women are not, by nature, revolutionaries. It has taken us hundreds of generations to get to where we are now; for there to be a majority (or a powerful and unopposed minority) which is in the position to instigate the creation of a new social order, and for the changes to happen which will facilitate the complete overturning of the status quo and the structure of a radical new style of society, will take a few more generations. Not as a short-lived experiment but as a permanent and positive move forward in human evolution.

They say that you should be careful what you wish for – in case your wish becomes true.

Over a hundred years ago Emmeline Pankhurst and her 'sister' Suffragettes struggled for, were imprisoned for, and even died for, the cause of enfranchisement; for women to have the right to vote. It was, to them, the first step towards true emancipation; a world where women could be acknowledged to have a status equal to that of men and thereby life opportunities equal to those of men.

Well, women got the vote; and, slowly, women's lives have been changing for the better; haven't they?

Now, less than a century later, in certain areas of most cities and large towns in the UK – particularly on a Friday or Saturday night – you will find numerous highly inebriated young women more scantily and more provocatively dressed than you could find a prostitute in any seaport in the world. These representatives of their gender are loud, aggressive and display sexually explicit behaviour. Frequently, they can be seen losing every semblance of their dignity as they rollick about drunkenly. Some will end up having 'cat fights' in the street, others will reach the nadir of their evening by falling comatose in the gutter. Down adjacent alleys, girls give their inebriated bodies in public acts of copulation. Their less intoxicated, or less liberated, 'sisters' await a slightly more discrete venue for their soon to be forgotten acts of depravity. They may represent a tiny minority of the young women of their generation but they are highly conspicuous by their behaviour.

Meanwhile, by daylight, in the business centres of those same cities, university educated women dressed in smart suits strut importantly to their professional destinies. They have all the intelligence and acumen to out-perform any male competitors, they bring their feminine attributes to the workplace and race up 'the greasy pole' of promotion with a velocity capable of shattering any 'glass ceiling'.

Then, seemingly inexplicably, this same once potent minority of young women become like some unstoppable laser-guided missile as they enthusiastically seek out their target. They willingly take their leave from the world of work and exchange it for the undeserved anonymity of the lifestyle of motherhood, for the allure of maternal duties.

In 2014 Kirsty Allsopp stirred up a real hornet's nest by stating that she would tell her daughter (and thus, by inference, all other young women) to abandon thoughts of higher education and a career path and to get married, get on the property ladder and have a baby by the time she is 27. A career path, she advised, could be followed later in life. Her suggestions caused a furore in the media and she was accused of being both sexist and patronising. However, there were also some substantial areas of support.

Management Today made some very interesting observations on this debate. They noted that Apple and Facebook were now offering to freeze their female staff's eggs so that they could continue to work until their 40s. Does this offer reflect a caring female-centred attitude or profit oriented companies manipulating or taking advantage of their female staff? The fact that they offer such a scheme certainly confirms and reinforces the stereotype of the strength of the draw for young women preferring a family over a career.

In the article, both Amanda Mackenzie, CMO of Aviva, and the Natural Fertility Centre, cite the health benefits of motherhood in the 20s. Further, three women who had their families first and their careers later in life are interviewed. They were Nikki King – chairman of Isuzu Trucks UK, Sally James – ex of UBS Investment Bank and now a director of three large companies, and Anne Owers – the former Chief Inspector of Prisons and now chairman of the Independent Police Complaints Commission. They jointly believe that there are three relevant factors (1) that women over-prioritise their careers and that being enticed into the virtues of a university degree course is not always the best route (2) that taking the career route when you are young is not the only option for success in business and (3) that both life and career changes are possible at any time of life.

Why is it that some women are initially driven to want to succeed in business and commerce, in what they perceive as a man's world? Their female networking will have already told them of its testosterone driven ways; they will all have heard the legend of the glass ceiling, they can sense the potential futility of their cause for themselves. Yet, they still appear compelled to seek admittance to this self-perpetuating, self-gratifying, patriarchy. Are they driven to change the system rather than to reinforce it? Do they believe that if they can gain entry into this exclusive club and become part of the inner sanctum that they will be in a position to instigate a revolution from within? In truth, they know that if they ever tried, the moment their insincerity was uncovered they would be rendered commercially impotent. Their young working life sacrificed for a futile symbolic gesture.

Instead of trying to emulate men, instead of trying to gain access to a man's world, why haven't women chosen to make men more like women; why haven't women inculcated feminine values into men? After all, men are only boys who got older. And, it is almost exclusively women who are in charge of creating the fundamental value systems for both girls and boys – from conception until, at least, the beginnings of secondary education. Mothers, grannies, aunts, friends, neighbours, primary school teachers – all women. Where's the problem, ladies? Why not start off by making sure that all boys are exposed to a growing-up process which develops an empathetic nature in each and every one of them; for their outlook to be substantially, if not totally, feminine biased? The Jesuits say that if you give them a child until it is seven years old they will give you the adult. Well, we're talking about a potential period of 11 years – that would allow 50 per cent more time than the Jesuits ask – for your indoctrination process to work.

But then, perhaps the truth is that 'equality issues' are, to paraphrase William Shakespeare, 'much ado about nothing'. Is it that there is just a tiny nucleus of social misfits, overtly feminist women, who enjoy causing all members of society – whatever their gender – to feel unrest, to make us all feel vulnerable. Are these feminists, in truth, just a vociferous group of radical activists trying to promote a feminine-centred version of anarchy?

With modern technology replacing much of the traditional need for the muscular strength of men, and with the relatively recent acknowledgement of women's ability to be at least mentally equal to (if not superior to) men in most areas of business, commerce and education, why is it that most women who have entered and risen in the world of business have subsequently chosen to opt out of its value system. It is not that they have chosen to make a concerted, long-term sacrifice – in an effort to get inside the system and from there to change the structure and methods of business – so that their 'sisters' following behind them will have an easier journey. A dedicated push in that direction could, in effect, create a self-perpetuating training scheme from which women could begin to change the commercial side of society. But, rather than doing that, once they have savoured the experience of this mystical man's world they have rejected its ethos, decided to turn their backs on it all and walk away – in the direction of the value system of a softer, feminine, maternal world.

Let's get our perspective right. Proportionally, there have hitherto only been a tiny minority of women who have specifically dedicated their life to achieving and maintaining a position of power or authority in any traditionally male dominated area of business, commerce or politics. There are even fewer men, indeed a minuscule number, who have ever tried to gain admittance to positions of control in the few areas of work which had previously been seen as 'female only' and thus inaccessible to men.

The number of either gender who have achieved their ambition of infiltrating 'enemy territory' or, who have been thwarted in their efforts to do so, has become the subject of urban myth. One side provides colourful anecdotes of women's efforts to gain equality of opportunity – some of which have allegedly been thwarted by grossly misogynist men whose like must surely be worthy of caricature; whilst the other side quotes statistics, government statistics, of young women unfairly out-performing young men – first at university and then in the professions. There are, for example, now more female than male doctors working in general practice – according to the General Medical Council's own website and their GP Register of Doctors; women 50.8 per cent. But then, we wouldn't want the truth to spoil a good story, would we?

Of course, the vast majority of men and women currently in employment in the UK did not go to university; their jobs are commonplace, they sit squarely in the middle of a 'norm referenced curve' (bell-curve) for just about every aspect of their lives. Generally, they perform roles which are seen as stereotypical for their gender.

Do both men and women actually feel more comfortable performing traditional gender roles in both the workplace and in social situations? Should the majority be made to feel uncomfortable by an activist minority, be pressurised to perform different gender roles? What exactly would be the purpose of doing so, why should anyone be coerced into becoming an unwilling participant in some perverse social experiment?

Is it not true to say that, in general, the vast majority of men and women willingly continue to perform gender specific roles in their employment, their leisure, socially and domestically; in exactly the same way as their parents and grandparents did and, for that matter, all their ancestors have done for generations before them? If so, how is it that this apparent stasis has persisted for so long and exactly why should it not remain the blueprint for society?

Men and women have inhabited the same world for millennia without any substantial signs of social dislocation. Mutual cooperation has been the unspoken byword for this evolutionary success. Until now. Does it really matter to the vast majority of people if this is the way the world is? Should we not just accept the current equilibrium of society, which is borne of traditions created over thousands of years, and ignore the 'agent-provocateurs' who are trying to disrupt this way of life. Aren't these people just feminist biased anarchists trying to impose an ill-fitting 'new order' on society – seeking to usurp the existing traditional and well-tried benevolent patriarchy and to replace it with all the insecurities of a radical, new and untested matriarchy. Change for change's sake; not for the overall benefit of each and every member of that society. Is 'equal opportunity' either a realistic or desirable goal? It seems that human nature has ensured that, in our society, it is usually the stronger or the better educated or the wealthier members who take greater advantage of 'opportunities', whatever they are. No-one has been asked if the public, in general, want to vote for these changes; indeed, no-one has even posed the question of the populous let alone suggested voting for or against it.

But, maybe it really is time for radical change. Perhaps, though, we should strive for absolute equality – above equal opportunity; that would be a more equitable process, produce a more fair outcome, wouldn't it? If men and women really are equal beings. Equality would have to be across gender, race, age, ethnicity, religion and sexual tendencies. To enforce it we would each have to be subject to a state-imposed proportionality of each and every role in society; no more, no less.

You see, we are now being told that one of the biggest problems of society – which has, apparently, been an unspoken truth since time began – is that, from the misguided male perspective, men and women have cohabited in our world relatively compatibly. Whereas, women have, seemingly, been coerced into a perpetual and near-silent acceptance of the male-imposed status quo and continued living in a parallel – no, a divergent – world in which their gender has always held opposing perspectives to men, forever constrained by illogical rules and irrelevant values.

History records that men and women have learned to coexist on virtually all the habitable surfaces of this globe and to perform mutually supportive roles within the various and varied societies thereon; they have come together as circumstances dictated, sometimes in harmony and sometimes in disharmony. The control of these societies has always been imposed by an elite minority on the majority with sets of rules which are generally accepted by, and adhered to by, each and every one of the members of that society. The observance of these criteria is necessary for social cohesion and therefore the continuation of that society. Sometimes, and usually only temporarily, individuals or groups of people benefit from, or are disadvantaged by, the benign operation of that society. The roles of both genders, and each of the individuals therein, appear predetermined and constrained by certain social parameters. Society has no intrinsic need for individualism; indeed excess is usually discouraged as being counter-productive. Cooperation has been paramount for the continued coexistence of both genders, and each member of those genders, within this model of society. It was always so.

This next raises the question of – to what extent do women, in general, really want to have equality of participation in all aspects of the world of work. And, if men really are currently in control, what, if anything, would cause them to relinquish this power; and, in the end, will that even be the men's decision to make?

I think that the fact that we have yet another very competent Queen on the throne and that we have in recent times had an extremely strong, forthright and controlling woman as Prime Minister would tend towards dousing the argument of the impossibility of power and control for women or that there really is an unbreakable glass ceiling in either politics or constitutional power. The rules of succession for royal families expressly include, rather than exclude, females. Centuries ago, Mary Queen of Scots was crowned as Queen of Scotland aged just nine months and then aged 16, and already married into the French nobility, she was crowned Queen of France too. And that in such a socially and gender divided society. And yet, none of these all-powerful women ever took steps to empower the women of their own generation; did they not believe them worthy of equality?

I am not saying that any woman determined to become a captain of industry, head of state or other position of absolute power would have an easy journey – but, then it wouldn't be easy for a man either. The male could not look for support on a gender basis whilst the female, nowadays, most certainly could. What if we were to make race, religion or disability the major factor in the equation instead of gender?

For a woman it may mean having to substitute the more tradi-tional roles she might have been brought up to believe would be hers (and which she had possibly even looked forward to) for a much more a male oriented working lifestyle. This may be the choice she would have to make. Yes, of course, it would also be possible to become pregnant and have a baby but not without the potential for it having an effect on some of her duties as either a business person or as a traditional mother.

And at this point I am looking at a juxtaposition of issues such as continuity of management and leadership, maternal duties, allegiances, relationships and emotions. Most bosses are, of necessity, addicted to their jobs and inured to the virtual exclusion of all else; thereby they are willing and able to make the appropriate sacrifices and to be constricted by the lifestyle their chosen role necessarily imposes.

If we bring into the equation the potential emotional stress and conflict of interests which the role of motherhood might induce I do not think any woman could (or should) ask of herself to be both a totally efficient and committed full-time business leader and to be a compassionate fully involved mother – unless we were to find a route by which all business, both national and international, as well as child-care arrangements, were done on a completely different basis.

In complete reverse, it would not be easy, indeed probably less easy, for a man to become a success at any of the roles traditionally dominated by women. And, whereas the woman aspiring to a leading role in what has traditionally been considered as a man's world might be thought of as a heroine, in the reverse situation a man would doubtless be thought of by his peers as 'lacking' or even deviant.

Nonetheless, I think that it could be reasonably argued that it is both necessary and desirable for the whole of the human race that we evolve into a more benign, egalitarian and humanist society.

If current feminine propaganda is to be believed women have never had, yet always sought, emancipation from employment, religious, legal, economic, sexual and political oppression. And, in many parts of the world, this is doubtless the current reality for most if not all women and there are those who continue to be persecuted for pursuing their just cause of women's rights.

But the evidence of history does not totally bear this out. There have been real women, and legends of women rulers, warriors, and even whole armies of women, as evidenced by things as diverse as Roman sculptures and Japanese woodcuts of the fighting Amazons. Civilisations as diverse as the Romans and the Celts gave women very significant and authoritative roles in their societies. Joan of Arc was a famously efficient soldier; and those who are or have been the rulers of tribes and of nations, such as Boadicea, Cleopatra, Queen Elizabeth I, Queen Elizabeth II, and Queen Victoria, Mary Queen of Scotland & France, and Maria Theresa, Archduchess of Austria; the present and past heads of state of countries such as Argentina, Australia, Bahamas, Bangladesh, Bolivia, Brazil, Burundi, Central African Republic, Chile, China, Costa Rica, Croatia, Cyprus (North), Denmark, Ecuador, Finland, Germany, Grenada, Haiti, Iceland, India, Indonesia, Ireland, Israel, Jamaica, Kosovo, Latvia, Liberia, Lithuania, Malawi, Malta, Mauritius, Mongolia, Namibia, Nicaragua, Norway, Panama, Philippines, Poland, San Marino, Senegal, Serbia, Slovenia, South Korea, St Lucia, Switzerland, Trinidad & Tobago. Women have been astronauts, pilots in the Royal Air Force's Red Arrows aerobatic team and heads of industry. Just look at the women in *The Sunday Times* Rich List or in *Forbes* magazine. And these lists are very far from exhaustive as a search on the Internet will confirm.

That 50 women have been awarded a Nobel Prize – with Marie Curie getting one twice – sounds quite good but less so when put into perspective by the fact that 860 individuals and 22 organisations have been awarded it in total.

Another, less exulted, example of a competent woman succeeding in a man's world is 'Fearless' Nikki Thomas who is a trained RAF weapons systems operator who, together with her pilot Juliette Fleming, became the first all-female crew of the two-seat Tornado ground-attack fighter aircraft. Now, Nikki Thomas (36) has become the first female Wing Commander in the Royal Air Force and is in control of the 16 10-million-pound Tornado aircraft and their crews who form 12 (B) Squadron. Equality of opportunity has truly given her wings.

Throughout time males have, in general, constructed and dominated most means of control – be they social, administrative or fiscal; and, they have always been dismissive of women having any influence in or on these institutions or of them even being a voice to be heard. The ebb and flow of influence exerted against and by women has, over thousands of years, caused supporters of women's equality to feel both despair and hope. Given the relatively short period of time between the 1960s and the present day, compared with the length of time that we as 'modern humans' have been around, the recent rate of change in the roles of females in western society has been nothing short of phenomenal. Maybe not as fast as some women would like, but, nonetheless, quite unprecedented.

CHAPTER 2
LOOKING BACK

You may wonder why there is a long chapter on the history of mankind, from a British perspective, in a book about gender equality; in truth, without it we cannot make sense of either how we got to where we are now or where things could go in the future. In this chapter I will take the reader on a journey, from our origins forward through layer upon layer of our history right into modern times, in an effort to offer an explanation for the historical domination of men over their apparently subservient women. Our behaviour is dictated by the social circumstances in which we find ourselves and, of course, by the effects of our hormones; this is as true now as it ever was, and both are gender biased. Our inherited male and female gender roles have always been there; they haunt us like omnipresent shadows.

Why do these differences between male and female life paths and behaviour patterns matter so much? Has the eternal indoctrination of dominant male behaviour patterns from generation to generation been part of some insidious, gender biased strategy for the control of women or is it, in truth, an inadvertent consequence of our divergent historical roles? Men no longer fight hand to hand whilst looking into the eyes of their enemies; they are no longer gruesomely mutilated and killed by their work or their soldiering; they are no longer likely to be captured and enslaved. Women are no longer liable to be tortured and diseased by consequence of their bearing children nor left as widows, abandoned, destitute and dependent on the generosity of family or clan – or left to rely on charity; victims of circumstance, without the protection of the modern social safety net, women and children were always condemned to suffer as an unintended consequence of the tribulations of their menfolk.

This retrospective, in conjunction with the information in chapters 3 and 4, clearly shows that whilst there have been some positive movements in the quest by women for gender equality over several centuries it is only in relatively recent decades that technological advances have allowed the potential for a reordering of gender roles. For the most part these opportunities have been seized upon, manipulated and exploited by a relatively small group of visionary women whose incremental efforts have mirrored these opportunities for social change.

Modern advances in medical technology, such as MRI scanners, have been adopted by researchers into human behaviour and as a result of their work we can now see a direct causal link between actions, behaviour and thought patterns and the consequential development of the physical structure of the brain and of its function. What we do and think affects how our brain will grow and how it will work; and this then affects how we behave in future. Sometimes a virtuous circle; sometimes a vicious circle. This process happens in just the same way that physical exercise will stimulate growth in our muscles and our flexibility of movement; our brain then remembers and reinforces the links. Because we have, as both genders, behaved in certain ways for thousands of years, so will our brains have been developing in their structure and their way of operating; thus, our behaviour and thought patterns are deeply engrained. If we want to change the way society works these long adopted modes of functioning of both genders will require substantial changes; unwanted behaviour patterns will have to be erased from our memory banks and new ones substituted; these processes will then need to be assimilated into the psyche of both the individual and of society. Social change and cerebral change are, we now know, interdependent.

*　*　*

Some may believe that, as modern 21st century humans, we have a necessity to reform our society – and to do it quickly. But, before we go down that road too far and too fast we need to get our human existence into some sort of perspective. We need to appreciate just how quickly things have actually been developing over the last 50 years compared to the more gradual way that humans have been evolving for many tens of thousands of years.

Let me share with you this illustration; it depicts the whole of time, as we understand it, as a 24-hour clock. Our concept of time starts with the initial creation of the world, goes through the very origin and development of each and every form of life right up until the present time and then looks forward until the predicted total demise of this planet.

Thus, if as we believe, planet Earth began 5 billion years ago and will, it is predicted, end in 5 billion years' time (when the sun is expected to expand so much that it will burn the Earth to a cinder) then we are, right now, exactly at midday.

Using this 24-hour time model, the earliest humanoid life-forms, which began five million years ago, would show up on the clock at 11.59.17; Neanderthals were 500,000 years ago and would be at 11.59.55; modern man at 140,000 years ago would be at 11.59.59; and every bit of history ever recorded by man would appear in the last one-tenth of a second – at 11.59.59.9. The afternoon and evening of this imaginary day – right up until midnight – is our planet's exciting (or scary, depending on your point of view) future. At this level, human history is not that long.

Chimpanzees and bonobos are very closely related to each other, they are different branches of one family tree; we humans are also a branch of that very same family tree. Genetically speaking, chimpanzees and bonobos are more closely related to humans than either of them is to a gorilla or, for that matter, to any other primate. We humans have been around for a very long time and started by living a pretty primitive lifestyle.

If we are to believe modern scientific research, the male of the human species has always been larger and physically stronger than the female. By virtue of his greater size and strength the male was the 'slayer of beasts' – be that for protection or for food. The female was the bearer and nurturer of the young and, a gatherer. Exactly how and why these physical developments may have come about will probably always be open to debate. But, when put into perspective, the origins of this hereditary size and strength differential seem to matter little now. Both roles were risky; life was risky.

The female would always have been the person with authority over child-rearing and would have developed an intimate knowledge about the seasonal fruits, berries and other crops which she harvested; she would be able to choose the most appropriate habitat in which to set up a home base according to these two intertwined needs. She would also have prepared and cooked the food. These would have been her decisions. (Modern scientific tests show that humans throughout the world still sense red foods, with their ripe berries association, to be sweeter than other colours.) When pregnant, giving birth or looking after young she was always vulnerable and being left alone whilst the male was away hunting or fighting exaggerated this vulnerability. The potential medical problems associated with pregnancy, childbirth and child-rearing in such a basic environment would have been immense; mortality rates would have been high. Fulfilling this arduous role would have been an all-consuming occupation and would have left little time or energy for other less immediate matters.

The male, in comparison, learned what and where to hunt and how best to protect his family from predators. His hunting trips to feed the family may have taken him away from their base-camp for many days at a time and were not always successful. He would have spent long periods alone and have faced frequent danger. His energy would have been spent in short intense bursts, whether for hunting or fighting. These energetic bouts would have been interspersed with longer periods of physical inactivity as he recuperated; this gave the male more time and opportunity to think and to mentally organise. Thus, the male was possibly in a better position to be able to make decisions based on his thoughts, rather than to always have to react to an external stimulus. Assuming that his thoughts would be discussed with his mate, by virtue of his greater size and strength, he could determine the outcome of an argument. Doubtless this is how the male, rather than the female, initially became the major decision maker. It was a sort of meritocracy based on physical strength and prowess.

This was an existence which we can readily understand just by observing much of the animal kingdom, and especially the primates. Individuals and couples must have worked out that by being together not only with their extended families but with other humans too would bring advantages in hunting, child-rearing and, of course, for protection. They must have developed a common language, created fresh blood ties through interbreeding, and enjoyed economic benefits.

To allow this to happen there would have been rules and a social contract between the members of the group.

For some humans, life changed little for millennia. For example, the lifestyles that the European explorers discovered when they first encountered the native North American Indian tribes or when parts of Africa, South America and Australia were first explored. Even today, at the beginning of the 21st century, there are still a few small pockets of the world where a primitive tribal hunter-gatherer life exists.

Most humans, however, evolved from this isolated hunter-gatherer life into a less nomadic and more socially organised grouping thus creating the basis for a type of society with which we can now easily identify. As these 'clans' developed they learned to herd and breed animals and to cultivate crops. More people from different families meant that the gene pool became enlarged and thus lessened the risks of interbreeding. A 'herd mentality' was developing in place of the previous insular model. Consequently, life became less risky and more productive from both a food and a human perspective.

For those more organised groups the advantages of becoming even bigger beckoned but, with that, antagonism between the individuals and the groups must have occurred and created new problems.

These doubtless caused feuds between groups, and subsequent pacts and allegiances. For the male, the battle with beasts was beginning to be substituted by battle within social groups and against members of his own species. The ingenuity of man soon allowed these growing societies to become more complex and for different technologies to develop to beneficially alter their lives.

Decorating our bodies with flowers, feathers, stones and bones was the earliest form of adornment; we also used to paint our faces and our bodies with natural dyes. We have used variations of these techniques and designs to make us look both more attractive to our mates and to look more scary to our foes. The phallus was also worshipped in many cultures and is thus a recurring image.

The earliest clothes were made from animal skins stitched together using bone needles threaded with animal sinews. Pelts with the fur or wool still attached gave better thermal protection. To soften the otherwise stiff animal skins they were treated and tanned and became leather; early methods, which are still used in some parts of the world today, included soaking them in urine. We know that some garments were embellished with decorative stitching patterns and with stones, bones and beads as further adornments. Jewellery, from all the historic periods through which leather was the main clothing material, was equally strong in its style, size and its manufacture; it denoted status and wealth and was also used as a lucky talisman to ward off bad spirits. Leather also became used for footwear, bags, water-bags, armour and weapon sheaths.

Our use of clothes, jewellery and cosmetics is as old as us; they reflect the society and the technology of the time. We have evidence that ancient civilizations had eye and lip enhancers, hair gel, fingernail stains, perfumes, breath fresheners and even anti-wrinkle preparations.

Woollen cloth making originated as a domestic process, using mostly basic wooden tools and technology to prepare, spin and weave it. The fabrics produced were fairly coarse in texture and of variable quality. One of the major benefits of taking the wool from a sheep or goat and making a fabric from it, as opposed to killing the animal and then wearing its skin, was that you still had a live animal which could be milked and that more wool would be produced every year. Its warmth made it a fabric most suitable for the climate of northern Europe.

Linen is a fabric made from the softened internal stem fibres of the flax plant and takes its name from the Latin name of that plant; it has been around for well over 10,000 years and that was long before woollen fibres were being spun and woven into cloth. Coarse linen could be used for sails; the finer the linen the softer it was to wear as clothing and the higher its cost and thus, the higher its status. Because it was virtually impossible to dye, it was worn in its natural off-white colour; sometimes the garments were embroidered. When new it could be scratchy to the skin but the more it was worn and washed, the more soft and comfortable it became; it was fairly easy to launder and dry and was a cool rather than warm fabric. It became the standard underclothing for those who could afford it and warmth was found in wearing a top layer of animal pelts, sheepskin, goatskin or, later, woollen fabric. The word lingerie is derived from the same base word as the one for linen. The lightness of both the colour and of the weight of this fabric led to more ornate and delicate designs of complementary jewellery being worn on it; brooches and belts were very fashionable and worn for decoration as much as for status. Linen was eventually replaced as underclothes by cotton or, for the very wealthy, by silk.

For several thousands of years there was an overland trade route along which camels and donkeys brought silk from China, and then Persia, through Asia and the Middle East to the shores of the Mediterranean Sea. The cloth was revered by many cultures, including the Romans, for its fine threads and its soft feel.

During a period since more than 2000 years BCE, and in different regions of the world, civilised cultures as diverse as the Chinese and the Aztecs, the Egyptians and the Mayans, had complex societies with religions, temples, pyramids, gold and jewels, planned cities with their associated infrastructures – including complex irrigation networks, mass production of food and, of course, large armies to protect all their assets. These societies were based on the concept of a hierarchical social network. During their prime most of these civilisations produced original thoughts and systems which were to become contributors to the structure and organisation of future civilisations worldwide. For instance, the Greeks had developed mathematics and geometry and could navigate by the stars; the Egyptians had developed a working form of air conditioning and later the Romans had forms of central heating and flushing toilets.

The Minoans were a civilization on Crete 5000 years ago which was only ended by the eruption of the Santorini volcano in 1500 BCE; Greek, as well as Egyptian, history also spans the last 5,000 years; the Phoenicians, and Moses and the Jews, also lived in complex civilizations, from around 1000 years BCE. And long after them, just over 2,000 years ago, came the Romans. In 'civilized' Rome there were over a million residents. They were crammed into a small geographical area such that the population density was 10-times that of modern cities like London. Almost half of the population were slaves – captured as a result of invasion or of war; there were slaves from what we now call the British Isles in Rome.

Cicero, writing to his friend Atticus in 55 BCE, jokes about the poor quality of the slaves captured by Caesar in his invasion of Great Britain: 'I think that you will not expect any of them to be learned in literature or music' (Cicero, *Letters to Atticus*).

There was a hierarchy within the slave community; some were well cared for domestic servants much like the 'below stairs' staff we might see in *Downton Abbey*, some were even teachers or bookkeepers, some were used for sexual gratification. But, most slaves were the workforce that did the heavy labour and the otherwise socially unacceptable jobs; or, they were to be human sacrifices, awaiting death for the amusement of the populous.

The majority of slaves were men and their lives and their labours were usually arduous, dangerous and eventually fatal; but, there were women slaves and child slaves too. The children of slaves were born as slaves; it was not unusual for a slave couple to kill their own children rather than give them into a life of slavery. Slaves were bought and sold in slave markets – where strong young men with the potential of a lifetime of hard work ahead of them fetched a good price; so too did cooks, as did sexually attractive young people of both genders.

The glory that was Rome, the relics of which we can still admire today, was built because they had vast numbers of captured men, slaves, to perform hard labour, to act like human machines. All the wonderful buildings were created by stone quarried, carved and erected with slave labour; they also slaved on the magnificent system of aqueducts which ran for many miles, from the springs in the hills, to bring fresh water to the city and on the vast sewerage system which washed the city's waste down to the river Tiber and out to sea. The sophistication of Roman bathhouses also relied on huge numbers of slaves to keep the water running and the temperature appropriate to the needs of the Roman elite.

The Colosseum was the centre of entertainment for the Romans. It was a multistorey building with underground pens secreted below the arena which held captive both animals and humans. It had man-powered lifts to propel these cages up through trap doors in the floor of the auditorium so that these victims appeared, almost magically, before an audience of up to 50,000 – fresh for their mortal combat. After each session of mutilation and carnage the dead and dying were dragged out of the arena by men and horses. It has been estimated that a total of half a million men (and it was mainly men) and a million animals were to die as part of these macabre floor shows. Life for the Roman elite was sophisticated; their pleasures were many and diverse. They loved beauty in all its forms, they loved good food and wines, they loved comfort and cleanliness, they loved clothes and jewellery, they loved poetry and music, they loved sex; and, they loved to watch humans and animals tearing each other apart. In every way, their lifestyle was paid for by their slaves.

The Romans came to conquer Britain and continued to live their cosseted lifestyle – at our expense. They subjugated us and then some of them interbred with us. They taught us their technologies, their values and their social structure; they inculcated their mindset on us. They even created a slave market in London. Slavery in Britain had existed before the Roman invasion and continued after they left; it was the forerunner of the feudal system and of serfdom which lasted until the Industrial Revolution. We have a history which was closely intertwined with, and therefore influenced by, the Roman form of society; they were a role-model for aspirational Britons. The Roman Empire spread across the whole of western Europe and to all the countries around the Mediterranean Sea; these countries were also subject to the same enduring Roman influences.

Historically, for the ruler and those few others who had money, influence, power and privilege it was always going to be a potentially good life. Immediately below this higher echelon – whilst protecting their interests and pandering to their needs – were a small number of advisers, military generals, priests, clerics and other 'hangers-on' whose lives could also be comfortable. These groups would eventually evolve into the aristocracy and the upper classes.

Since the very earliest of records, all civilisations have been party to slavery. In Britain there are records of it dating back to before the Viking invasions. People were seen as one of the spoils of war – no different from any other booty. It was actually recorded in 1086, in the Doomsday Book that 10 per cent of the English population were slaves.

Slavery in England and across much of Europe continued, at some level, until the 18th century – and in a few European countries until the mid-19th century. Slaves were often treated badly; they were fed and sheltered in exchange for their work and they could own nothing – except their hunger. They were bought and sold in markets like cattle.

We, as a nation, have been both slaves and enslavers; those enslaved lost everything, including their dignity; some, as slave traders or slave owners made enormous fortunes which have been handed down generation upon generation and that inherited wealth continues to bring privilege to some today.

The next up the social ladder, and the most numerous social group, were the various levels of serfs.

Each family was allotted a small parcel of land which they would cultivate so that they could use it to grow their own food crops and raise a few domesticated animals; they could also build a dwelling and outbuildings. They usually owned a few belongings but were rarely in the position to be able to amass much in the way of individual wealth; they had no other freedoms but, at least they could not be bought or sold. The children of serfs automatically became subject to a life of serfdom. Their payment for these privileges was to work for their liege lord, a manorial baron or knight, as he directed; usually it was in a seasonal way – cultivating his crops and tending his land. They would also be his foot soldiers as and when necessary. In return, he allowed them to live on his land and would pledge to protect them from robbers and villains. The word to describe this relationship between the serf and his feudal lord was known as bondage. Serfs (from the Latin word for slaves) were not allowed to leave their village area without a specific reason and having had permission granted by their liege; and, they had to return to their village when they had fulfilled their purpose. The only exception was people going on a religious pilgrimage. Thus, strangers were immediately apparent; people who had abandoned or been cast from their village communities were called vagrants, they were trusted by no-one and led a hard and hazardous life resorting to begging and stealing to survive. In a village type of environment it is easier for a society, mainly through family and friends, to control behaviour, particularly sexual behaviour. This social structure was to remain the situation for all the periods prior to the Industrial Revolution. The social group which were originally serfs was, over centuries, to become what we now know as the working class.

The top 10 per cent of commoners were the Freemen. They either owned their land or paid a monetary rental for it as a tenant farmer; they did not work on the land of the local baron. Their land was used to grow crops and rear livestock which could be sold at market and provide an independent income for them. This was the beginning of the middle classes.

Across all civilisations it has always been the leaders who determined what was allowed and what was not and it was their underlings who applied these laws.

The historic system of English law – also known as common law – originated in an organic way and was often not written down. The precedent was tradition, the way things had always been but, with the judges allowed the freedom to interpret and modify the laws, to be arbiters. This legal system, because of the British colonisation of so many countries and their peoples, now represents almost half of the legal structure of the world.

The other system is known as the civil – or Roman – law. It originates with the emperors of the Roman dynasty and contains an almost limitless number of statutes; definitive written laws which judges apply without modification. This system was prevalent in countries with a history of Catholicism and accounts for most of the remainder of the legal systems worldwide.

Nowadays, many counties have adapted their legal systems to take account of what they believe to be the best out of their existing system and merge it with the best bits of the other system. It used to be said, rather tongue in cheek, that in Britain unless there is a law which says that you can do something then you cannot. Whereas, in most of Europe, you can do what you want unless the law says that you can't.

For the majority of the population, who toiled under duress to provide the benefits for their betters, it was a hard and short life. It had always been so; and little changed for the ordinary man over the centuries – other than by a very slow evolution. Survival was, of itself, a victory. And, for millennia, these hierarchical relationships and systems remained unchanged.

Wars were frequent and unimaginably brutal. Being in another shire or county seemed almost as far away and as strange as being in a foreign land; foot soldiers marched for days or weeks – sometimes straight from another battle. There were few roads other than those created by the Romans. A 'high way' was just that, a path over high ground avoiding the boggy marshes.

To stand in a battle-field with a sword in one hand and perhaps a shield in the other – with hundreds of other men similarly armed and standing next to you – ready and willing to inflict grievous wounds that would ensure a tortured and often prolonged death on your foe. And they, your foe, standing only feet away facing you – similarly armed and with similar intent. Somewhere nearby – heavy horses, the tanks of their day, ready to crash through the hoard crushing and creating havoc in their wake.

Archers set to shower a deluge of deadly arrows. And these were the well-armed professional soldiers. The masses were feudal serfs with home-made weapons and little or no expertise. And little or no option but to 'do and die'. Somewhere behind were the women-folk tending to the needs of the soldiers and serfs alike.

What mindset must you have to go into a situation like that knowing that you are unlikely to be other than mutilated and left to die a slow and painful death? Or, perhaps to have a limb amputated without skill and without anaesthetics and face a life unable to work; an emotional and financial drain on all your loved ones. And, if you survived intact, bearing the knowledge of how awful it was and aware that you would, almost without doubt, be called upon to do it again. That was the reality of war.

Men were brought up knowing that it would be almost a certainty that this would be asked of them at some stage in their lives. By today's standards, the numbers killed may seem fairly insignificant compared to those of the two World Wars; but, they must be taken as a percentage of the population as it was then – and it was a pretty small population. The only possible strategies for coping could be bravado, a hardness, a coldness, detachment from the value of a life – and a lot of liquor. The word soldier used to be spelled 'souldier', it was derived from the French verb *souler* to be drunk; you must have needed to be anaesthetised with alcohol to numb your senses. Hard men for hard times; scared men for scary times? A permanent imprint on the psyche of all males.

For women, their battle was with childbirth. The rates of attrition for them were simply staggering. Mortality in childbirth was commonplace – for either or both, mother and child. A breech birth or similar complication condemned a mother and her baby to an agonising end.

Life in a rural setting may have conferred some benefits but would not have always been ideal for the delivery of a child. However, it compared favourably to a life in a squalid and overcrowded ghetto in an industrialised city as an environment for safe childbirth. For a few, money may have brought the advantages of improved nutrition and better cleanliness but, obstetrics were not necessarily much better for the wealthy. For most women, the nutrition and general healthcare we expect today were left to chance or the generosity of others.

A child without a mother was unlikely to survive and if they did, could look forward to a life of abject poverty. For many thousands of women across the world this sort of scenario is still their reality. Even in 2013, according to the United Nations Population Fund, almost 290,000 women worldwide are known to have died as a direct consequence of childbirth – that's 800 per day. They do not have any records for many remote areas. This vulnerability must surely have left permanent imprint on the psyche of women.

For the poorest of women, prior to the benefits brought about by the Industrial Revolution, their clothes would have been home-made from coarsely woven fabrics with little colour and decoration. More wealthy women had access to better quality, more colourful, more sophisticated fabrics like fine linen, woollen cloth and silks and more ornate decoration and jewellery.

Knowledge of silk may have been brought back to England from the Holy Lands by returning crusaders. Silk, as a raw material, is already a thread and so just needs to be twisted before being ready for weaving. Silk, in any form was always expensive; raw silk was difficult to obtain but, nevertheless, manufacturing centres were created in southern France and in Italy. Eventually, it was to be manufactured in England too. For thousands of years, silk has been the preferred thread for embroidery, a method of decorating fabric with coloured stitch-work, which was popular in many cultures. English embroidery was first noted as an expensive adornment on the clothes of the clergy and the royalty of England in the middle ages; contemporary English embroidery skills gained an excellent reputation throughout Europe. Lace-like tied work has been iden-tified from as long ago as 1000 years BCE but modern 'bobbin' lace seems to have begun in the 12th and 13th centuries, initially as part of the regalia for clerics. From there, it gained popularity and in the Industrial Revolution some more basic forms were machine made.

Knitting seems to have been first seen in Muslim workshops in Spain in the 12th and 13th centuries; it created items of clothing which were favoured by the Spanish aristocracy. The technique soon spread across Europe; it was a way of producing fabric and clothing in the home using the most basic of technology and did not demand the more fine threads used for weaving cloth. Wool was also knitted, initially, as a cottage industry and later by machines in factories; it was used mainly for making socks and cheaper stockings. The best stockings were made by knitting silk; Queen Elizabeth I wore only hand knitted silk stockings. Woollen yarn was also used to make tapestry wall hangings which were popular in the castles and manors of the middle ages.

Medieval jewellery, for those with wealth and power, was made from gold, silver and precious gems whereas for the less well-off copper and pewter were the usual metals used. These items were made to stand out against the coarse dark fabrics of the time and displayed a quality of workmanship, considering the tools and technology available, which was quite astonishing. Cosmetics, although actively discouraged by the clergy during this period, remained popular with the wealthy.

The quality, availability and cost of clothes, jewellery and make-up has always reflected each historical period and the social status of the women, and to a lesser extent the men. Technological improvements decreased the prices and increased the range and quality. Social fashions and sometimes restrictions drove or limited their adoption.

Apart from a few scribes and the like, for most, work was manual. It depended on physical labour which, because of his greater size and strength, was the forte of the male. Even after the invention and adoption of machines, men did the heavy work, normally as hired labour. Some, might be skilled – as a stone mason, wheelwright or blacksmith – some, might work on the land or as labourers. And, as frequently happened in this era, most of the men were taken off to fight in someone else's war as and when it was deemed appropriate. Women, meanwhile, did the generally less physically arduous work – in kitchens, cleaning and on the land; though, by today's standards, we would consider it a harsh lifestyle. Between them the couple would also try to raise some kind of produce for their family. It was literally a 'hand to mouth' survival.

A woman's position in society was totally subservient to men. Being 12years old was the accepted norm for a girl to be ready for sex, to get married or at least to begin breeding, although it was known that childbirth before the mid-teens was more dangerous. And these ages did not only apply to the poor; royals and nobility followed the same practices. Some women, but certainly not all, were treated little better than cattle. Women were even sold; only a few hundred years ago there were still 'wife sales' – events much like cattle auctions. A nagging wife could be forced by her husband to wear a 'scold's bridle' (an iron headpiece with a metal plate entering her mouth to restrain her tongue and often with a barb on it) and be paraded in public. A woman who killed her husband was not committing murder but the offence of Treason and, if found guilty, could be burned at the stake.

Life was unbelievably severe in the period sometimes known, and not without good reason, as the Dark Ages. Take, for instance, the ferocious campaign which became known as 'The Harrying of the North'. In 1066, the Battle of Hastings caused the death of King Harold and the defeat of the English army by William the Conqueror's Norman army. The Normans took over England and ran the country from their bases in the south of England. Soon afterwards, some of the Norman troops rode north to convert and subdue the northern barbarian hoards. But, the northerners repelled the Norman army and slayed many of them. As a result, rebellion soon spread around England – as far south as Devon. The Normans were badly defeated by the rebels on several occasions and in various parts of the country but then retaliated and killed all of their opponents they could find in an effort to quell these local uprisings.

The Harrying of the North was carried out by William the Conqueror to rout and to subjugate the Anglo – Dutch – Viking population in the north of England. This indigenous population had lived in an area north of an imaginary line drawn between the Humber Estuary and Liverpool and up to the Scottish border region. The north was remote from the south by virtue of the poor road systems and their condition – mainly as a result of the local geography. Thus, the sea route was the preferred method of trade and of transporting goods between the north and the south.

During the winter of 1069–1070 William's army attacked the northern rebels. They arrived, not by the sea route as may have been expected, but by marching north on the roads. His army destroyed crops, animals and food stores; they burnt villages to the ground and slaughtered all the inhabitants of all ages; men, women and children. The few who had somehow escaped the killing would have been condemned to a death by starvation because there was no food left. The population of the whole of England at that time was just over two million; 100,000 people, in total, were estimated to have been killed by the Normans. Twenty years later the Doomsday Book officially recorded vast areas of the north as 'wastelands'. From then on, the Normans ruled the whole of the north of England. Perhaps this was the origin of the modern north-south divide.

To put this into perspective with our modern 21st century life-style: if you accept the average lifespan to be about 70 years, this all happened just 13 lifetimes ago. Nowadays, when we hear of atrocities like this anywhere in the world we are outraged by their barbarity and there is worldwide condemnation; the perpetrators would be prosecuted in international courts.

It was in 1348, towards the end of the Middle Ages, that the Black Death arrived in Bristol. It was, at this time, England's largest port and our second city, after London whose population was almost 100,000. Within two years the Black Death had spread across most of the country and into Ireland. Overall, it killed nearly 50 per cent of the population and in some places almost wiped out entire villages and towns. As a consequence there was a severe dearth of labour in every sector and as a direct result of that wages went up to attract workers. This bade well for women who were fit, able and willing to do the work which had erstwhile been solely the province of men. They immediately gained both financially and in status – although it seems that this was not sustained for very many years and fell back as young males became old enough and strong enough to work and thus to displace the women.

Ever since the Black Death there had been intermittent bouts of plague-like deaths; there was still no sanitation and the streets of towns and cities were strewn with human and animal excrement. Although its severity was less than that of the Black Death, the Great Plague (1665–1666) still had, in many places, almost halved the population and labour was in short supply. The Plague killed priests and clergy just as frequently as it killed the parishioners; the Bishop of Bath could not raise enough priests to hear confessions and extended the duties of priests to ordinary parishioners or, in extremis, he would allow women to hear confessions; 50 per cent of children died before they reached their 15th birthday. This tragedy was then followed by the Fire of London which occurred between 2nd–6th September 1666; one sixth of the population of London died and 13,000 buildings were destroyed. In those days there were 20,000 shops in London and the population was around 700,000 which was one in 10 of the whole population of England.

By the mid-18th century manufacturing and some agricultural production was already beginning to be mechanised. The division of labour between men and women, both paid and unpaid, had varied little over time. One of the big differences was that agricultural work was seasonal and thus it was neither continuous nor well paid. On the other hand, factory work was a constant source of better paid employment. Men did the heavier work and were frequently appointed as the supervisors whilst the women worked on the looms and carding machines. Life expectancy was still fairly short with disease and injury both prevalent. The majority of the women were under 30 years old and would often leave their youngest children in the care of the grandmother who would, of necessity, become the substitute carer for much of the time thus allowing the parents to work. There were also women who stayed at home and took other working women's children into their houses in exchange for payment – in an early form of crèche, just as we see today.

Life for the more wealthy woman was somewhat different; it revolved around their social life. They lived in overtly sumptuous surroundings and wore beautiful clothes. From the 17th century, with the advent of softer, more sophisticated fabrics manufactured in a wide range of colours and designs, jewellery styles developed and there was a fashion to replicate foliage and floral shapes. New technologies had also allowed better enamelling techniques and advances in the cutting of gemstones; the 'brilliant cut' diamond was seen for the first time in the mid-1700s. It was also the fashion, for a while, for small jewels and other adornments to be sewn onto dresses. A sun tanned skin was seen as a sign that you were so poor that you had to work in the fields and thus the highest fashion dictated as pale a skin as possible; white powder, often made from lead and arsenic derivatives, was liberally applied to exposed skin and other make-up applied on top of this early form of foundation.

Looking at contemporary records, www.british-genealogy.com estimates that at least 3 per cent of teenage girls and young women became pregnant and gave birth out of wedlock – usually hoping or expecting to marry the father before the child was born but frequently, and for quite a variety of reasons, this did not happen. Having been born a 'bastard' imposed both legal and social exclusions; it also reflected on the mother and her family. This social situation is referred to in the writings of both Dickens and Anthony Trollope amongst others. In the 18th century illegitimacy in the mill towns of the north rose but so did marriage – and at younger ages than before; this was an urban phenomenon. The girls were part of a relatively well paid workforce and by continuing to work after the birth of their baby they could afford to pay someone else to look after the child. In rural areas or where there were no factories having a child out of wedlock and not subsequently marrying the father was a social and financial disgrace.

For those working and living in service it was a disaster; they would lose both their job and their accommodation. Therefore, the number of new-born babies taken to the foundling hospitals or abandoned on the steps of churches was very large. Even during the Victorian era one quarter of all babies born did not live to see their first birthday and half of those surviving babies did not live beyond 15; disease and accidents were rife.

With money, a woman's life could be much more pleasant; they could enjoy their leisure and dress in ways which reflected their social status. As time advanced, women had more and more designs of jewellery available to them; many were very expensive pieces but, eventually, there were also ones using cheaper materials which could be more readily afforded. The only limits were the artisan's skills and his client's purse. Because of the high value of gold, silver and gemstones, as fashions changed jewellery would often be melted down and reformed into new styles. For much of the mid to late 19th century fashions changed and became more 'sober' and any make-up, other than a light dusting of pale foundation, was out of fashion; rouge was associated with being provocative and thought to denote being a 'lady of the night'.

By the early 19th century the Industrial Revolution was really taking hold; new roads were being built for the first time since those created by the Romans, canals were being dug, and more and more machines were being invented and used in manufacturing and farming. The horse, as it had been for centuries, remained a highly important source of power and motive force. These developments may have reduced some of the reliance on human physical strength, particularly in factories and mills, but certainly not all of it.

Before the early 1700s there had been numerous small commercial mills manufacturing woollen fabrics using large hand weaving looms but soon, due to the numerous technical advances of the mid to late 18th century, water-driven mills were positioned alongside the fast flowing streams and rivers of the Pennines. Mills were becoming ever larger and their products, being more fine and more evenly woven, found ready markets. The workforces were drawn from the towns and villages and destroyed the home weaving culture. By the beginning of the 19th century there were numerous large steam-driven, coal-fired, mills whose location was no longer dependent for their source of power on being next to flowing water. These large mills carried out all the pro-cesses, including chemical dyeing, required to produce quality woollen cloth in huge quantities; one machine could produce over fifty yards of cloth a day and, each worker looked after numerous machines. Mainly via the docks in Liverpool, English woollen fabrics and products were shipped all over the world – at the rate of 1,000 tons per day or, ten thousand loaded ships per year.

The return cargo for the ships exporting English woollen cloth and other products was often cotton; initially, it was manufactured cotton from India and later just the raw material for processing and manufacture, mostly in the north of England. Eventually, cotton would be sourced from the southern states of America. The cold, damp climate of the north of England was of benefit to the manu-facturing process as it meant that the fine filaments of cotton were less likely to snap under pressure than in warmer, drier climates. Cotton was soon very popular because of its cheapness, light weight, its ability to take colour and patterns and, because it was easier to launder than either linen or wool.

The mindless, automated pace of these machines was of incalculable benefit for the factory owners; they determined and drove the rate at which work was done. Profit was the proof of the potency of the manufacturing process. The mill owners made fortunes.

The mill workers, including the children, had a hard life. It wasn't until the 1833 Factory Act that children under nine were no longer allowed to work in the mills; children up to 13 could work a maximum of nine hours and those up to 18, 12 hours. Later, children of eight to 13 were only allowed to work a half-day of six and a half hours. The small children were really useful at working under the machines, keeping the area clean and retrieving missing items. Because the parents needed the income from their children's work they often colluded with the factory owners so that the children could work outside the law; there were few factory inspectors so most of them got away with it most of the time.

The regular money that could be earned by working in a factory in a city was much greater than in the countryside. Money was a tremendous incentive to work in industry as opposed to on the land. At the beginning of the 19th century about a fifth of England's population already worked in factories in cities from Manchester to London; by 1850 it was almost 50 per cent of the population. And industrialisation was having an effect on every town throughout the land and throughout the industrialised parts Europe.

In an area of just half a square mile in east London there were 2,000 prostitutes known to the police. In cities, far from familial roots, it is easier to be anonymous or to reinvent yourself and thus to enjoy greater promiscuity without condemnation. This post-Industrial Revolution behaviour caused a shift in morals. As production increased so reproduction increased; there were more mouths to feed. All these people massed together in urban conurbations needed food but had neither the time nor space to grow their own. Thus an industry built up in bringing produce from the countryside to people in the towns and taking away the unwanted by-products. In London, Thames barges brought food produce from the east coast counties to the capital and took away mountains of horse manure from the streets.

In cities, homes could not be heated by wood; we did not have enough trees to feed the demand, wood needs seasoning before it is good to burn and wood is too bulky to easily transport. Coal became the standard fuel for heating and cooking. It was less smoky than wood but, we now know that its smoke was more dangerous, it contained tiny carbon particles which were easily inhaled and would have been very bad for health. These particles were drawn into the lungs and caused respiratory disease. Consumption was a prevalent disease; it is now believed that the ingestion of carbon particles from coal dust was a major contributor to the increase in incidences of consumption. This is evidence which has come to light as a result of modern technological research.

By the mid-1800s the railway was beginning to provide a faster and cheaper system of transport than canal barges or horse-drawn carts. It moved people around the country quickly and easily, be it over short or long distance and, it provided women a form of escape from their immediate environment without the need for a male to drive a horse-drawn carriage.

Children had a vital part to play in the new industries; they would often be alongside a family member as they learned the routine and worked all day, just like the adults. Sunday was the only day off – for children in particular.

Robert Raikes (1736–1811), the editor of the *Gloucester Journal*, was credited as being the founder of the 'Sunday Schools' movement. His scheme used the Bible as the educational tool and was supported by members of his local Church of England clergy but it was he who funded four women, including a Mrs Meredith, to act as the teachers – initially in their own homes. He wrote articles about his scheme and had them published in various newspapers and journals in London and around the country. The idea quickly spread and became a church based, nationwide network of Sunday Schools. In 1811, the year of Raikes' death, the National Society for the Promotion of Education of the Poor in the Principles of the Established Church was formed; it still exists today but is known as The National Society. It is said that the majority of children attended a Sunday School and that the movement had a total of five million beneficiaries thanks to the auspices of both the 'Church of England' and the non-conformist churches. In 1870, The Education Act made education compulsory for all children between the ages of 5 and ten. The pay for teachers was poor and, because men could earn more in other forms of employment, women became the mainstay of the teaching profession.

The dexterity of women (and too frequently children) could be a useful attribute in looking after the 'lighter' requirements of the machines. Thus, mothers would work in the factories all day, every day. Men did the heavier work or became the overseers or supervisors. As ever, when thought vital, the majority of the men were sent to fight wars. In their absence, their work did not stop; women adopted most of their men's roles.

In the mid-1800s shipbuilding for the English navy was changing from wood to iron. As they learned new skills and tried new methods, the workers were subjected to many new types of injuries. The environment was hot, dirty, noisy and dangerous. When Charles Dickens visited the dockyard at Chatham to see the building of the new iron ships, he described it as 'a living hell'.

Because their new found skills were in such demand the workers were highly valued and therefore well paid.

However, frequently injuries resulted in absence from work and a subsequent loss of production; and, there was no NHS or Social Security as a safety net for the workers. In those days medical help was often from friends and family or unqualified amateur physicians because the cost of being treated by a trained and qualified doctor or surgeon was beyond the means of any working man. Both employer and employee would be the losers in the event of injury.

So, the national government took a new and radical step at Chatham dockyard in dealing with the workers' injuries and their consequences. Their strategy comprised two levels: firstly, the surgeons of the Royal Navy, who had an enviable reputation, would treat all the dockyard workers' injuries. Secondly, workers who were temporarily unable to work as a result injury, and who were likely to return to work in the dockyard, were given half-pay during their absence. Most of the injuries were caused by heavy sheets of iron, hot components and processes, and shards of iron penetrating the skin and the eyes. Thus, the doctors had to find new methods of treatment and surgery. A shard of metal through the skin or, more urgently, in the eye needed immediate and innovative intervention. Pulling with tweezers was not the answer. Necessity became the mother of invention; a hand-held magnet, of great power, was created to draw the iron shard from the body or eye of the patient. It employed non-invasive surgery, no pulling and tugging; the shard could exit the patient via the same route that it had entered.

This was the first instance of healthcare being sponsored by the national government albeit that it was initiated for their own benefit and was only available to the male employees. It was almost a hundred years after medical and financial benefits were first offered to the workers at Chatham dockyard that they became available to everyone through the National Health Service and the Social Security benefits system. Yet another instance of war instigating invention and social change.

The Quakers, or Society of Friends, which has its origins in the middle of the 17th century, advocates peace, equality, truth and simplicity which they have brought about by adopting a charitable attitude to their dealings with the rest of the world. There are many Quakers who have been influential and whose names are part of our British culture. They include the confectionery manufacturers Cadbury, Rowntree and Fry; biscuit manufacturers Jacob and Carr; Clark's shoes; Sturge and Pease, associated with the first commercial railway from Stockton to Darlington; the builder of the world's first iron bridge and the origins of the bankers Lloyds, Barclays and Friends Provident. The evangelist churches, such as the Methodists, and the Church of England also gained a higher profile in relation to charitable giving and acts of philanthropy during the 19th century.

Since the mid-Victorian era there had been some of these factory owners who appeared more enlightened and benevolent than their peers by providing things such as new housing estates with facilities as diverse as open spaces, libraries and swimming pools. However, this may not have been such a philanthropic gesture as it may at first appear. Perhaps it was just that they had realised that if you looked after workers they would be more compliant, that you would get better productivity; and that made good commercial sense. Just like keeping a wheel greased so that it will turn for longer, and run quieter and smoother.

Of course, women worked too; mainly in service, in offices and at light, and sometimes not so light, factory work. For both men and women working in service had, since the early 19th century, been the third biggest employer in England – after working in the factories and the mills of industry – and in agriculture. Women worked to keep families alive; not as a lifestyle choice, not just for luxuries. But, there were more luxuries available to women due to a combination of improving technology and a change away from the austere Victorian fashions. As the 20th century dawned, advances in the production of cosmetics made them more affordable and that helped them to regain their popularity. With the exception of the periods during both World Wars when there was a dearth of these products, the use of cosmetics has flourished as time has advanced; the range of products and their availability has grown ever greater whilst their relative cost continues to diminish. It has been exactly the same story with both clothing and jewellery.

The First World War (1914–1918) was to affect everyone in Europe and many beyond. Killing technology had not advanced greatly since the previous century so it was reliant on men with rifles and heavy guns pulled by horses, plus the new guns capable of firing rapidly. In the Battle of the Somme, which was just one of many actions in the First World War, there were over one million heavy shells used – plus all the small arms ammunition. A total of one million men were said to have perished as a result of just this one battle. Our ammunition was manufactured in the UK by women working in munitions factories – doing work erstwhile done by men. Whilst ever grateful for the armaments, it did not go unnoticed that 30 per cent of these munitions failed to function properly (or not fire at all) due to poor manufacturing and quality control. It was a cause of frustration to the troops that they were trying to fight with 'dud' ammunition. But, however unjustly, it also proved to be a boost to the self-worth for those men in the trenches with little else to cheer them – that the women, when left to do a man's job, were not entirely up to it!

Mechanised transport was rare. This was to be the first time tanks were ever used in battle – and they were British; horses were used for just about everything else. There were many battles which were long stalemates fought from the trenches where neither side lost or gained much in the way of territory – but in which many men died. By the end of this four year war 10 million men were estimated to have been killed. The effect on the countries involved of losing most of a generation of young men was immense. They were all someone's sweetheart, husband, father, son or brother. Towards the end of the war, Spanish Influenza struck Europe. In just one year it killed more people than had died in four years of the Black Death. Between early 1918 and 1920 it is estimated to have killed over 50 million people worldwide. The First World War had killed approximately 17 million soldiers and civilians. In the UK a quarter of the population were estimated to have been infected at some level with fatalities of at least 225,000 civilians and 30,000 troops. Whilst we hear much of the two World Wars few remember the devastating effects of the 'Spanish Flu'; history seems to have almost erased it.

Then came the Second World War and again, just like during the First World War (and all those wars for centuries before), the men who were deemed fit went off to fight and the women took over the once male dominated workplace producing both armaments and the absolute necessities of a wartime life. An often overlooked statistic is that 500,000 females were also conscripted into the forces during the Second World War and there were, in total, an estimated seven million women working in some direct way towards the war effort.

This war relied much more heavily on technology than the previous one. Little need for horses – transport was mechanised. Planes were no longer made from wood, paper and string and used just for reconnaissance; they were fast killing machines, some capable of firing automatic machine guns, others of carrying tons of bombs. And they could fly far into enemy territory and still have the fuel to get home. Army tanks were large, speedy and had immense firepower. Guns of all types were more reliable, could fire further and faster. Communication was via radio – not a man on horseback nor even a pigeon.

The conflict spread through Europe and around the world; with new and sophisticated methods of waging war and killing people the death toll by the end of the war was estimated to be 55 million globally. There were 50,000 men in Bomber Command alone during the Second World War and most, aged only just in their early twenties, were killed. They trained on, and usually fought in, smaller fighter aircraft before transferring to bombers. The majority of the fatalities and casualties of war were men of working age.

For the six years of war, women worked alongside those men not conscripted into the armed forces and tilled the land to feed the nation, made bombs and bullets and aircraft and everything else a country needs to survive during a war. At Bletchley Park, women were used, by preference, as researchers for the decoding work necessary for the Enigma machine. When the war was over, those men who had survived to return to the UK, and were still able to work, returned to their former jobs. The women – often reluctantly – returned to more mundane work or to the home. It was seen that a job was the right of a returning hero.

For that generation life must sometimes have seemed unfair. The Second World War during that century had not long ended, they had fought in it, lost comrades along the way and now, as the victors, they had to exist on rations for almost a decade. Not the hero's return of their imagination.

To have good health, the security of a job for life, and to have a pension too, were the greatest things any working man could ask for; and, a time of peace. That all, eventually, came about; as did the National Health Service, Social Services and the benefits system. According to the Office for National Statistics, in 1900 the 'Life Expectancy at Birth' (approx.) was 45 years for men and 48 years for women; in 1945 it was 58 years for men and 63 years for women; in 2010 it was 79 years for men and 83 years for women. The end of the Second World War in 1945 and the return of the soldiers created what was to become a 'baby boom'. With lots of children growing up in a safe world there was hope.

Things had changed; and the war had, directly or indirectly, caused many of these changes. Nothing develops technology like war. Men had travelled and seen things; Americans had bases in the UK and were provided with all the attributes of their lifestyle 'back home'. As rationing became less stringent, society began to feel more egalitarian, technology made more things available and at a price that was not always out of reach of the ordinary family.

Work in the home had always been hard; apart from, perhaps, a gas cooker instead of a solid fuel range there were almost no domestic appliances in British homes; washing clothes meant using a 'copper', a large water filled metal bowl with a fire under it, bringing the water almost to boiling before a bar of hard soap was used for scrubbing clothes clean by hand. Because the work was so arduous and domestic staff so cheap to employ, many middle-class homes had a servant or two.

It was not until the end of rationing that refrigerators, electric kettles, toasters, washing machines and vacuum cleaners started to become readily available. These domestic appliances helped to reduce women's traditional 12-hour daily drudge of keeping a home clean and feeding a family. Now women had more time and more energy; more opportunities, more options.

Slowly people went from having a wireless to having a television (black and white in those days), a car or a motorcycle combination instead of a bike and public transport, a telephone for some, and new houses all had inside toilets. Even if you couldn't have these new things right now you knew you would probably be able to have them soon. And there was the 'never-never', the beginnings of people buying things on credit and without the same social stigma as before the war. As Harold MacMillan, the then Prime Minister, said in 1957, 'most of our people have never had it so good'. Things were different; almost everything had changed or was changing. For the children born in that post-war baby boom anything seemed possible. Whether, in the longer term, things will be deemed to have really been better – or just different, only history will tell us. Since the end of the Second World War we have enjoyed the longest ever period of sustained peace in Europe.

But, there was still a generation alive who had spent most of their lives before this headlong rush into the future. They had lived through the First World War and seen family and friends killed; they had struggled through the financial quagmire of the depression in the 1930s, only to find themselves in the second World War of their lifetime. These were the generation of people who still held many of the reins of the country (in government, banking and industry) and as tightly as possible, afraid of the consequences of going too far too fast. So, it took the structures which control society longer to change their rules and regulations, their way of doing business, than it did for the 'man in the street' to change his mindset.

For young men excitement, freedom and adventure were often bought at a high price. In 1960 alone 14,000 young men were killed in motorcycle accidents. As a result of the antics of some young motorcyclists, generally known as Rockers because of their love of rock music, leather jackets were banned from coffee bars, pubs and shops. As a direct result, and in direct opposition to groups like the Hell's Angels, the 59 Club was formed as a Christian club for motorcyclists and helped redeem their image. Eventually, and after numerous bloody street battles between them, the Rockers were to be replaced by the newly emerged and fashion conscious Mods on their scooters.

Many of the older generation blamed each and every social or fiscal problem on the recent more covert relaxed attitudes towards both moral and ethical codes; a lack of respect for authority, the ending of conscription; the easing of divorce laws. They thought that television had brought a new and not always positive perspective into more and more homes.

But, whatever the negatives some might wish to attribute to 'progress' there was radical but really quite positive change happening in society by the time the 1960s were upon us. Once, there had been very strictly observed lines drawn between the classes, between genders; between what was acceptable behaviour and what was not; what was morally right and what was morally wrong. Now, almost inexplicably, more and more people were adopting a more liberal and indeed more liberated lifestyle.

By the 1960s women's lifestyles were changing radically – through technological advances and improved wages leaving families with more disposable income. Not only were there new machines capable of reducing much of the arduous or tedious work in the home – and in the kitchen in particular – but, since the end of rationing, basic foods had become more readily available and now manufacturers were creating new food products to tempt the housewife. A survey done in the 1960s revealed that 70 per cent of married women were stay-at-home housewives. If at all possible a woman, ideally, needed to be at home; looking after her family; shopping – and shopping was all in small individual shops, spread across the often wet and windy town – preparing the food and cooking it, washing and ironing, and cleaning. Even with her new appliances, it was a day-long series of arduous and boring tasks; all day, every day, and that meant seven days a week.

The new foods were appealing on two levels; they brought new flavours and textures, which was a positive experience for all the family and, because they often did not need much preparation and were easy to cook, they helped to release women from some of their drudgery. But, these products were not that cheap to buy and up until the mid-1960s the prices of food, drink and other household necessities had their retail prices fixed by the manufacturers; there was no competition between retailers based on price, no discounts, no economies of scale. Shopping had always necessitated visits to numerous small shops each with its own restricted range of products. Whilst the likes of Sainsbury's and Tesco already existed and were expanding the size of their stores there were no large supermarkets – not as we know them now. In December 1961, Tesco had opened the first proper supermarket, in Leicester; it was the largest one in Europe. Even with their immense buying power Tesco were not allowed by law to discount the retail price of the manufactured goods which they sold. They, and other vested interests, lobbied the government. Ted Heath, the then President of the Board of Trade, convinced the government of the benefits of ending retail price fixing. By 1964 the Resale Prices Act was enacted. Retailers, for the first time ever, were allowed to sell a manufacturer's products at a discount on the 'recommended retail price'.

The benefit for the government was that living costs appeared to have reduced during their time in office. The big retail players, with their superior buying power had created a whole new consumer experience with a vast range of products, most of which were discounted, and in one location – no more traipsing around the town to individual shops in the wind and rain. Another massive step in releasing women from some of their workload. For those having to shop with their children alongside them the problems associated with 'pester power' began. For all the benefits of supermarkets for the housewife, by the end of the decade smaller shops were beginning to close. Nowadays, 14 per cent of the entire workforce is employed at some level in the groceries retailing business. With more disposable income and a greater range and availability of food the public developed a willingness to try new things and thereby helped to support the emergence of small restaurants in every town. These establishments had not existed to any very great extent before but now eating out became an affordable 'treat' and a culinary adventure. The cuisine was both national and international with Italian, Chinese and Indian becoming favourites; this helped to spawn the development of takeaway food establishments, the first real alternative to fish and chips. Hairdressers proliferated as women used their spare time and money to pamper themselves; new coffee bars and tea rooms became social meeting places – although a woman would never enter a pub unless accompanied – because pubs could legally refuse to serve an unaccompanied woman (because she would be considered as likely to be a prostitute touting for business) and non-food shopping became an enjoyable diversion.

Some middle-class women were apparently actively choosing independence; no longer satisfied to be 'just' mothers and/or housewives, they made a lifestyle choice to go out to work – usually as well as, rather than instead of, being a home-maker, wife and mother. People wanted 'things' which they had been convinced (by the influences of television, radio, magazines and other advertising) would bring them eternal happiness.

Another massive set of technological advances which were to begin to revolutionise the lives of women in the 1960s and 1970s were the advances in contraception – the effects of which, I will look at in-depth in a later chapter. Also, women began to wear 'slacks', not just in the home at weekends but, out in the street and, eventually, to work. Nowadays, they may seem like almost laughably minor changes but at the time they were items worthy of extensive news coverage in the media. The fact was that society was no longer one, almost homogeneous, mass where individuals were afraid to be seen as being 'different'. Now you could more easily be whoever you wanted to be and to reflect this in your style of dress, as can be seen in film footage of people on the streets of London in the 1960s. However, the dress code for most businesses remained, much as it still does today, uniformly sober and uncontroversial. Society had become acquisitive – the various media advertised and promoted all the things that were now available and at the same time the apparently appealing lifestyle of those with money, especially 'new money', was highlighted in the press. We wanted some of the same – whatever the cost.

In modern times governments have provided easy money for people. The initial intention was good – financial support for the elderly and those unable to work through illness or temporary unemployment – but, over time, some people have seen it, and used it – as a source of income without the necessity to work. Manipulation of the system, untruthful information being used in form filling and dishonesty at any level all being useful steps in securing this financial benefit. Don't get me wrong, for those with a genuine need it has become an essential source of income and is a reflection of a caring society.

There is, according a joint paper published by the Uppsala University, Sweden and the Ministry of Finance of the Swedish government, a direct correlation between the amount of benefit paid – relative to the national wage – and the rate of unemployment. The greater the social benefit and the easier the access to it, the higher the unemployment rate. It is a phenomenon which can be found in countries across Europe and the other structured economies of the world.

Countries like Spain and France have large numbers of people claiming benefits. It makes a large drain on the public purse – over 50 per cent of government spending. To pay for it, the employer's contribution to the state is around 50 per cent of the employee's salary – a wage of a 1,000 euros means the employer must pay 500 euros to the state for social contributions for that employee. Because it is so expensive to employ people, he keeps his workforce as small as possible and looks for other ways to cut costs whilst still producing his goods and services. Meanwhile, with high outgoings on social benefits and a low tax revenue from a smaller workforce and less profits from companies, the government struggles to survive. With much time and little to do, a claimant's boredom is expressed in social unrest, the black economy and crime thrive and these cause the government to spend money combating them. It is a vicious circle.

In countries with high levels of benefit and low levels of social stigma the number of single mums rises dramatically. In some Scandinavian countries over half of all children are born out of wedlock whilst in countries like Italy, where the social benefit system does not offer such strong support of single mums and where there is a social stigma against having children out of wedlock, the numbers are substantially lower.

For some, mobility was upward and onwards – geographically, financially and socially. For another, less fortunate, sector of the workforce the spiral was in a less positive direction. For every action there is an equal and opposite reaction. In the manufacturing workplace automation had increased productivity and profitability but, at the expense of the jobs of less skilled workers. Overall, it was certainly a good thing that so many heavy, dirty, dangerous and monotonous tasks could be eliminated. At the same time other countries with much cheaper labour costs and manufacturing overheads were evolving, their presence felt by their undercutting the prices of our own domestic producers. Men's (and it mostly was men's) jobs were becoming less secure. As one generation was looking forward to retiring gracefully another generation was looking to have to re-skill, move industry and often to be forced to move towns. The unions rebelled on behalf of their workers; there was industrial unrest and there were strikes. It was the same in offices; initially secretaries gave way to the dictating machine, then typing pools disappeared as typewriters gave way to word processors, carbon paper and duplicator machines disappeared as photocopiers arrived, telephone switchboards became automated, the need for filing, and paperwork in general, began shrinking as the 'paperless society' became, if not an immediate reality, a more likely future.

So, is the rapid change in the structures of both employment in particular and of society in general, which we have seen evolving in the last 50 years, merely a consequential and inevitable reaction to the benefits conferred by our continually advancing technology? Have these changes, in themselves, afforded an unforeseen opportunity for their own manipulation to allow us to gain more control and thereby to satisfy some latent urge to re-order society at both a class and a gender level? Were these changes, and would future changes, be male or female centred? Have these changes, and the subsequent aspirations, caused or just permitted a 'sea change' in perceived gender roles and values, and if so how? Or, conversely, is it merely a coincidence that an organic change in society has been brought about at this exact same time by an unrelated evolution in general attitudes?

I would suggest that it has been as a result of the technological advances since the end of the Second World War that changes in social constructs have occurred and that these have allowed the potential for the re-ordering of some gender roles to become a reality. Further, that before these latest developments in social structures and in technology, it would not have been credible for society to even begin to imagine the possibility of changing in such a way or at such a speed as it has done since the mid-20th century. One facet of the social structures I refer to is that which created both the National Health Service and the social benefits system – both initiated in the late 1940s. Between them they have formed a safety net, a social 'insurance' for those whose lives fall upon hard times; an unexpected consequence has been their developing ability to allow people to make lifestyle changes without them being constrained by financial issues. Before this, as it still is in most countries around the world, having lots of children was a necessity. Also, more reliable methods of contraception allowed pregnancy to be planned, controlled.

The traditional reason for large families was twofold – firstly, women needed to bear lots of children because the survival rate of babies into adulthood was so poor; and secondly, all families needed plenty of young, fit adults. This new generation would then become the financial and practical carers for those of their own family members who became unable to work for age or health related reasons; each new generation would be responsible for providing for, and caring for, the older generation as they became infirm. This is still the reality in certain parts of the world today.

Thus, gradually, since the beginning of the 1960s, there has been less pressure on women to produce lots of babies. Those babies they did have were more likely to survive because of the level of healthcare available to all; and, for adults in general, pensions and benefits became the financial safety net instead of the support of family members. Statistics from the National Centre for Biotechnology Information states that in England in the later part of the 19th century families with six or more children were commonplace – and they had no domestic appliances; by the 1930s, they say, the number had dropped to around three and nowadays two to three children is the norm. Thereby, women have slowly been able to have more time and energy for other things. The extended family was no longer a practical necessity; it was losing its social value. Subsequent to these changes, women have started to become more self-assured, more assertive; they have made better use of the education system and taken on a wider range of occupations. Divorce laws have changed and now favour the women and the child carers, child-benefits have been created and increased, government support systems like the CSA were created. Whilst perhaps not a perfect set of systems, the advances in favour of women during the last 50 years are unparalleled.

Further, it is only from this 'new order', permitted by the advances generated by the current technological and sociological revolution, that there has come the potential of a more realistic chance for women to choose to have a greater participation in the control and organisation of workplaces and of the structure of western society in general. And, very interestingly, the early stages of this 'technological revolution' were, for the most part, initiated and developed by men for industrial applications. The ability for the subsequent technological advances to become used as catalysts for a female based reordering of social mores was an unintentional by-product.

It has been women who have taken advantage of the potential created by these technological advances to act as a springboard for revolutionary changes in equality in particular and society in general. These developments devalued the traditional strengths of men at every level. Our past reflects into our future.

CHAPTER 3
WOMEN'S SELF-DETERMINATION – THE EARLY DAYS

There have always been individual women, groups of women and even some men, who have made a stand against the sexist mores of our male dominated society. Some have been more high profile than others, some have been more successful than others; social status has always had a distinct advantage.

The trouble with identifying these women and their deeds is that all we have to rely on are a few contemporary documents, accounts, diaries, memoirs, newspaper reports– usually hidden in the storage vaults of museums – and history books; and, almost all of them have been written for and by men. There are also a few paintings and drawings but the artist's patron would have invariably been a man. And, men are not going to promote female dissension in a positive way.

Latterly, the camera has allowed an immediate and therefore a rather more truthful perspective of people and events.

Women have traditionally been expected to be subservient and to dedicate their lives to the needs and well-being of their menfolk first, and then to the remainder of their family and household. Doing anything other than that has always been thought of as antisocial and deviant.

Below are accounts of some notable individuals whose actions have been significant enough to be recorded.

Remember, these are not value-free observations and often say as much about the persons recording them and their values as they do about the women who are the subjects of the writings.

A is for Amazon

The Amazons were a mystical race of women warriors whose images have been seen in early Greek sculpture and on their pottery; there are stories of Greek encounters with them. Some believed them to be real, some thought that they were creatures of myth and legend; historically, there was too much smoke and not enough fire.

These Amazons are thought to have lived their nomadic life around 2000 years BCE and were based in the Black Sea, Pontus region in what was part of Persia and what we now call Anatolia in the Asian part of Turkey. Greek mythology says they were the daughters of Ares, and that Achilles, having attacked one of them in a battle of the Trojan Wars fell in love with her dying body. Some used to credit the word Amazon as being derived from the word 'Mazon meaning breast and the 'A' meaning without. The story was that they removed their own right breast to make it easier to fire their bows; there is no actual evidence to support this quite bizarre and rather fanciful theory. If the association with the word Mazon meaning breast has any credence it is likely to be the association of warriors with breasts. Even the contemporary representations of Amazons, most of which seem to have been created by their Greek opponents, show them with both breasts intact.

The Amazons were believed to be a man-hating, feminist sisterhood who only had occasional relationships with men so that they could breed. Girl children were then raised as trainee warriors and legend had it that they either killed the baby boys or gave them to their fathers. A more truthful perspective may have been that they practiced 'fosterage', an ancient custom of giving your son to a member of another tribe for them to bring up; it was a mark of trust and respect between both parties and had the benefit of reducing the incidence of incest by increasing the gene pool, and was treated in a not dissimilar way to arranged marriages. Sometimes cattle, horses or other livestock were also exchanged as part of the deal. Fosterage remained a normal practice across Europe, including in England, Scotland, Wales and Ireland until the middle ages. It is probable that the Amazons were actually a female warrior force which was a peripheral part of a larger heterosexual society. There were also other cultures of Amazon-like warrior women in Libya, India and China.

But now, with the benefits of modern methods of archaeology and anthropology, we have found burial sites, some not that far from the Pontus region of Anatolia, with artefacts which point to women warriors buried with their swords, daggers, double-headed battle axes and short bows with barbed arrows. Further excavations, and other evidence, shows that they were skilled horsewomen who fired their short bows and fought with their other weapons whilst riding on horseback; they had tattoos for decoration and status, drank a milk-based alcohol, smoked marijuana using a hot-boxing tent and wore trousers or leggings made from sewn fabric. In those days Greeks wore rectangles of cloth pinned together either as loin-cloths or as togas; leggings were a completely new phenomenon.

All this was found, according to The Smithsonian Institute and the *National Geographic*, in the 1990s joint Russian and American team excavation of numerous burial mounds called Kurgans near Pokrovka in the southern Ural Steppes near to the border with Kazakhstan. They found around 150 graves of warrior women buried with their weapons including bows, arrows and daggers and the other artefacts and in some cases with their horses. They are estimated to have been five feet six inches tall which makes them very tall for that time. About a third had 'battle wounds'. The overall area now seems to extend from the Black Sea through to Mongolia. In those days the general area would have been known as Scythia and their descendants were probably the Scythian speaking Samaritans. Greek legends had always placed them in that area (amongst many other areas) so these discoveries are tending to legitimize the credibility of many of the ancient legends of Amazons. The Queen of Sheba lived in what we now know as Ethiopia and allegedly had bands of female warriors. A significant number of modern Ethiopians apparently have up to a 50 per cent gene correlation with peoples from Europe Major (Caucasians). There is much historic evidence of African warrior queens from the 16th century like Queen Turunku from an area around modern Niger and Libya to Yaa Asantewaa (1850–1921) from Asante in Ghana who, until she was eventually captured, had a series of battles with the British. In 2006 archaeologists found a burial in Moche, Peru of a woman buried with war clubs and spear throwers. And now, we have modern Kurdish women fighting against the IS. For those interested to find further information on such matters there is a seemingly unending resource in Academia.edu the on-line platform for academic research papers (it is a dry collection, like an old-fashioned academic library but on-line – the clue is in the name) and also in the collected works of Eric Edwards.

In the 13th century BCE Lady Fu Hao, one of the many wives of the Chinese Emperor Wu Ding, was an army general of the Shang Dynasty. In her first notable campaign she led an army of 3,000 men into battle and later in her life, in a battle against the Ha people, she led an army of 13,000 men. Her burial chamber was filled with numerous weapons including a battle-axe.

In the 18th–19th century in Dahomey, West Africa (Benin) there was an army of Amazons (called Mino). They were the fully armed and dangerous bodyguard of each king and were 'notionally' his wives; each king usually had hundreds of wives. It was a highly trained, well-armed, well-paid, high status social position; most were virgins and they were not permitted to have sex with men.

They were sometimes women who had been the wives or daughters of prominent men who had 'donated' these particular women to the king's bodyguard. The size of the unit was variously estimated as anywhere between 1,000–5,000 women strong.

Queen Gwendolen

According to Geoffrey of Monmouth, in the 11th century BCE the British (Albion) Queen Gwendolen, the daughter of a warrior of King Brutus of Troy, fought her husband Locrinus, a son of the House of Brutus, in a battle for the throne. She won and so, allegedly, became the first female reigning British monarch.

Eleanor de Montfort

King John was an unpopular English medieval monarch and part of the Angevin dynasty whose ancestors originated from Anjou in France. He died in October 1216, a year after putting his seal on Magna Carta at Runnymede. The barons of the north and east of England had long disagreed with King John about the way he was trying to rule the country, their lack of autonomy and the taxes imposed on them and, as a result, a war ensued between the supporters of the king and those of the barons; it became known as the First Baron's War.

Magna Carta was essentially the King's peace agreement with the barons; it was never intended to have any effect on the poor. It stated that all 'free men' (not serfs) should be protected from illegal imprisonment, always have access to justice, that there should be no taxation without consent; and, that the King should not be above the law. From a female perspective, it allowed women of status who had been widowed or, in some cases, had been divorced, to keep their fair share of their husband's money for their own and their estate's upkeep. However, they were not allowed to marry thereafter without the specific agreement of the King. This gave him control of where the money went and when and how political and financial alliances were made. It was an extension of the concept of the 'Charter of Liberties' agreed between the baron's forebears and King Henry I a century before. At that time, parts of southern England were in the hands of King Philip of France, and later his son King Louis VIII. King John had spent most of his personal wealth and the money received from the taxes he had levied, in fighting wars.

King John's widow was Isabella of Angoulême, France. It had been a marriage of convenience, like most were; uniting lands, bringing wealth and forming links with other royal families. When they were married Isabella was just 12 years old with blue eyes and blonde hair; she was described as beautiful. The King was alleged to be besotted by her and to have spent most mornings, until lunchtime, in bed with her. Because she was already betrothed to the son of the Count of La Marche, King Philip II of France became so enraged that he confiscated their lands in France and as a consequence there was a war between the two nations.

His eldest son Henry, aged just nine years, succeeded him. He became Henry III; his adviser was King John's adviser, the elderly

– but, very wealthy – William Marshal (or, William the Marshal). Just like his father the young King was advised to keep his mother, Isabella, without sufficient funds to be able to do other than just survive, thus ensuring that she was unable to become a source of concern. Under French law she was not to have access to her personal family fortune in France as long as she was married to King John and living in England. As a result, the actuality was that, after his death, she spent most of her time in her homeland. Her children were brought up and educated in England by other families, subjects loyal to the King – a well-established system called fosterage – as was the norm for wealthy families in those days.

Although he signed the Great Charter of 1225 which limited his power, King Henry III continued to rule as before; he, like his father, was an unpopular monarch. In 1224 Henry's sister Eleanor, then aged almost nine, was married to William Marshal the Younger who was 25 years her senior and who was probably the wealthiest and most influential man in England. There would be great benefits for the King from this alliance. England was spending much on wars and needed cash. The marriage was short but apparently happy. William died in 1231.

Eleanor, now aged 16, took a religious vow of celibacy at Canterbury and accepted the 'Ring of Christ'. Eleanor was to be provided for by property given to her by the King and more property and income from the assets of the estate of her late husband, William Marshal. These types of settlement, a dower, were usual and widows in receipt of them were known as dowagers. She was potentially a very wealthy woman. However, the brother of her late husband denied her the dower. As a result, Eleanor had to borrow monies from Jewish money lenders to tide her over. She still had a retinue of staff and 15 properties to keep and was technically a Lord. She had to learn about agriculture, crops, stock and the farming year. Her 21st birthday present from her brother was Odiham Castle, a Royal residence in Hampshire built by their father, King John. She spent her days managing the estates, looking after the lands and her staff, at prayer and doing good deeds. In 1236 King Henry III married Eleanor of Provence. It was a political and financial marriage. She was 12 years old, he was 28. As time progressed she had five children. She was said to be the stronger personality of the two.

In 1238 Eleanor met Simon de Montfort, a member of a French noble family, at her brother's court. He had come to England to claim his rights to the Earldom of Leicester; his grandmother had been married to the previous Earl and the position was vacant. He was personable and was soon accepted by the King at his court. He originally pursued the daughters of two wealthy European kings but was rebutted. Eleanor was apparently feeling 'broody' and she was attracted to Simon de Montfort. They wanted to wed.

Although it would be marrying below her, brother King Henry agreed; but things were kept quiet because of her previous vow of celibacy. When news of the marriage became public it was not well received. So, Simon went to see the Pope with a considerable gift of money and eventually she was released from her vows and the marriage was ratified. Simon was granted the Earldom of Leicester, and Eleanor was pregnant. Simon went on a crusade for the King – partly in repayment of all the monies the King had spent on them because her dower had still not been settled. At one point Simon borrowed monies naming the King as surety. When the King and his advisers found out they were furious. The de Montforts were both accused of using their closeness to the King for their own advantage and, in a fit of temper, Simon was even accused of having seduced Eleanor. The King tried to imprison Simon in the Tower but he and Eleanor escaped to France, his homeland. They left their son Henry with another family; Eleanor was pregnant again.

It was after a period of two years and with the intercession of Henry's French mother that Simon and Eleanor were accepted back into the King's court and provided for. Simon was given a role as the governor of Gascony in France which was an English protectorate at that time. Simon, being French and having contacts and influence in France, made him the obvious choice. When not with him in France, Eleanor was running their estates in England; they had over 200 permanent staff and numerous properties.

Henry III had money problems; he was spending too much, particularly on his wife's French family and his French half-brothers.

He began to seek big rises in taxes in an effort to raise funds. This caused more friction with his subjects and with many of the barons. At the Oxford Parliament they moved to force the King to deport aliens – including his family members – as a way of lowering the Royal expenses. Twenty-four barons were involved and Simon was the key player. This was with the support of his wife Eleanor, the King's sister. Somehow, Simon and Eleanor had their continuing claim for Eleanor's still unpaid dower to be brought into the same negotiations. It had been a thorn in the side of both Eleanor and Simon and was, by then, getting to the stage of being a festering wound.

The wars with France, which had been ongoing since the days of King John, were probably the greatest drain on the Royal purse. Simon was appointed to try to negotiate a peace with King Louis IX, the French King. To Henry it seemed a logical appointment.

Part of King Louis' demands, before peace could be declared, included the lands in France currently controlled by members of the English royal family being returned to French ownership. King Henry assured King Louis that they would do so but Eleanor refused to return her lands. To her it was a potent lever to force the settlement of her dower – owed since the death of her first husband, Marshal, the interest on it, and the expenses incurred. The Treaty of Paris – as the war deal was known – was held up because of this. Feeling powerful, the de Montforts increased their demands to a point where the English King himself could not afford to pay them. But, in the end Henry did agree to pay his sister, the de Montforts capitulated, and so the Treaty was signed.

But, King Henry reneged on the deal with his sister and her husband; he did not pay them. He made promises, but never paid. Subsequently, the barons split into two factions; one supporting the King, another supporting Simon de Montfort and his group of 'Reformers'. War ensued – the Second Baron's War.

King Henry's forces took Dover Castle which belonged to the de Montforts; but, the King was soon to be defeated and captured, together with his brother Richard of Cornwall, at the Battle of Lewes. The eldest sons of each man, Lord Edward and young Henry surrendered themselves as hostages in lieu of their fathers. King

Henry's wife left France and returned to England to try to raise support for her husband and the royalist cause.

The royal hostages were the 'guests' of Eleanor – whilst Simon was elsewhere with the Reformers. She was trusted for her abilities and for being a motivated supporter of the cause. The 'guests' were moved around to make their rescue less likely. But, when not directly in Eleanor's care, Lord Edward managed to escape.

The Royalists had reorganised and were now pursuing the Reformers. Simon and his followers were cornered by an army of Royalists three times the size of his own. Lord Edward (later to become King Edward) was there and selected a group of 12 knights whose sole mission was to kill Simon and his eldest son Henry de Montfort – whatever the cost. After the death of Simon de Montfort and his son, the Royalists hunted down any Reformer they could find and killed them; they gave no quarter.

Eleanor de Montfort and her daughter fled to France and were soon joined by her sons. All Simon de Montfort's lands and properties in England – together with his title Earl of Leicester – were given to the King's grandson. Eleanor made retreat to a Dominican nunnery, founded by her late husband's sister, where she was to remain. With the support of the French King and Queen she continued to pursue her dower and other inheritances both in France and England. To her it was a matter of honour that she should receive that which she was entitled to and also it would provide for her children for their lifetimes.

A peace broker was sent from the English royal court to negotiate with the de Montfort children in Europe but he was killed, allegedly by the surviving brothers. They were pursued by the authorities and one was put under house arrest – but with a family member, another died of other causes and the third, who had spent his life as a religious recluse, had an alibi. In 1272 King Henry died and was succeeded by his son Edward. On his trips to France, King Edward met with Eleanor, his aunt, and agreed to give her funds and to pursue her Marshal dower on her behalf. Eleanor, the daughter of Simon and Eleanor de Montfort, married a long-term friend of the family from Wales; she became the first Princess of Wales. Eleanor de Montfort died at her nunnery in 1275, aged 60.

Eleanor was not unlike her formidable grandmother and namesake, Eleanor of Aquitaine, who had first been the wife of the French King Louis VII and then the English King Henry II. Eleanor de Montfort had also led the life of a strong woman; she was frequently taken advantage of by the actions or lack of action, of others. Her brother and her late husband Marshal's family had failed to honour her dower. She, and later her husband Simon de Montfort, pursued these honourable debts for all of their lives. As a result of the non-payment of the dower they had a permanent need for money which they tried to resolve however they could. For her time, she was a radical woman in taking on so very many male roles and male opponents; people had tried to treat her as insignificant just as they would have done to any ordinary woman. But Eleanor would not let the injustices done to her rest. She fought until her dying days for their resolution.

Virtually all of the records, which were written by and for her male opponents, agree on the facts and her pursuit of her just cause. They do not portray her as overbearing, grasping or demonic. She spent her life fighting for her family and for what she believed to be a righteous cause – the well-being of her children and their future. She used her connection to her brother, the English King, as a bargaining chip whenever she felt it necessary but, she fought adversity and did not lead or pursue an extravagant lifestyle for herself.

It is difficult to find another woman of such sustained strength and resolution in medieval England.

Even in royal households, women were to be subservient and were without rights; they were told how to behave and who to marry – they were chattels. Well dressed and elegant, but possessions of their menfolk and without redress to wrongdoings. It was frequently espoused that for a woman to disobey a man was a crime in the eyes of God. This God-fearing woman was not going to be made the servant of any man.

Jane Ingelby (1601–1651) was born at Ripley Castle, near Harrogate, North Yorkshire into a papist and staunchly Royalist family whose generations have lived there from 1309 to the present day. The family fought for the Royalist cause against the troops of Oliver

Cromwell in the First English Civil War (1642–1646). It was an often ferocious war which turned family member against family member and was responsible for killing one in 10 of all adult males in England and wounding many more (as a percentage of the adult male population that is five times more than were killed during the Second World War).

In 1644 Jane Ingelby disguised herself as a man, donned a suit of armour and went off to fight alongside her brother, Sir William Ingelby, for the Royalists in the nearby Battle of Marston Moor. Three hundred Roundheads and 3,000 Royalists were said to have died in that one battle. Defeated, the siblings returned home but were aware that the Roundhead troops would be looking for any Royalist soldiers. Sir William hid in the priest hole in their castle but Jane had no reason to hide as no-one would suspect that, as a woman, she had been fighting in the battle.

Oliver Cromwell came to Ripley Castle, the nearest house of substance, looking for Royalists, and for refreshment and rest. Fearing that Cromwell would search the castle, looking for her brother, Jane managed to keep Cromwell at bay in the library all night by sitting with him and guarding him, and her dignity, with two loaded pistols on her lap. In the morning Cromwell left – having not discovered Sir William. Ever since, because of her acts of bravery, she has been known as 'Trooper Jane'.

The Levellers

As the English Civil War (1642–9) was drawing to a close a new political movement came to the fore. Its highest profile members, John Lilburne, Richard Overton, Thomas Prince, Major John Wildman and William Walwyn, were educated middle-class men who advocated religious toleration, human rights and constitutional reform. Their demands included a new form of government based on a reformed House of Commons with an elected membership, abolition of the House of Lords, equality before the law for all men, for ordinary men (but not women) to have the vote, and for free trade. They wanted the MPs to be elected every two years by their constituents and for the constituencies to be of a similar size. These they said were Natural Rights – rights which had been enshrined in Magna Carta – and had been the accepted laws of the land since before the time of William the Conqueror but which had never been enacted. Had their demands been acceded to it would have given England a form of democracy. Thanks to the printing press, they were probably the first activist group to print leaflets; they were also the first to lobby Parliament and to gather signatures in a petition. John Lilburne was the first of them to be imprisoned – for criticizing MPs for living in comfort whilst poorly paid soldiers fought their battles for them. Needless to say, this gave the Levellers rising support for their cause from the army, whose pay was already in arrears. The consequences of a dissatisfied army and their potential for mutiny greatly worried Oliver Cromwell.

This group of would-be political and constitutional reformers became known as the 'Levellers' because many people mistakenly believed that what they really wanted was for a levelling of wealth, for it to be evenly distributed across society. A further misunderstanding, which acted to their disadvantage, was that there was another group known as the 'True Levellers' or 'Diggers', led by Gerrard Winstanley, who considered themselves true radicals. It was they who caused civil unrest in pursuit of their cause; they wanted land ownership for all men – through property rights being totally reformed. This got the Levellers an undeserved bad name and, as a consequence of monied society's paranoia about the potential loss of their property, their members were frequently harried and imprisoned.

When Charles I escaped imprisonment and headed towards France, Oliver Cromwell had a reason to get back at the army. There was a brief mutiny by army officers who formed the core supporters of the Levellers; this was quickly followed by the arrest of most of the alleged ringleaders and the death of one.

Eventually, after the trial and execution of Charles I, Cromwell established the Commonwealth and Protectorate and again the Levellers were in dispute with the Council of State of the Rump Parliament of the government. They were imprisoned as a result of their actions and demands; John Lilburne was sentenced to death.

Throughout their efforts to change the system and to enfranchise the ordinary man the Levellers were supported by their wives. When the men were in prison the women continued their menfolk's work whilst lobbying to get them released. These women were mothers and carried out these acts on behalf of their husbands whilst still looking after their families and their homes. We know that one, Catherine Chidley, was mother to seven children and had all the work which that entailed in those days as well as supporting her husband's cause whilst he was incarcerated.

The main female protagonists were Elizabeth Lilburn, Mary Overton and Catherine Chidley. Their initial demands reflected those of their husbands. For their troubles these and other middle and upper class members of the protest groups were publicly belittled but with their actual punishment left to the discretion of their husbands or fathers. For the middle and lower class members the punishments frequently included being beaten, imprisoned or even put into workhouses or mental institutions. Just like a modern political faction they held mass demonstrations, leafleted, created petitions and lobbied the MPs. This is the first recorded instance of women becoming involved in political agitation. Given the possible penalties and the social stigma it was an amazingly brave stance for these potentially vulnerable women to take.

Since 'The Lawes Resolutions of Women's Rights 1632' a woman's legal position depended solely on the goodwill of the dominant male of her household. The father – for a child or unmarried woman; the husband for a married woman. Otherwise, for instance, in the rare situation of a widow or unmarried woman who was not part of a household which had a man at its head, the law did not recognise her existence.

Because the main protagonists were well brought up and edu-cated women their documents were always very well written, the points well argued. They understood the political and social systems and how to best use them. One Eleanor Davies, a woman of some substance, had dared to criticize Charles I on several occasions and had been imprisoned for her effrontery. She subsequently wrote a book promoting women as worthwhile individuals in their own right; she paid for the book to be printed, published and distrib-uted. For her endeavours, she was convicted of 'circulation of false prophesies' and was given the then enormous fine of £3,000 and also imprisoned. It was in 1649 that the Leveller women raised a petition to Parliament which was signed by 10,000 women (in its day, this was a very large proportion of the female population of England) this time demanding equal rights for 'all classes' of women and equality with men. This was a first; a demand for emancipation for women. Sadly, it was rejected and no reform followed.

Mary Astell (1666–1731) was born in Newcastle upon Tyne into an upper middle-class family. Her father was the manager of a coal company; he died when she was just 12. He left provision for her brother's education but there was very little left for her and her mother's upkeep. Thus, her mother decided to live with an aunt. By the time she was 22 her mother and aunt had died. She then decided to move to Chelsea, London, where she had more affluent connections, to develop her writing skills. In London, there were influential people who were willing to act as her patrons and she soon made good social networks including with the Archbishop of Canterbury, William Sancroft, who assisted her financially and with developing her writing skills. In 1694 she published her work *A Serious Proposal to the Ladies for the Advancement of their True and Greatest Interest*; it promoted, amongst other things, the idea of a 'ladies only' academic college. A work of this nature would be controversial enough if published by a man but, for a woman to have an opinion, a dissenting opinion, was shocking. In 1700 she brought out *Some Reflections on Marriage* which looked at marriage from the point of view of a woman and she proposed that for a woman to have an education equal to that of a man would help to bring about a more equal partnership. Whilst she gained some support from Daniel Defoe she was satirised in *The Tatler* by Jonathan Swift – in part, because she was a woman who had never married. In 1709 she gained enough support to found a charitable girls-only school. Over time, she became more and more reclusive; she was diagnosed with cancer in her right breast and had a mastectomy, after which she remained in her room sitting alongside her own coffin until eventually she died. She is remembered as a free-thinking, cross-gender philosopher, writer and debater: the first English feminist. Her most famous line was: 'If all men are born free, how is it that all women are born slaves?'

Fanny (Frances) Burney (1752–1840) was born in what we now know as Kings Lynn. Her father was a charming and talented organist, musician, composer and writer who had moved there from London for health reasons. In 1760 he decided that it was time to return to London, initially to Soho and later to Westminster, for its social and financial benefits. When Fanny was just 10 her mother, a French emigré, died; her mother's life and death were to have a lifelong effect on her. Four years later her father married an old family friend from Kings Lynn; she was not well thought of by Fanny or the rest of the family. Fanny was seen as being plain, shy, serious and short-sighted. Unlike her siblings, Fanny was not formally educated, indeed she was considered a 'slow learner' but with the help of the playwright and family friend, Samuel Crisp, and her access to her father's extensive library, her education flourished. She wrote letters to Crisp and began to develop her own style full of humorous, satirical observations of the people and life she saw around her. Her first book Evelina was a sensational success, although it was published anonymously and her identity was hidden for some time. The book, just like her subsequent books *Cecilia* and *Camilla*, satirised the characters, lives and social mores of the aristocracy. She was feted by the likes of Joshua Reynolds, Sheridan, David Garrick, Edmund Burke, Jane Austen and Thackeray and by the socially influential 'Blue Stockings'. We know that her book *Camilla*, netted her £2,000 which was an enormous sum in those days. At the age of 34 and unmarried Fanny met King George III and Queen Charlotte and as a result was offered the position of 'Keeper of the Robes'. She accepted the role, believing that it would have a positive effect of her social position but, within a short time, was feeling stressed and unwell such that she had to ask to be relieved of the responsibility of the position. She received a small pension of £200 per annum (about £12,000 by today's values) and was able to maintain a good relationship with the royal family. At the time of the French Revolution (1789) she became friendly with a group of French exiles living in England. She soon began to be drawn to the penniless General Alexandre D'Arblay and against her father's advice they were married in 1793; her father did not attend the wedding. This was when she had her financial success with her book *Camilla*; the funds allowed them to have a house built to their specification which they called 'Camilla Cottage'. In 1801 Alexandre was offered a position of service with the French government under Napoleon Bonaparte; they moved to live on the outskirts of Paris. Soon after, France and England were at war; for a period of almost 10 years she was an exile herself in a hostile country and had no access to either her family or her monies.

Next, she was diagnosed with breast cancer. She was operated on by a group of seven surgeons to remove her right breast – an operation she endured with no more anaesthetic than a glass or two of wine. She tells vividly of the excruciating pain of the operation in her writings. Her father died in 1814 and a year later Napoleon was defeated. The couple returned to England together and lived in Bath where she began writing about their experiences. By 1818 Alexandre had cancer and he then died. Alone, she dedicated her life to writing a three volume tome *The Memoirs of Doctor Burney* a tribute to her father. She died in 1840. In an age when women were not expected to be in the public eye, let alone be very successful published authors, she was an extraordinary woman, a trailblazer. In her lifetime she wrote four novels, eight plays and decades of journals; she depicted social cameos with satirical and humorous observations of her subjects. She was, said Virginia Woolf – 'the Mother of English Fiction'.

Mary Wollstonecraft was born in London in 1759, the second of seven children. Her father had once been rich but was now relatively poor, abusive and a drunkard – who beat his wife. He spent the family fortune on loss-making forays into business and as a result the family were forever having to move houses – further down-market each time. In an act of desperation, he even forced his youngest daughter Mary, to give him the monies she should have inherited when she became 21 years old.

Mary Wollstonecraft formed two close friendships originating in her childhood – with Jane Arden and Fanny Blood; she had developed strong attachments to both of them – which some have suggested may have shown lesbian tendencies. She was just 19 when she first felt compelled to leave home; she left to become a ladies companion in Bath, before eventually returning home to nurse her dying mother.

In 1780, when she was just 21, her mother died. Still disenchanted with the oppression of living with her father, she decided to leave home again; to be able to control her life and to earn her own living. Together with Eliza, her sister, and her best friend Fanny she set up a school at Newington Green, London for the daughters of merchants. Five years later her friend Fanny died. Devastated, Mary moved to Ireland to work as a governess and to have the 'space' to mourn her dear friend.

Her life-experiences promoted her, in 1787, to write her first paper – *Thoughts on the Education of Daughters*. She soon returned to London where she learned French and German and began work as a translator for a well-known radical publisher and through his magazine had several articles published. This was when she first met William Godwin, a renowned philosopher.

In 1792 she published what was to become her most high profile work – *A Vindication of the Rights of Women* – in which she refuted the image of women as just ornaments. It was directed at middle-class women. She described women as 'gentle domestic brutes' and believed that their life confined to the home made them tyrannical with both their children and their servants. Equal access to education was, she suggested, the remedy; with equal education, men and women would be on an equal footing. In her book *Maria – The Wrongs of Women* she said that women were creatures with strong sexual desires and that to not accept this was degrading to women. Needless to say it was, in those days, an exceedingly radical thing to be said by anyone – let alone in public and by an educated woman.

During this period she had formed a strong romantic attachment to a married artist and proposed that, together with his wife, the three of them live together in a form of ménage à trois. It all ended before it began – with embarrassment all-round.

It was whilst visiting friends in Paris, France in 1792, just weeks before Louis XVI was guillotined, that Mary met the American adventurer Captain Gilbert Imlay. She fell in love with him or at least her image of him. Very soon she was pregnant. She continued to write, including a paper outlining the effects of the French

Revolution (1789) and a record of her subsequent travels to Scandinavia with Imlay. England declared war on France and English citizens were being imprisoned or guillotined. Now living in Le Havre, they pretended to be married so that she would be thought of as American not English. Their fragile relationship was already breaking down – she became 'too maternal' for his liking – thus, he left her before the child was born and moved to London. He had always made plain that he was not the marrying type. She gave birth to a daughter whom she called Fanny – after her close friend who had died. She returned to London seeking out Imlay; he rejected her and she attempted suicide. She returned to Scandinavia with just her child and a maid in an effort to impress him. On her return to London she realised it was hopeless and, in another suicide attempt, threw herself into the Thames – but, she was rescued.

She slowly returned to writing and to her old circle of literary friends, including the philosopher William Godwin. By 1797 she had been courted by, married and had a daughter by William Godwin – he was the philosopher who was the founder of the anarchism movement. They both lived, happily, each in one of a pair of houses – thus giving each other freedom and independence. Just ten days after the birth of their daughter she died from complications. Her remains now, thanks to her grandson (Sir Percy Florence Shelley), have been moved from a graveyard in St Pancras to lie in the Shelley family tomb in Bournemouth. Mary and William's daughter, Mary, was to become Mary Shelley, and was renowned for being the author of *Frankenstein*.

As an act of love, William Godwin, who had previously rejected the concept of marriage, published the life story of his wife, Mary Wollstonecraft. It was detailed and intimate; he wanted the world to love every part of her just as he had. It laid her bare; it detailed her feelings, her lack of religious belief, her love affairs, her child born out of wedlock, her suicide attempts and her vulnerabilities. It was a life too radical for its time. The world saw the book as an unnecessary and too revealing exposure of her personal life; a life which was, to many of them, too shocking. The poets Robert Southey, Robert Browning and William Roscoe each had their say on her life and his exposure of its detail.

Her erstwhile reputation, amongst the literati and the public now lay shattered. Since those days most people, apart from the likes of Elizabeth Barrett Browning, Lucretia Mott and George Elliot, have read her life story but disregarded her books and other papers – for over 150 years. It has taken members of the feminist movement of the last 50 years to realise how far in advance of her time both her writing and her lifestyle were and therefore how important she is to the history of the women's movement.

The Peterloo Massacre

The Napoleonic Wars ended in 1815; a fortune had been spent fighting these battles and the country's coffers were nearly empty. The Corn Laws had been invoked stopping grain imports and thereby keeping English grain prices artificially high. At the same time that the population was growing, jobs were diminishing and food was becoming prohibitively expensive. Because of the strength of their position as employers the industrial mill owners reduced their workers' wages. Little work and little food were a recipe for social unrest.

In those days, to be eligible to vote you needed to own freehold property or land and receive an income from it. Voting was verbal – not an anonymous cross on a piece of paper – and only took place in one town in each constituency. Because of the speed with which the Industrial Revolution had redistributed much of the population of England, the new industrial towns were not yet distinct constituencies and therefore did not have their own member of parliament. The number of men eligible to vote and the number of MPs bore no relationship to each other. For example, in the Old Sarum constituency in Wiltshire (near Salisbury) there were two MPs but only one man eligible to vote. These unjust constituencies became known as Rotten Boroughs. Manchester and its surrounding area had over a million inhabitants but the whole county of Lancashire, including the city of Manchester, was represented by just two MPs.

In the mill towns of the North civil unrest was growing and calls for reform were becoming louder. That so few men could vote, and thus be in a position to change the laws, was a great source of political agitation. The Manchester Patriotic Union was formed by a group of radical reformers.

They planned a large public meeting in St Peter's Field, Manchester on 9th August 1819 and asked the militant orator Henry Hunt to be the main speaker; William Cobbett would also attend. The government had located spies in this area and they soon became aware of the meeting. This allowed the government to prepare their reaction well in advance. They banned the meeting organised for 9th August 1819. In response, the reformers changed the date to 16th August – too late for the government to react by banning it and thus the meeting went ahead. Previously, meetings of this type were small, disorganised and ineffective. The organisers were determined to make this meeting large, well organised and effective.

On the day, the local magistrates located themselves in a building with a full view of St Peter's Field. They had a force comprising 600 Hussars, hundreds of infantry men, one unit of the Royal Horse Artillery complete with two six-pounder field guns, 400 Cheshire Yeomanry, 400 Special Constables and 120 members of the Manchester and Salford Yeomanry. This last group were described by the press as 'not regular soldiers' but as 'a group of "licensed" amateurs... young Tory activists... set against the reformers... a local Mafia on horseback'.

When the crowd began to gather it was plain to see that they were in orderly and well organised groups dressed in their 'Sunday best', and behaving themselves. Whole families were there, father, mother and children. It was, in some cases, treated more like a social day out; there was dancing and a carnival atmosphere. There were numerous women's societies with their members dressed symbolically in white and carrying the banners of their associations. In just one group of men and women, from the Oldham area, there were 10,000 people. It was estimated the total was around 100,000 men, women and children.

Henry Hunt was due to arrive to speak at 1pm. A short while before, several hundred Special Constables tried to create a 'corridor' through the crowd. Many of the demonstrators believed this was an action to enable the authorities to easily get at Henry Hunt when he arrived, arrest him and remove him. Against this, the crowd formed a protective cordon around the speaker's rostrum.

When Hunt arrived he got a tumultuous reception. Seeing this, the Magistrates issued a warrant for his arrest. The Cavalry were summoned and, swords drawn, they began to enter the crowd in an effort to get to the rostrum and arrest Hunt. The mass of the crowd was so great that the Cavalry soon became stuck. In panic they began to slash with their swords. Unintentionally, this caused such a diversion that the Chief Constable was able to get another contingent of men to arrest Hunt and others. Stones were being picked up and thrown at the Cavalry who were becoming even more aggressive with the use of their swords and slashing at people randomly with them. Now the Hussars, professional soldiers, formed into a line and charged into the crowd. The exit from St Peter's Field was blocked by other soldiers with bayonets fixed. A peaceful civil demonstration was being treated by the authorities as a military battle. Sheer panic gave the crowd the impetus to disperse within just ten minutes. Behind them, in St Peter's Field, lay 600 injured and 11 dead. The 'walking wounded' were trying to hide their wounds and flee the scene for fear of retribution by the authorities. A two-year-old child was the very first victim; struck by a member of the Manchester Yeomanry whilst in his mother's arms. Four of the 11 dead were women. One hundred and sixty-eight of the 'listed' casualties were women.

The enormity of the importance of this meeting was such that it was attended by numerous journalists from cities all over England and therefore there was a good independent record of what actually happened. In an ironic to reference to the Duke of Wellington's glorious victory at Waterloo just four years earlier James Wroe, of *The Manchester Observer*, headlined the tragedy as 'The Peterloo Massacre'.

The sad result of all this was not apology and reform but that the government cracked down even harder on any radical reformers or their proponents. Wroe was arrested for sedition because of his newspaper article, fined £100 and imprisoned for a year. *The Manchester Observer* and its editors were hounded by the police and regularly shut down; as a consequence it was finally forced to close in February 1820. *The Manchester Guardian* was created subsequently and still flourishes today.

Hunt and 10 others were tried at York, having been charged with sedition; five were acquitted but Hunt was given a jail sentence of 30 months. Members of the military involved on the day were brought before a court – but, acquitted. By the end of 1820 every male supporter of radical reform had been hunted down and imprisoned.

The government's draconian measures were seen by the populous as proof of their fear and their insecurity. This was proven true, although it took a long time to remedy; as the century advanced so, slowly, did acts of reform.

The Chartists

As Queen Victoria's reign began, tens of thousands of men were being 'laid off' – there just wasn't enough work for everybody. And, that number of men was, in those days, an enormous proportion of the male working population. This was not a consequential outcome of the Industrial Revolution; it had come about because of the reduction in the market for English exports around the world.

The Corn Laws had already banned cheap imported wheat from entering the country and as a result even fresh bread became unaffordable for many poor people. Working class anger was reaching boiling point and the only solution they could envisage was for them to live in a benign democracy where their opinions and their votes could change their lives; they would no longer remain passive or be victims at the mercy of the laws passed by an undemocratic parliament. Because their demands were set out in a written document they called the People's Charter its supporters became known as Chartists.

The Reform Act of 1832 had already disenfranchised numerous 'rotten boroughs' (a constituency with very few electors – often just the members of one influential family) and lowered the financial property requirements for male enfranchisement by 50 per cent thereby letting most members of the upper middle-classes into the electorate. But, there were no votes for the working classes.

In May 1838 the People's Charter was published as a draft parliamentary bill. It outlined six distinct proposals: Manhood Suffrage; the Ballot; the Abolition of Property Qualifications for MPs; Payment of MPs; Equal Electoral Districts; Annual Elections.

William Lovett was its principal author. William Lovett, in his book *Social & Political Morality*, wrote that it was only fair that men and women should have equal rights – but, at the same time stated that their roles in life were different. He saw men as the providers for the family and women as being in charge of the household duties. The wealthy heads of industry, politicians and landowners considered that the Chartists were just another unruly mob who were set on destroying the stability of society; everyone, they said, just needed to be patient and wait for international trade to strengthen and then there would be good times again. But, the working classes were diseased and starving and that was a remedy they felt that they could not wait for.

The tenets of their Charter were eventually addressed in a draft Act of Parliament. The Chartists believed that their demands were so just that they could achieve change purely by the powers of logic and persuasion – although they also believed so strongly in their cause that, if necessary, they would fight to achieve it.

The Chartists had similar political aspirations to those of the Levellers 200 years earlier. It soon became a very large organisation with its main power-base in Yorkshire, Lancashire and the Midlands. The cities and most large towns in these areas had branches which held regular meetings. And, most of these branches had women's sections. In Birmingham alone there were in excess of 2,000 active female members.

The women held, and spoke at, their own meetings, sent out press releases, donated money, made banners for their own women's groups and marched under them alongside their menfolk. They raised the money to pay the legal costs of men who needed representation, collected names on petitions and took part in marches, demonstrations and strikes. Their efforts were to promote the rights of their husbands to enfranchisement as this was the main policy of the movement. A Mrs Legge of Aberdeen and a group of like-minded women was recorded, although only locally, as having publicly demanded votes for women; 'votes for all' and 'universal suffrage' were common chants on their marches. When the initial charter was first drafted it had included women's enfranchisement though this demand was soon dropped as it was thought so radical that it would lower the chance of the main charter being accepted.

At that time most women just wanted their menfolk to earn enough so that they did not need to go to work too. The National Female Charter worried about the effects of women having jobs and working whilst there was no work for their men – who consequently stayed at home. Women's suffrage was definitely on the back-burner at that time. Women were simply looking for an escape from a life of abject poverty.

History notes two prominent women activists, Miss Susannah Inge and Miss Mary Anne Walker – both of whom remain absolute mysteries, save for the information that they were young educated members of the City of London Female Chartists. In both their written addresses and face to face encounters with prominent males at their meetings, they more than just suggest suffrage for women. When one of these ladies was taunted by one male speaker, a Mr Cohen, who said that women were 'domestic ornaments... not physically intended to take part in political rights', and further added, that if she were to become a member of parliament, that, because of her womanly weaknesses, she would not be able to stick to her principles because she would doubtless find eligible male members of the opposition too much of a distraction to her – she gave him short shrift, much to the amusement of the other ladies present. It was a noteworthy enough encounter to get into *The Times* the next day. Both women soon became inspirational lecturers on the Chartist Women's circuit.

In pursuance of the aims of the Chartist movement thousands of people had attended rallies all around the country and gave their support; many were imprisoned for their actions; some were transported to Australia and 22 were shot by soldiers. The new Poor Law of 1834, which penalised the working classes and trade unions, inspired the Chartist activist and Member of Parliament, Feargus O'Connor, into fomenting physical disobedience in support of the cause and as a result he soon became known as the 'Lion of Freedom'.

A huge rally was held at Kennington Common in London on 10th April 1848 and was attended by an estimated 150,000 Chartists carrying banners and wearing rosettes or ribbons in green, red and white – the colours of the Chartist movement. It was the largest political demonstration that the world had ever seen – even though it poured with rain. Their latest petition was alleged to have over five million signatures on it but in reality there were just over two million verifiable signatories. It was taken from this rally directly to Parliament; it was so large that it filled three hansom cabs. There had been three Chartist petitions to Parliament – in 1839, in 1842 and this one in 1848.

Knowing that this rally was about to happen, Queen Victoria was sent to the safety of the Isle of Wight and the Duke of Wellington stood by with thousands of troops and special constables, and even had canons positioned at strategic locations like Buckingham Palace, Parliament and the Tower of London – ready to protect the capital from the demonstrators' anger. In the end, as photographs of the period show, the whole event passed off peacefully.

The petitions did not achieve their purpose. Feargus O'Connor MP had begun to see the merits of changing the lot of the working man by changing his environment. A movement emerged whereby members could club together and raise donations to buy small plots of land on which to build homes with gardens large enough to support a self-sufficient lifestyle. The women's branch of the Chartists were great advocates of the idea.

Prince Albert saw the idea as positive and in the Great Exhibition of 1850 had a display of 'model lodgings' constructed. He was active in trying to help working families achieve better conditions both at home and at work. By this time international trade was beginning to build up substantially and the desperate circumstances of working families was being relieved.

After the 1848 petition the female membership of the Chartists began to fall dramatically, probably as a result of the increase of work available in production and the improved finances for working families. With more money and less time for promoting the cause, it lost its potency. The Sheffield Female Radical Association, a Chartist support group, remained active until 1851. Ann Knight, a Quaker and anti-slavery activist had been at the London World Convention in 1840 and as a result became an avid supporter of women's suffrage. She and the Sheffield Association instigated a petition to be put before Parliament proposing women's enfranchisement. This was noted in the *Northern Star,* a Chartist magazine. They formed links with French women revolutionaries and started the National Women's Rights Association.

The Reform Act of 1867 lowered the limit for the financial property requirements for male enfranchisement doubling the electorate to two million male voters. The Reform Act of 1884 lowered the limits again which increased the electorate to five million men.

None of the initial 'sparks' created at the beginning of the Chartist movement were ever given the chance to develop properly. The principles of enfranchisement for women which were always there, although not the main movement's highest priority, continued to engender much female support. Women sacrificed their needs for the more immediate benefits for their menfolk. The principle of universal enfranchisement did not disappear it lay smouldering for the next activists in the women's movement.

The Ladies Land League

By the early 1800s Ireland's population had exploded to eight million from only two million just two centuries previously. The same small croft buildings and the same amount of land producing the same amount of crops – for quadruple the population. There was work and money in cities such as Dublin and Belfast and in the busy international ports too but, the rest of the country was rural, isolated and desperately poor. The country's diet was based on potatoes and then more potatoes; 10–15 pounds of potatoes per person per day, each and every day. Life for the poor of rural Ireland had always been that way.

In 1845, an airborne potato disease called 'potato blight' blew first into the west of Ireland and soon got blown all over Ireland. It took only days before the crops began to look unhealthy and just a week or two before the potato tubers fruiting in the ground had turned into an inedible mushy mess. The potato was the staple food of the poor and it was rotting before their eyes. They went from hunger to starvation within days. Meanwhile, the rich gentleman farmers with hundreds of acres of oats producing thousands of tons of grain per year were exporting their crops via the ports and making a good profit, thank you. An Englishman called Charles Trevelyan at the Home Office in Whitehall, London would not allow any of these Irish grown oats to be eaten by the population of Ireland; every grain had to be exported. And every grain exported was taxed and produced an income for the English government.

At first, mainly through the charitable acts of churches, soup kitchens appeared; but, they stood no chance of coping with a disaster of this magnitude. The workhouse became the only refuge; offering just one small inadequate bowl of unappetising food a day. To be eligible to enter you had to leave behind your rented home and land and everything that was in it. Husbands were separated from their wives and children. Oh, how happy the landlords were; they were getting back their tenanted land and using it to breed and fatten sheep and cattle. Far more lucrative and less trouble than renting it out to a poor tenant farmer. If a tenant got behind with the rent he was quickly evicted and then the building was pulled down so that neither the tenant nor anyone else could come back and reoccupy it. There were even rumours that the landlords had somehow caused the potato blight just so that they could get their land back.

Death and disease was everywhere. Babies were dying faster than priests could baptise and bury them. An un-baptised baby could not be buried in consecrated ground and would not be worthy to go to heaven. Fathers had to bury their dead babies wherever they could.

Those who could scrape enough money together for one or perhaps two members of the family to buy a passage on a boat and get out of Ireland did so; some to Canada, some to America, some to Australia, some to South Africa. Anywhere was better than famine and disease ridden Ireland. Families were torn apart. Husbands and wives separated; parents and children separated – never to see each other again. It wasn't a choice; it was a necessity. There was no other way of ensuring that some would survive. By the end of the famine two million people had emigrated; and, there were over a million dead.

This did not happen without a struggle to survive. The Land War (1872–1879), as it became known, was to be one of the major steps toward Irish independence. The main activists were Charles Stuart Parnell (MP) the leader of the Irish Parliamentary Party and also an Anglo-Irish landlord, and Michael Davitt a former Fenian and agrarian reformer.

Those who had survived the potato famine and were still scraping through on their tenanted land were facing an uphill struggle; and there were over a million of them. Then, for several years in the 1870s the weather was so wet that, like the potato blight before, it was causing rot and poor harvests in the potato crop. Starvation, destitution and eviction were constant pressures on the tenant farmers. Failed crops caused reduced incomes and made affording the rents virtually impossible.

In 1879, in County Mayo, Ireland, the National Irish Land League was formed and amalgamated with other support groups. It tried to highlight the tenants' predicament and pleaded with the landlords to reduce the rents whilst the situation lasted. The League asked for 'the three F's' – fair rent, fixity of tenure, free sale. These were already the basis of an informal agreement in one area and called 'the Custom of Ulster'.

Parnell intended to use the unrest as a weapon for change; to create a popular movement which would help to diminish British colonial control in Ireland. He was an outspoken proponent of Irish Home Rule. Davitt was aligned to the Clan na Gael grouping and would have liked to see Irish land ownership virtually nationalised as Ireland threw off the shackles of their colonial rulers; and they would not mind using force if necessary.

In 1880 Parnell and Davitt made a promotional tour of North America, paid for by the American branch of Clan na Gael, in an effort to raise funds from sympathetic Irish immigrants. Parnell travelled over 16,000 miles, spoke at meetings in over 60 towns and cities and even addressed a session of Congress. He helped form the American Land League in New York in 1880. They did indeed raise a great deal of funds, over $3,000.

Parnell's sister Anna, lived in America with their mother, Delia, and sister, Fanny. They were already working as activists for the American headquarters of the Ladies Land League which had swiftly opened branches all over the country and was raising substantial amounts of money for relief in Ireland.

An interesting side effect of this organisation was to unite the immigrant Irish women, raise their feelings of self-worth and to give them a more respectable social status. In Ireland, before they had managed to emigrate, most of them had been poor subsistence tenant farmers, they had left their home country because of the potato famine. They were neither well educated nor well off and because of their background were considered by some as of low social status. That is why they were so sympathetic to the Land League cause. The word 'Ladies' in the title of their organisation was chosen specifically for that effect. In America, Irish men had gained the negative reputation of being hard drinkers and aggressive; therefore being an Irishman's wife had negative connotations.

Substantial numbers of Irish men, and often the ministers of the churches favoured by the Irish Catholics, felt threatened by the success of the Ladies Land League and said that it was not a woman's place to seek political influence. Some American literature of the time was postulating the 'four cardinal virtues' for women: piety, purity, submissiveness and domesticity. Perhaps the disquiet in some men was because one faction of these women wanted not just to support the Irish situation but to begin to change their own role within American society. But, the women diverted criticism by saying that it was a woman's nature to look after the whole family and that the disadvantaged people in Ireland were, to them, members of their greater family.

Davitt had suggested an 'Irish Ladies Land League' to carry on the work of the men when they had been imprisoned for their acts of civil unrest. The women could, he said, perform charity work, support evicted tenants, relieve distress and keep up the administration. He did not want or expect them to become activists.

During their American fund-raising trip, Davitt had been impressed by Anna's work and as a result they persuaded her to return to Ireland to head up the Ladies Land League campaign. He believed that the women, for the sake of attracting international sympathy for the cause, would be immune to the existing British government controls which were curtailing the work of the men. Unfortunately, just as she arrived in Ireland, on 31st January 1881, Davitt was imprisoned for his political activities.

The Ladies Land League was the first substantial national women's political group in Ireland. Irish women had already created anti-slavery societies, worked to change aspects of the Married Women's Property Act, revised education entry systems for women and even started women's suffrage societies but they were generally much smaller and more locally based organisations. They were being deliberately neutralised. Under the auspices of women from the Quaker movement they were able to raise the awareness of the Irish people to the horrors of slavery through the Hibernian Ladies' Negroes' Friend Society of the mid-1830s and the Cork Ladies' Anti-Slavery Society 1845–1847 and a few similar organisations but their efforts to amend the Married Women's Property Act and their support of suffrage were being seen as too divisive. All the nationalist organisations were male controlled and thus specifically banned women from membership of such organisations. The Ladies Land League was controversial and seen by some as threatening because it ran counter to this edict.

Anna toured the country and gave passionate speeches motivating the women's groups – meetings which frequently had large numbers of men present too. Had a man done what she did he would have been imprisoned. She wanted copies of all legal documents served on the members; all writs, actions and process documents. She wanted them sent to the headquarters in Dublin where they could be collated. She persuaded her women volunteers that work experience of that nature would be good training for those able to subsequently work in an office environment. Soon there were over 400 branches across the country.

With the entire male Central Executive of the Land League imprisoned in Kilmainham Gaol, Dublin in 1881 the work of the Ladies became essential to the continuance of the cause. Any remaining male activists, or even uncooperative male tenant farmers, were likely to be put in jail at the slightest provocation.

As they grew in strength the Ladies were not solely recording the events but had become physically involved in trying to protect the tenants from being evicted. In the end they were finding themselves physically attacked by both the authorities and the landlord's men. Many of these women were injured, some seriously; some were even killed – shot or 'run through' by swords.

Soon the Dublin office had a complex system recording and cross-referencing all the occurrences relating to any of the actions by their members or against their members. The men had never been this organised. It was like the coordinated efforts of a resistance movement in an occupied country. The women even had to write, print and publish the nationalist newspaper *United Ireland*. To keep one step ahead of the authorities, who were trying to shut the paper down, they moved its printing from London to Liverpool to Manchester and even to Paris. They were creative in their running of the whole organisation. When the women were arrested it was not as political activists – as that would have afforded them positive publicity – it was under legislation usually used for prostitutes.

The works and organisational skills of the Ladies Land League produced results which were so potent that eventually William Gladstone, the Prime Minister, began negotiations with Parnell. This led to the release of all Land League members from prison and gave protection to tenant farmers in arrears with their rent in exchange for a cessation of violence and the Land League's activities being terminated. Also, Parnell's political party formed an alliance with Gladstone's party. Parnell had moved from the original purpose of the League to using its influence to achieve Home Rule which, for him, had always been the eventual goal. By 1882 he ceased land reform activities and concentrated on the Parliamentary campaign for Home Rule in Ireland. In his plan to achieve this he had the members of the League who were not totally supportive of his goals, including the Ladies Land League, removed from the group.

The Ladies Land League had not been privy to these negotiations until after they had been completed. The men's Land League told the Ladies Land League to disband as they were no longer necessary. The women refused. The men then accused them of having embezzled the funds to the tune of £70,000 – a very substantial amount of money – even though they had full accounts to show where the money had come in from and how and where it had been spent (which was more than the men had ever done). Soon, the name was changed to The Irish National League (thus omitting the word 'land' from its title) and it described itself as '...an open organization in which ladies will not take part...'

Subsequently, at the end of the campaign, all the records which the Ladies Land League had created were mislaid or destroyed; a suspiciously convenient coincidence.

The Ladies Land League had improved the overall organisation such that it ran in a better fashion than the men had managed; they had a scale, influence and organisation new to Irish political movements. Although Parnell and Davitt had a good fundraising tour of North America it was actually Parnell's sister Fanny who, whilst living in North America, was the main person to raise money for their cause through her unending works with the North American Ladies Land League. It was the funds which she raised which allowed the Irish National Land League to function, for them to continue their works. Women, in those days, were not usually political activists. They and their members had been subjected to ridicule, public humiliation, physical assault, imprisonment and some had even died for the cause.

The Ladies Land League was disbanded in 1882. Anna never again spoke to her brother. The same year Fanny died of a heart attack. Shattered, Anna retreated to England and spent the rest of her days in obscurity, and under an assumed name, in Cornwall. She died in a swimming accident in 1911.

Both sisters, in their own individual and very diverse ways, were effective militant activists and were equally important; they promoted their cause to its ultimate conclusion. They were not what the 19th century normally expected of well brought up and educated young ladies. They were ahead of their time. However history may record them, they were a substantial and active force in the road to Irish freedom from English rule.

Most histories of the Irish Land War and the work of the Irish Land League movement were male accounts and either ignored the work of the Ladies Land League or dismissed it as irrelevant.

However, and most significantly, Michael Davitt himself was to say in *The Fall of Feudalism in Ireland* (1904): 'Everything recommended, attempted or done in the way of defeating the ordinary law and asserting the unwritten law of the League…was more systematically carried out under the direction of the Ladies' Executive than by its predecessor'.

In 1909 Anna Parnell wrote a detailed account of what had happened in the days of the Ladies Land League which challenged the 'official' account. But publishers were all men in those days and so, no-one would publish it. It lay forgotten for over a century. Now discovered, it is throwing a new and informative light on this period of Irish History. After the disbanding of the movement Henry George, the American correspondent for *The Irish World*, said of the Ladies Land League '…They have done a great deal better than the men would have done…'

Other Early Equality Protagonists

Jeremy Bentham (1748–1832) was an English philosopher and social reformer and a man born way ahead of his time. He was the 'father of welfarism' (economic welfare – not the modern concept of the word); he believed that political policies and rules should be evaluated on the basis of their potential consequences. In 1817 he publicly stated that women should have complete equality with men and that women's current legal position of inferiority was intolerable. He believed strongly in both individual and economic freedom, the church not having influence on the state, equal rights for women, easier access to divorce, the abolition of slavery, the death penalty and corporal punishment and the reform of laws on homosexuality. He even left his body to medical research. Sadly, his efforts at reform were to fall on stony ground.

Lord Hardwicke's Marriage Act 1753 caused minors (under 21years of age) to require the consent of their parents or guardians before being legally entitled to get married; however, this law only applied to England and Wales. In Scotland the legalities of marriage were not changed and thus the age of personal consent to marriage remained at 12 years old for girls and 14 years old for boys and the consent of parents or guardians were still not necessary. Here began the romantic tales of young runaway lovers and marriage at Gretna Green.

William Thompson (1775–1833) was a wealthy Irish writer and social reformer who was born and lived in Cork. He was a non-smoking teetotaller and a vegetarian, and he was a man with ideas – which were acknowledged as influencing the Cooperative movement, the Trades Union movement, the Chartists and Karl Marx; he even supported contraception in his Irish homeland. What was probably his seminal book was *An Enquiry into the Principles of the Distribution of Wealth* which was published in1824. He was also an influential thinker on the subject of women's equality issues. In 1825 he published *An Appeal of One Half of the Human Race, Women, Against the Pretensions of the other Half, Men.* It was based on the theories and beliefs of Anna Wheeler – as he rightly acknowledges. It refutes the roles and values that had traditionally been expected of women and of their subservience in marriage. It acknowledges a woman's intelligence, needs and rights as being equal to those of men and says that marriage should be a partnership between equals. It is filled with what were then radical beliefs, ideals which are the tenets of feminism. It was the first ever English language book outlining women's rights and feminist beliefs. It includes a chapter 'Introductory Letter to Mrs Wheeler' in which he credits her with much of his inspiration and describes himself as her 'interpreter and scribe of your sentiments'. In 1830 he wrote another book called *Practical Directions for the Establishment of Communities.*

Anna Doyle Wheeler – née Walker (1785–1848) was born in County Tipperary, Ireland to a Church of Ireland clergyman and his wife. She was home educated and learned to speak, read and write French. At the age of 15 she married 19-year-old Francis Wheeler, who was part of the family of Baron Massy. They moved to Limerick where she was soon to give birth to two daughters. He became an abusive alcoholic so the marriage only lasted for 12 years. At this point, in 1812, she moved to Guernsey to live with her uncle Sir John Doyle, the Lieutenant of Guernsey. She remained there until 1815 when she decided to move to London to benefit her daughters' upbringing and

DAVID deVIRE

to widen her social circle. She was virtually penniless and lived with and relied on the generosity of family and friends and some translation work. Her husband died in 1820. She led a fairly nomadic life; she journeyed through France and variously lived in London, Dublin, Caen and Paris.

She was the first woman to publicly campaign for women's rights; she is noted for her spirited and controversial public addresses on the tenets of what were to become known as feminist issues. Of particular note was a lecture given from the pulpit of a chapel near Finsbury Square. In the 1830s she wrote articles for the French publication *Tribune des Femmes* which was originally known as *La Femme Libre*; it was a journal which only accepted articles written by women. About the same time she also had an article called 'The Rights of Women' published in *The British Co-operator* which was a publication sponsored by Robert Owen the 'Father of British Socialism' and the founder of the Co-operative movement. Because of her strong beliefs in women's rights she was given the nickname of 'Vlasta' by some people. Vlasta was the legendary 16th century Swedish head of an army of women who fought against their men's oppression. In 1833 she published a work under the title *A Letter from Vlasta*. By 1840 she had to retire due to ill health but continued to support the cause at a lesser level. She died in 1848.

James Barry (1792 or 1795–1865) led an extraordinary life which has been recorded by the Science Museum and others. He was born as Margaret Ann Bulkley in Cork, Ireland; her father was Jeremiah Bulkley, a grocer, and her mother, Mary-Ann, was the sister of James Barry the celebrated Irish artist and Professor of Arts at the Royal Academy. Because her father allowed the family to get into debt her mother sought the financial and strategic advice of her brother and his wealthy and individual friends. It appears that a bizarre and clandestine solution to their problems was agreed upon. In 1806, when Jeremiah was sent to prison for his debt the plan was put into action; unfortunately, that same year Mary-Ann's brother James died – but, his friends continued to help her. With monies left to her, Mary-Ann took her daughter Margaret to live in London so that she could continue her studies; this was also where her brother's support network was based.

In 1809 mother and daughter boarded a ship bound for Edinburgh; this is where the practical subterfuge began. Margaret boarded dressed as a boy; the change had been made between their home and the ship in order not to arouse suspicion. On arrival at Edinburgh, it was not a mother and her 'son' who landed, they had assumed new identities for themselves, they were now adopting the roles of aunt and nephew. To be able to ensure that they were never to be found out they cut off all ties with families and friends; he always wore a greatcoat and lied about his age. The newly created James Barry entered Edinburgh University and studied medicine; he graduated in 1812. They then moved back to London where he worked in St Thomas's Hospital for six months before enlisting in the army as a doctor. He was noted as being the first surgeon to perform a caesarean operation which was successful for both mother and baby. For 46 years he travelled the world as he performed his army role.

He saw service in India and South Africa and eventually rose to the rank of Inspector General and in that position was in charge of military hospitals. It was only after death that the truth was revealed by the woman who laid him out; but, they didn't know who this person originally was. According to *The New Scientist*, this was to be revealed by letters, still in their original envelopes, retained by a meticulous solicitor. An envelope in his handwriting noted on the outside that it was from Mary Bulkley but the letter was signed by Dr James Barry. The handwriting of this letter has been compared to handwriting known to be of Margaret Bulkley as a teenage girl by an expert graphologist from the UK Forensic Science Service. And, thus the mystery of this remarkable life was solved.

Elizabeth Gaskell (1810–1865) was born Elizabeth Stevenson in 1810, the only surviving daughter of a Unitarian family living in Chelsea, London. Her mother died a year after her birth and as a result she was sent to Cheshire to be brought up by relatives. At the age of 22 she married a Unitarian minister, William Gaskell, and a year later she had a stillborn daughter and then a son who lived for just one year.

As a therapy to counter her grief she began writing a book. She had become so affected by the problems she saw being faced by the poor working class that she wrote a novel to bring their plight to the attention of the educated classes. *Mary Barton*, as it was titled, was a tale about the lives of working people in Manchester. She painted a vivid picture of the conditions they endured in their so very basic homes, the oppression at their places of work and the misery that these conditions imposed on the whole family.

In her research she visited their homes, places of work, the gin palaces and the dark back alleys. To her educated and genteel readers, she had painted a picture of what seemed a foreign land with its own foreign language; an alien culture. She frequently used the word 'clemmed', – a street language word for starving, to describe them. It was her honest belief that by bringing this world to the attention of her influential readers she could improve the lot of working families.

The book was published anonymously. It soon became successful as a work of literature and was praised by both Charles Dickens and Thomas Carlyle, amongst others. Like much of her work it has subsequently become a resource for social historians. She continued her writings which were popular and, as a result, she soon became part of an influential social circle which included the likes of Dickens, Carlyle and John Ruskin; she was a close friend of Charlotte Brontë upon whose death she was asked by the family to write her biography. She had *Cranford* published by Dickens in his journal *Household Words* in 1853 and another *North and South* in 1854. Her work *Wives and Daughters* was published in *Cornhill Magazine* from 1864 to 1866 as a serial but she died not long before it was completed. It was finished by Frederick Greenwood, a professional writer and author. Her lifetime writing portfolio included numerous novels and short stories; she died in 1865.

Angela Georgina Burdett-Coutts (1814–1906), 1st Baroness Burdett-Coutts, was the youngest of the six children of Sir Francis Burdett, the radical MP, and his wife Sophia Coutts. So, she was born into the exceedingly wealthy Coutts banking family. Before her birth her father had been having an affair with Jane Harvey,

Countess of Oxford. Angela was apparently conceived as an act of reconciliation. At the same time her grandfather, Sophia's father, was having an affair with a young actress called Harriot Mellon whom he later married. In 1822 he died. His now very wealthy young widow then married the 9th Duke of St Albans who was 23 years younger than her.

Angela, like most wealthy young women of that age was educated at home before going on a tour of Europe. Her grandfather's money and social connections ensured that wherever she went she met the right people; when in Paris she met members of the royal family including the future King Louis-Philippe.

When Harriot Mellon Coutts, Duchess of St Albans died in 1837 it became apparent that she had left the vast majority of her fortune to Angela – provided she did not marry a foreigner; it amounted to approximately £1.8 million (almost £200 million in 2016). She was now said to be the second richest woman in the country, after Queen Victoria.

She bought a new house in Piccadilly and gave allowances to members of her family. She was inundated with offers of marriage; rumours were rife. She was introduced to Charles Dickens and, like many of her contemporaries was attracted to him. He sought her financial help with the Ragged Schools (based on an extension of the Sunday School model). She supported the cause most generously. At about the same time she was to meet and become friendly with the Duke of Wellington. In January 1844, when she was just 30 years old, her mother died; 11 days later her father died too.

Because of the location of her London house she became aware of the problem of prostitution so, when Dickens wrote her a long letter suggesting the setting up of refuges for prostitutes she was immediately keen on the idea even though the Duke of Wellington expressed his reservations.

Her relationship with Wellington grew ever closer and it was rumoured in society that perhaps they were lovers or would get married. In February 1847 she proposed marriage to him; she was 33 and he was 78. The next day he sent her a letter which effectively, but charmingly, declined on account of his fondness for her and the potential pain that the age difference would cause. It was subsequently revealed that, over time, he had sent her more than 800 letters.

That same year the refuges for the prostitutes began to be used and she and Dickens shared many discussions on the details of their operation. Angela tried to spend much time with Wellington too but he was feeling his age and even chastised her, telling her to remember that he was now 82 not 28 years old. He died in 1852 when she was 38.

Angela heard about Florence Nightingale's efforts in the Crimea and donated medical supplies and equipment, including a clothes drying machine, in an effort to help the cause. Inspired and supported by Dickens she was also to get involved in the design, building and funding of social housing in London.

Dickens' marriage was breaking up and it was complicated and messy; it was also very public. As a result, Angela decided to sever her personal and philanthropic relationship with him. She continued to press-on with her social housing building projects.

During her lifetime she donated money to a seemingly endless number of other charitable causes; some of the more notable ones include: numerous endowments, including to South Africa, Australia and Canada; she supported scholarships; paid for the building of two churches; supported the RSPCA and helped to found the NSPCC; she was the President of The Goat Society; she supported cancer research through the Royal Marsden and the Brompton Cancer Hospital; she paid for the memorial in Edinburgh to Greyfriars Bobby (the terrier who supposedly guarded his owner's grave until his own death). She was the first woman to be made a peer as a result of her charitable works; she was given the freedom of both London and Edinburgh.

By the time she was 66 she had lost her lifelong friend and companion Hannah Brown. Her sole support, she felt, was her secretary William Ashmead-Bartlett whom she had known since he was a child. Very soon she decided to marry him; she was 66 and he was 29. Her own bank, members of her social network and even Queen Victoria were all surprised and worried. They were married in 1881 when she was 68 years old and he was 31. Because he was born in America he was classed as an alien and, as a result, she lost her entire inheritance to her sister; all she got was an annual allowance. In 1885 her husband was elected as the Conservative Member of Parliament for Westminster. She died in 1906. Her body lay in state for two days and an estimated 30,000 people came to pay their respects; she was buried in Westminster Abbey. Her husband continued to support her good works after her death. In the press and throughout society she was remembered as 'The Queen of the Poor'.

The Married Women's Property Acts 1870, 1882 and 1893

These acts were exceedingly significant changes in the legal status of women in England; the first for nearly a thousand years. The 1870 Act allowed women to keep and use their own earnings; the 1882 Act allowed them to own property; the 1893 Act allowed them to keep any property acquired during the marriage.

When the Normans invaded and conquered Britain nearly a thousand years ago they brought their laws with them too; one of them lasted right through until the Married Women's Property Acts of 1870, 1882 and 1893. This law was called 'coverture' (or, to use the correct Norman term, 'Couverture'). Under this law a 'Feme Sole' was an unmarried woman who had some control of her own property. When she married she became a 'Feme Covert'. Thus the name of the law being the Law of Coverture.

In 1756 Sir William Blackstone SL KC, an English judge and Tory politician wrote a book *Commentaries on the Laws of England*. In it he describes the law of 'Coverture' thus: 'By marriage, the husband and wife are one person in law: that is, the very being or legal existence of the woman is suspended during marriage, or at least incorporated and consolidated into that of the husband: under whose wing, protection, and cover, she performs everything'. He elaborated: 'A man cannot grant anything to his wife, or enter into a covenant with her: for the grant would be to suppose her separate existence; and to covenant with her would be only to covenant with himself'. Further, Common Law said that he had the legal right to beat her with a stick – provided it was no thicker than his thumb;

that women could be imprisoned for refusing to have sex with their husband; that the children of a marriage belonged to the male.

In 1836 **Caroline Sheridan** and her husband George Norton, a barrister and Member of Parliament for Guildford, separated. He was commonly known to be an objectionable man and a drunkard who became unable to make enough money to support his family to the best of standards. His mental and physical abuse was the reason that Caroline left him. Earlier during their marriage she had established herself as a popular society hostess; she was beautiful and entertaining, though her opinions and behaviour sometimes raised eyebrows, nonetheless she had many admirers. Her husband was very happy for her to entertain in this way as he believed that her social contacts would bring him more legal work.

Her husband would not divorce her and in those days a woman could not divorce her husband. He was of the belief that she was having an affair with Lord Melbourne, the Prime Minister, and took him to court for 'Criminal Conversation' as the offence was called then. Adultery was seen as trespass of the wife's body which belonged to the husband. Norton lost the case but it caused much trouble for both Lord Melbourne and his government.

George Norton did not provide for his wife or his three sons who were living with her at the time, so Caroline wrote poetry, prose and fiction and was able to make a small living from it. When Norton realised this he successfully took her to court so that he could take these monies for himself. A woman could legally own nothing on her own account, it all belonged to her husband. In a clever move she then lived on credit and directed her creditors to her husband for payment – her debt was his legal responsibility. She had played him at his own game. Norton abducted his own sons and hid them away with members of his family and denied her access. He had the legal right to do so because children were the property of the man. A man even had the right to enter the house of another person to forcibly take his wife back.

After the death of her youngest son whilst in his custody, Caroline Sheridan began a crusade for what she believed to be issues of social justice. Using her contacts and influence she was able to help create the Custody of Infants Act 1839 which would allow a mother to keep her children with her until the age of seven and to have regular access to them thereafter. Unfortunately, if the arrangement was not agreed to by the husband, pursuing a legal case would have put justice beyond the financial means of most women. She also worked towards the Matrimonial Clauses Act 1857 which made marriage a legal contract and gave more rights to women especially in relation to divorce and custody of their children. The Married Women's Property Act 1870 allowed women their own legal 'identity'; they were no longer the property of their husband.

Caroline was to be the model for a painting in the House of Lords depicting 'Justice'. She was apparently chosen because society believed that she was a victim of a poor judicial system.

Whilst feted by many as a feminist because of her actions and the changes of law in favour of women's rights that she was able to influence, she said in an interview with *The Times* newspaper that she thought the correct position of women was to be inferior to men, that it was God's will and that mankind should not try to change it; and, further, that equality was a wild and dangerous doctrine.

Although she had various liaisons and affairs she was not free to marry until her husband died in 1875. She remarried a close friend in 1877 but died three months later. By this time all her children had already died.

In 1830 **John Stuart Mills**, a Member of Parliament, went to a dinner party where he first met Harriet Taylor; it was love at first sight. She was a writer and a poet – and in an unhappy marriage. They were both victims of unhappy, loveless marriages. He often made the point to her that even a slave who is mistreated can be excused escape from his overbearing master. But, in those days divorce was extremely rare and depended on adultery by either party being either admitted or proven; apart from death, there was no other means of escape from a loveless marriage. Marriage was so often used solely as a vehicle for the transfer of power and property. Love was not part of the deal. Men could, and frequently did, find satisfaction outside their marriage and this was socially acceptable; to many men, women did not matter.

John Mills eventually became a widower though it was not until almost 20 years after they first met that Harriet Taylor's husband also died. They married. He renounced all rights over her property – it was a matter of principle for both of them. They both shared strong political views and believed that women should have equal pay for equal work and that they should also have the vote; after all, women were half the population of the country. By 1867 male householders had the vote. In parliament he proposed the vote for women and gained the support of 73 MPs; the vote was lost. Harriet, with the help and support of her husband, wrote a book titled *On the Subjection of Women*. It was politically and socially radical and its publication would have caused a strong reaction – they did not publish it. In 1869, after Harriet's death, John Mills had her book printed, published and distributed; it achieved much of the desired effect.

Queen Victoria wrote a diary from the age of 13 (1832) until weeks before her death in 1901. During her lifetime she wrote letters too, lots of letters. She is said to have written an average of 2,500 words each day; she was noted for being both frank, and at times forceful, in airing her opinions. Perhaps it was a cathartic process for her in contrast to her controlled life and environment? Those letters which have, thankfully, survived have become significant historical and social documents.

Her family were not so happy about her outpourings and could see the dangers of their existence. After her death her daughter, Beatrice, is thought to have edited her journals because they were too frank – a process which, because there was enough material to fill 700 volumes, apparently took her decades to complete; the original censored words were destroyed.

The 300 letters which she wrote to Alexander Profeit, her Balmoral estate manager, including comment about her favoured John Brown, were inherited by his son, George Profeit, who made it known that he was considering making them public. In 1904, apparently at the request of King Edward VII, they were purchased from George Profeit and destroyed.

Queen Victoria wrote a book *Leaves from the Journal of Our Lives in the Highlands* which sold 100,000 copies. This inspired her to write even more. A great number of her letters survive and are archived, but some of her more high profile written thoughts, which are frequently quoted in the media, cannot all be directly attributed to her; but, many are certainly in the spirit of her writings.

Having heard that Viscountess Amberley had become the President of The Bristol and West of England Women's Suffrage Society, and in that capacity had addressed a public meeting on the subject, Queen Victoria felt driven to write to Sir Theodore Martin, author, translator and solicitor, in 1870 and said: 'I am most anxious to enlist everyone who can speak or write to join in checking this mad, wicked folly of Women's Rights, with all its attendant horrors, on which her poor feeble sex is bent, forgetting every sense of womanly feelings and propriety. Feminists ought to get a good whipping. Were women to "unsex" themselves by claiming equality with men, they would become the most hateful, heathen and disgusting of beings and would surely perish without male protection'.

From the British Library we have her writing, again in 1870, in denial of equal voting rights for women: 'Let women be what God intended, a helpmate for man, but with totally different duties and vocations'. Further comments include: 'The Queen is most anxious to enlist everyone in checking this mad, wicked folly of Women's Rights. It is a subject which makes the Queen so furious that she cannot contain herself' and 'Women should perform the work appropriate to the strengths of their gender' and 'It is indecent for a woman to see a man naked – let alone to be allowed to operate on them'. Hopefully, times and attitudes have changed.

Elizabeth Garrett Anderson 1836–1917 was born to Newson Garrett and Louisa (née Dunnell); at that time they lived and worked in Commercial Road, Whitechapel, east London whilst her father was running a pawnbrokers shop for his father-in-law. She was the second of 12 children. He was fairly successful and ended up silversmithing and running a much larger pawnbrokers.

In 1841 Newson decided to move back to Leiston, East Suffolk where his family originated from; they were a family of well-respected engineers. He, however, decided to buy a corn and coal merchants business and built The Maltings at Snape (now a popular arts complex famous for the Aldeburgh Music Festival) and later, as a result of his successful move into the railway and shipping businesses too had a mansion, Alde House, built for the family. So, in the end, Elizabeth was brought up in a privileged environment and for a while was educated at home by a governess.

At the age of 13 she and her elder sister (15 years) were sent to a boarding school which was run by the aunts of Robert Browning in Blackheath on the outskirts of London. In 1854, together with her sister, she visited a school friend at Gateshead and there met Emily Davis who was to become a renowned feminist and founder of Girton College, Cambridge. This meeting was to be the beginning of a lifelong friendship.

It is thought that Elizabeth read, in the first edition of *The English-woman's Journal* in 1858, of the visit to London the following year of Dr Elizabeth Blackwell a woman who was born in England but been brought up in America and had qualified as a medical doctor. A speech by her in London titled 'Medicine as a Profession for Ladies' had been organised by The Society for Promoting the Employment of Women. Elizabeth was inspired by this talk to pursue a life in medicine and soon gathered the moral and financial support of her father.

She was also becoming more and more active in the women's rights movement, supported by Emily Davis and her sister Millicent (later to become Dame Millicent Garrett Fawcett, a renowned activist of the constitutional suffrage campaign) and, together with other notable women in the movement formed the influential Kensington Society.

In her efforts to enter the medical profession as a doctor she spent 6 months as a surgery nurse at The Middlesex Hospital where she was allowed to attend her first operation. Her attempts to enrol at the hospital's medical school were thwarted. However, this did not stop her ambitions and through self-funded private tuition she learned the appropriate Latin, human anatomy and physiology and gained entry to the dissection room and to lectures. Her moves were continually being blocked until the point at which she was asked to leave the establishment. She was, at least, given a certificate in recognition of her studies and her works.

She subsequently applied to numerous medical schools including at London, Oxford, Cambridge and Edinburgh. She eventually entered the world of professional medicine by a rather 'back-door' route – by qualifying as a Licentiate member of The Society of Apothecaries (LSA). On the day of her examination there were a total of seven candidates of whom only three passed. Elizabeth was the student with the highest marks. The Society immediately moved to subsequently ban all women from taking their entrance examination. But, now legitimately qualified, her name was entered on the British Medical Register. The Medical Act 1876 legislated to allow suitably qualified persons of all genders to be officially recognised as 'Registered Medical Practitioners'. Elizabeth Garrett Anderson was to remain the only registered female member for almost two decades.

However, although now professionally qualified she was still not allowed to take up a post in any hospital; so, she set up her first private medical practice in the now famous Harley Street area of London and in 1866 she also began a charitable venture 'St Mary's Dispensary for Women and Children' in Marylebone, London which had 3,000 patients in its first year.

Having heard that it would be possible to gain a medical degree in France she temporarily moved to Paris and took and passed the examinations and was therefore awarded her full medical qualification by the University of Paris. She was pivotal in creating the London School of Medicine for Women (which was later a part of the University of London) she became a member of its Council, taught there and eventually became the Dean. It was the first institution to allow women to qualify for a degree.

In 1871 she married James Anderson a director of The Orient Steamship Company but did not take a 'vow of obedience' as part of the marriage ceremony. They had three children but the middle child, a daughter, died of meningitis.

As a wife and a mother she continued to practice medicine on her own account and to promote the furtherance of women in medicine wherever and whenever she could. She was also a Member of the British Women's Suffrage Committee but because of her professional commitments was unable to dedicate as much time to it as she would have liked. She and her husband retired in 1902 to her old family home at Alde House in Aldeburgh; he became the Mayor and, after his death, she followed in his steps and became the next

Mayor. She was the first female Mayor in England. Retirement also gave her some more time to spread the word about women's suffrage and she even, in her dotage, led a delegation to speak to Herbert Asquith the then Prime Minister. She resigned from the Women's Social and Political Union soon afterwards because she disagreed with the notion of using militant tactics to achieve emancipation for women. Her surviving daughter was, in adulthood, to qualify as a Doctor of Medicine and she also wrote her mother's biography.

Whitelands College was founded in 1841 by the Church of England's National Society in Chelsea for teacher training for women. Then, in 1869 Gerton College, Cambridge opened its doors as a women only college; it was the first institution of its kind to offer the freedom to women to be educated at this level. Newnham followed in 1871 with the co-founder being the Suffragette activist Millicent Garrett Fawcett. In 1897 Philippa Fawcett, the daughter of the co-founder, passed the Cambridge exams with the highest mark – way above all the men. The achievement was national and international news – that a woman could not only be educated at that level but that she could far exceed the performance of any male. Unfortunately, whilst women could attend lectures and sit the exams they could not be awarded a degree. It was not until 1948 that they could gain a full degree and wear the cap and gown.

Lily Maxwell, in 1867, was a shopkeeper and ratepayer in Manchester. Her name was erroneously entered on the voters' roll of ratepayers for a local by-election. She attended the polling and cast her vote; but, her vote was soon disallowed and by the following year there was legislation specifically banning all women from voting. Lily Maxwell was not alone in being a woman erroneously granted a vote; like her, all women who found themselves in a similar situation were treated as imposters and their votes made null and void. She is remembered as the first woman to legally cast her vote.

Annie Besant was, in the late 1800s, drawn to work in the slums of cities as times again became hard, jobs disappeared and feeding your family became nearly impossible; a life of work for the poor could easily become substituted by a life of sin and crime. She gave free contraceptive advice to women in the hope of reducing the ever growing number of mouths to be fed. As a result of her good deeds the courts saw her as an unfit mother and she lost the custody of her young daughter. Her achievement on behalf of the 'matchgirls' of the Bryant & May factory was in getting the company to stop using the chemicals which had already been outlawed by other manufacturers. The phosphorous which they used in the manufacture of their matches was the cause of a facially disfiguring disease which affected the women working in the factory; it became known as 'fossy jaw'. The phosphorous rotted the jawbone from inside. The company was making good profits for its investors, who included the church, whilst the girls were poorly paid. Annie Besant got the results she wanted by getting the girls to strike – and had somehow raised the funds to agree to pay them during the strike. George Bernard Shaw was one of her supporters and worked alongside her on this campaign. In the end the company gave in to their demands. In 1888 she campaigned to have herself adopted by the Tower Hamlets school board. By this time she, and her works were well known and she won – with 15,000 votes.

In the 1880s to 1890s **Queen Victoria** made efforts to be seen to press Gladstone, the then Prime Minister, to do more about alleviating the housing problems of the poor. She disliked and distrusted Gladstone but when, in 1887, a new project called 'The People's Palace' in Mile End Road was completed she travelled there to officially open it. More projects to alleviate the problems of slums slowly followed. Her interest was doubtless in memory of her beloved late husband, Prince Albert, who had championed this cause. In their normal lives the educated classes never saw, and were virtually unaware of, the unemployed and in particular the one-third of the population of London who were homeless. As a result of her pressure there was a Royal Commission.

Bicycles becoming popular had an oft overlooked effect of technology on the life of women in the late 19th century. They gave freedom to the women able to afford them and the ability to cover what were then substantial distances and, without a chaperone – just as the railways had done. Post boxes allowed women to be able to write to another person without members of their household knowing.

Before the advent of this aspect of the postal service women would have had to have given a letter to either their husband or a member of the household staff for collection by the postman or delivering it to the Post Office; they were not allowed to do so themselves.

The Suffragettes: Towards the end of the Victorian era there was, throughout much of the developed world, a small but growing movement promoting women getting the vote. There had long been a fight, by women of privilege, against the traditional control of their lives by men. Women had always been seen as being the 'property' of the males in their lives; firstly as the daughter of their father (or other dominant male of the family) and, after that, as the wife of their husband. This system had, for centuries, not allowed women to own or control property of any type – from their clothes and jewellery – to inherited land. And, women in general certainly had no overt influence outside the home. Men had always taken advantage of this situation to allow them to accumulate money, property and land; and, through these acquisitions, power and influence. The 'costs' were borne by the women; 'marriages of convenience' were commonplace vehicles for this acquisitive social engineering.

Interestingly, to this very day and throughout much of the western world, many women unwittingly choose to continue to symbolically reinforce their traditional position of subjugation when they expect to be 'given away' by their father in their wedding ceremony.

It was mainly the socially privileged women members of the international Suffragette community – frequently exposing themselves to social disgrace, danger and even death – whose political agitation ensured the freedoms and powers that were eventually granted to all British women through the right to vote. They are the real heroines of women's emancipation.

Back in 1903, in Nelson Street, Manchester lived the Pankhurst family. Dr Richard Pankhurst was a barrister and his wife, Emmeline, had a small shop and was the Registrar for Births and Deaths in Manchester; she was born in Moss Side Manchester, had been well brought up and was sent away to be educated in Paris. The whole family were all, at some level, ardent followers and promoters of the Suffragette cause. Emmeline Pankhurst was probably the woman who gained the highest profile in the Suffragette movement but, her daughters Christabel and Sylvia (Estelle) and, to a much lesser extent, the youngest daughter Adela were also active and militant supporters of the cause; even their father was supportive of his wife and daughter's good works. It was Sylvia's imprisonment, in 1905, for her pro-Suffragette activities, which spurred Emmeline to a much greater level of action. The Pankhursts began the Women's Social and Political Union (WSPU) as the organisational core of the movement for enfranchisement for women. The Suffragettes raised money for their cause by diverse means including selling home-made produce, posters which they had printed and they even devised and sold a Suffragette board game. Later, women who were imprisoned for their efforts in support of the Suffragette cause were each given a large and ornate certificate by the Suffragette organisation in acknowledgement of their endeavours and sacrifices.

The government said that the Suffragettes were just a small group of radicals and that they did not have popular support. To prove their strong supporter base the WSPU organised a march in central London for Sunday 21st June 1908 to culminate in a rally in Hyde Park. It was to be the largest demonstration seen in the country to date; there was an estimated gathering of over 250,000 women – an immense number for that time when the population was smaller and communications and travel were less developed. Even the Pankhurst family were amazed at the turnout. Shops ran out of white dresses and white, purple and green ribbons. The Suffragette colours were purple for Dignity, white for being Chaste and green for Hope. Temporary stands were erected in the park for the 80 speakers to address the ladies. It was to become known as 'Women's Sunday'.

As a result, the new Liberal government created the Conciliation Bill intended to give women – but only those with wealth and influence – the vote. The Bill reached its second reading in the House of Commons but the Prime Minister, Asquith, reneged on his word and put a stop to it.

In protest, on Friday 18th November 1910, the WSPU sent a delegation of about 300 women to Parliament to protest. They were met with an aggressive response from the authorities; the women were beaten, hit with truncheons , kicked and sexually assaulted by the police. It has not been reported if this was a spontaneous reaction by the police or whether they had been instructed to use these particularly demeaning tactics. It was the first recorded incident of the Suffragettes being assaulted by the police. Almost half the women were arrested and it is recorded that two women died from their injuries.

The press and their photographers were in attendance and recorded the whole demonstration and had photos of the assaults and of the women's injuries. The authorities tried to stop publication and confiscate the photos but, by the next day, it was front page news – and Asquith and the government were condemned whilst the Suffragettes gained much public sympathy. It became known as Black Friday.

The Home Secretary refused to allow an enquiry into the events of Black Friday. His name was Winston Churchill.

Because this was the first time such violence had been used on the Suffragettes they had to re-evaluate their strategy and the responses they were likely to get in future. Initially, there were numerous unsolicited instances of women throwing stones to break windows in public buildings – it soon became a widespread tactic. One woman, Mary Clarke, was arrested for breaking a window and was imprisoned and she went on hunger strike. She was force-fed and eventually discharged from prison on Christmas Day but died a few days later as a result of both her starvation and her prison treatment. She was the sister of Emmeline Pankhurst.

Whether intentional or not, the use of different tactics – from lobbying to demonstrations, to mass rallies, to marches, to guerrilla attacks – meant that the authorities had to be ever vigilant, prepared for action from the Suffragettes at all levels. It used up precious police resources and energy.

The Suffragettes used civil disobedience to further their cause. They forced their way into many government and local council buildings and into official meetings intent on causing as much disturbance as possible. They chained themselves to chairs and to railings; they caused criminal damage, severed telephone cables, committed arson and even planted bombs.

In 1912, as a result of a raid on the headquarters of the WSPU and the arrest of her mother, Christabel Pankhurst fled England and sought refuge in Paris. Whilst there she wrote a paper 'Votes for Women – Chastity for Men' which was to become a slogan of the Suffragettes. The premise seems to be that if men do not give women the vote then women will not give men any sexual favours.

This has become an interesting stand to make – in the light of a recently discovered diary, written by WSPU member Mary Blathwayt. Articles quoting Professor Martin Pugh, of Liverpool John Moores University, indicate that there are numerous entries referring to lesbian relationships of and between leading members of the WSPU including both generations of the Pankhurst family. An interesting and erstwhile unconfirmed perspective.

The Pankhurst sisters were quite different beings from each other. Sylvia Pankhurst was born in 1882 and named Estelle Sylvia. She was their second daughter, after Christabel (born1880) and before Adela (born 1885); there were two brothers the first of whom died in childhood, aged four, and the second who died in 1910 at the age of 21; nothing more is known about them . Their distant but adored father, Dr Richard, was a reformist barrister, a pacifist and a radical socialist, he was also a strong supporter of the new Independent Labour Party; he was 23 years older than his wife Emmeline. At their home they would frequently have visitors who were prominent 'movers and shakers' of their day, including Keir Hardy and William Morris.

Sylvia was a talented artist and designer who was trained at the Royal College of Art. Politically, she aligned with her father's ideas; she was an eccentric, a pacifist and a staunch and radical socialist, perhaps even bordering on communism. Indeed, Lenin said of her that she was far too left wing. When the Independent Labour Party funded the building of a meeting hall in Salford, Manchester it was decided to name it Pankhurst Hall after Dr Richard Pankhurst; Sylvia was invited to create many of the internal paintings. However, neither she, nor any other woman, was allowed into the building as a visitor. It is said that this was a factor which boosted Emmeline Pankhurst's passion for the Women's Social and Political Union.

Sylvia spent much of her time and energy doing social work in east London and was a member of the local socialists. As a Suffragette, she was imprisoned more frequently than any other member.

By this time her mother and elder sister were being drawn to Conservatism and as a result of their political differences the family was being torn apart; youngest daughter Adela was given £20 by her mother and forcibly sent to Australia because she showed dissent for some of the WSPU tactics. Sylvia was supported in her social work by Keir Hardy; they soon became close and, even though he was 26 years her senior and married, they began a long-term and committed love affair.

In her forties, she met and fell in love with an Italian political radical and journalist, Silvio Corio; she moved from Bow so that they could live together in a cottage, which she re-named 'Red Cottage', opposite the Horse & Well public house in Woodford, E18 – which in those days was right on the edge of Epping Forest. In 1927 they had a son called Richard, named after her beloved father, and six years later they moved to a larger house near Woodford railway station where they stayed until Silvio died in 1954; they never married which was seen by both her family and locals as improper. Whilst in Woodford, as a result of the 1932 air attack on Ethiopia directed by Mussolini, she produced and published a set of works including *Ethiopian News*; she wanted to do all that she could to save Ethiopia from conquest by fascist Italy.

In 1956, two years after Silvio had died, she was invited by the Emperor of Ethiopia, Haile Selassie, to live and work in his country. She accepted the offer and remained there until her death in 1960 in Addis Ababa. She was given a state funeral, rather ironically in a coffin draped in a gold cloth, in recognition of all she had done for the country.

Christabel was beautiful, elegant, intelligent and socially adept and, as the first child, had a special relationship with both of her parents. All three sisters went to Manchester High School for Girls and she went on to qualify as a lawyer, like her father, but being a woman was not allowed to practice. For a while, she went to live in Geneva but returned to the family home in 1898 when her father died, an event which deeply touched her. These circumstances greatly strengthened the bond between mother and daughter. She was more of what we would call 'a right wing activist' whereas Sylvia was a socialist; Christabel is reported by her sister as saying that the women's movement had no need of working class women – that their lives were too busy to have the time or energy to help and that they were too ill-educated; she believed they needed only monied, educated and influential women in their movement to stand a realistic chance of effecting change. Christabel was to continue working for both the Conservatives and full emancipation. In 1921 she moved to America and became an evangelist preacher linked to both the Plymouth Brethren and the Adventists. By the 1950s the arrival of television had given her a new image; she was seen on chat shows depicted as an elderly eccentric Englishwoman who had once been a Suffragette and was now an evangelical Christian. She also gave lectures. She died in 1958, aged 77, in Santa Monica.

Adela was always a 'sickly' child and not really expected to live a very long life. She wore splints until the age of three; she was later partially educated at the Studley Horticultural College She was considered bright and was recommended to get a scholarship to Oxford but her mother would not allow it. She was sent to Switzerland for a while and returned wanting to be a teacher; this she did. Being the youngest, she seemingly lived in the shadow of her elder sisters but was still involved in supporting the Suffrage cause. Her 'mission' was to disrupt all of Winston Churchill's meetings – a cause for which she was arrested and sent to prison; but, the authorities decided that at seven stone she was too thin and feeble to withstand it and thus sent her home. By 1905 the disruptive tactics of the WSPU were failing to achieve their aim and so many members began resorting to various forms of more aggressive demonstration. Adela was against such violence. After a family dispute over the tactics of the suffragist movement her mother bought her a one-way ticket for a boat to Australia, gave her £20 and sent her away. That family split was never resolved. In Australia she was a strong anti-war campaigner and a member of the Women's Peace Army; she opposed both war and conscription and wrote a book *Put Up the Sword*. In her lifetime she supported many causes and at one time was a founding member of The Communist Party of Australia from which she was expelled and then, later, a right wing Nationalist member of the Australia First Movement. Little more is known about her.

The period from 1910 to 1914 was the 'Great Unrest'. The working class was in a mood for social unrest with workers attending rallies and marching – spurred on by socialist organisations. Wages were stagnant, prices were rising and thus the standard of living for the working man was getting worse by the day – and employers were all the time wanting more produced by fewer workers. Meanwhile, the rich were getting richer. The government was extremely worried by the social unrest and took drastic actions to try to quell it. Sylvia was all for the working classes and their rights whilst Christabel was on the side of the employers – and thus the government. The differences between the sisters was getting greater and eventually Christabel moved to get her sister expelled from the WSPU.

David Lloyd George had been an admirer and supporter of the views of John Stuart Mills and others, and as a result, when in opposition had always been a prominent supporter of women's rights but when in government, as the Chancellor of the Exchequer, he had failed to put these beliefs into practice. As a result, the WSPU placed two bombs at a house he was having built; one caused £500 worth of damage but the other failed to go off. There were no physical injuries. At a meeting of the WSPU at Cory Hall, Cardiff Emmeline Pankhurst suggested that her actions had doubtless incited the bombers but, in the end, no-one was prosecuted for the offence by the Police.

On 4th June 1913 Emily Wilding Davison, an active supporter of the Suffragettes for seven years, bought a return rail ticket from London to Epsom so that she could attend the horse racing at Epsom racecourse. It was the day of the Derby, the most prominent horse race of the time. That morning, she had wrapped a Suffragette poster around her body under her coat and was carrying a furled protest banner. She positioned herself against the rails at the edge of the racecourse at Tattenham Corner. Once the race had started and King's horse came close she rushed out and tried to grab its reins. The horse fell on her; several days later she died of her injuries. It has been said that the fact that she had purchased a return ticket was proof that she had only intended to make a protest, not that she had started the day with the intention of sacrificing herself in such a way. Whatever the truth, she immediately became a martyr for the cause of all Suffragettes.

In the summer of 1913, just before the First World War, Suffragettes from all over the country marched towards London to attend a mass protest in Hyde Park; an estimated 50,000 women attended. There were followers from all over the nation and even an Asian contingent. The rally ended in the Albert Hall with speeches from the prime movers; it became known as 'The Great March'. These marches were often quite civilized upper and middle-class affairs with stops en route for tea and sandwiches on the lawns of supporters' homes.

Emmeline Pankhurst, along with her daughters, had been high profile instigators of the movement. She was also one of the many protesters to be taken before a court of law and subsequently imprisoned for her acts of civil disobedience. Christabel had to remove herself to Paris to avoid imprisonment and only returned because of the threat of imminent war.

But there was another side to the cause of enfranchisement for women. Those who believed that political manoeuvres towards parliamentary reform, rather than radical activism, was the best route by which to achieve the change. Millicent Garrett Fawcett was one of these women. She was a suffragist and a feminist; she was the co-founder of Newnham College, Cambridge and President of the National Union of Women's Suffrage Societies (she also performed many other similar roles in her life). She was married to Henry Fawcett the blind Liberal Member of Parliament for Hackney (and formerly for Brighton). Her sister was Elizabeth Garrett, the first woman to qualify as a surgeon and her daughter a brilliant scholar at Cambridge University. She was an advocate of the work of John Stuart Mills and whilst she did not agree with the tactics of Emmeline Pankhurst she did admire her. In truth, both styles of approach to achieving the vote for women were valid and were complementary.

Once they were imprisoned, the Suffragettes usually went on hunger strike. The initial official reaction was to force-feed the women; this was a process that had hitherto been reserved for the insane. There was a public backlash to this treatment and, as a result, it was stopped.

The official response then changed; the authorities allowed the women to go on hunger strike until they became very weak but, the legal system then acted before the women would be likely to die. Too weak and feeble to be of any further trouble to the authorities, the women were released on compassionate grounds. This way the cause of the Suffragettes did not get the publicity and public sympathy borne of women dying in prison as martyrs. It was in Exeter Prison that Emmeline Pankhurst went on hunger strike in December of 1913; as a result of her weakened state and because of the publicity she was getting, she too was let out of jail.

Over the next few months there was a diminishing in the level of support for the Suffragette movement. The timing of this coincided with the fear of the likelihood of war; interest soon died away and, as war began, all women diverted their energies into support for their country and for the soldiers. The good works of women during the four years of war – supporting the country by working in factories, working on farms and caring for the soldiers injured in the fighting – were to become a more potent catalyst for the imminent emancipation of women than their previous civil disobedience had ever been.

The end of the First World War was to bring enfranchisement to all men over 21 years of age and to women over 30 years of age with property. By 1927 Emmeline Pankhurst was a pillar of society and she was adopted as the Conservative candidate for Stepney in east London. The following year, on 2nd July, the Representation of the People Act 1928 extended the vote to all women over 21 years of age; it was what the Suffragettes has always been fighting for. Emmeline Pankhurst died on 14th June 1928 and did not live to see this new law enacted.

As far as women legitimately getting the vote is concerned it was Wyoming in America who led the way; in 1869 it was the first place where women were given the right to vote and where they could serve on juries. But, it wasn't that the Wyoming legislature were social reformers who showed a political mission to give women equal rights in law, it was much more devious than that. Wyoming was a territory which wanted to become a State and, to be able to do so, they needed to fulfil the appropriate population requirement. By giving women the vote they were able to show that they had enough citizens eligible to vote (a large enough electorate) to be awarded the status of becoming a member State of the United States of America; in 1870 the population of Wyoming was 9,118; a decade later it was over 20,000. Initially, Wyoming became known as the 'Suffrage State' and it is now known as the 'Equality State'. Wyoming still has the smallest population of all US mainland States at around 600,000 whilst in California the population is 38 million.

When it comes to nations awarding suffrage to women it was New Zealand that was the early adopter, back in 1893; Australia followed suit the next year. In Russia it was 1917 after the Revolution and in the UK it was at the end of the First World War, in 1918. It also gave them the theoretical right to become a member of parliament. It took another 10 years for the government to be persuaded to give the vote to all women in the UK. In Canada it was 1919 and the USA it was 1920. Perhaps most surprising of all is that it took neutral Switzerland until 1971 to give women the vote.

Suffrage was not the same as equality – just a step upon a long and winding road. All women in Great Britain might have won the right to vote – but, sadly, not all use it. According to the government (yougov.co.uk & ipsos MORI statistics) at the 2015 General Election 67 per cent of eligible men voted and 66 per cent of eligible women voted. But, and this is interesting, according to the Electoral Commission 'Gender & Political Participation' survey women are 'significantly more likely to vote if represented by a woman but are generally less likely to be involved in campaign-oriented activities'. Four per cent more women than men vote for a female candidate. Seven per cent fewer women are likely to vote if the candidate is a man. In answer to the statement 'the government benefits me' 49 per cent of women agree if the candidate is female; eight per cent agree if the candidate is male. Further, in the 2015 election women (particularly those under 50) were more likely to vote Labour than men; this is a reversal of all the post-war statistics.

In **1919** the father of MP Waldorf Astor died; Waldorf inherited his father's title, Lord Astor, and moved from the House of Commons to the House of Lords. He persuaded his wife, the American born Nancy Langhorne, to stand for his outgoing constituency at Plymouth, Devon. She won the seat and remained an MP until 1945; Nancy Astor was the first woman to take her seat in the House of Commons as a Member of Parliament.

In **1911** a government census reported over 50 per cent of all men worked in jobs that were never performed by, or even open to, women. By today's standards there are, theoretically, no jobs that women are not capable of performing.

In **1914**, the Women's Police Service was created by two women to support the efforts for the First World War. The members were all volunteers and were, at a practical level, persuaders – they did not have any of the legal powers of male police officers.

It was the early days of the First World War and the town of Grantham in Lincolnshire had a problem. Fourteen thousand newly enlisted soldiers had been moved to army camps created on the outskirts of the town for their initial training. These young men, were about to leave the UK for France where they believed they would enjoy a new and exciting period of their lives. Grantham was where their new adventures would begin and a rite of passage was to lose their virginity – hopefully before they left. Hundreds of young women, intent on facilitating the young soldiers needs in exchange for money, moved into the area.

All these high-spirited young men, testosterone rushing through their bodies, were easy prey. The Army were aware of the potential problems and tried to keep the number of men allowed out of the barracks at low as possible but, in reality, could not keep them all contained all the time. In the short term the Army did not want disreputable behaviour of any kind to blacken their name and in the longer term they did not want to have to deal with the effects of hundreds of men with venereal disease.

In 1915 Edith Smith, a widow and ex-midwife, was appointed by the authorities for Grantham as the very first paid Woman Police Officer and given the power of arrest. Her specific role was to control the women who had made themselves available to the young soldiers. For two years she worked every day of every week in an effort to fulfil her role.

At the time of her appointment the Home Office opposed Grantham Council's appointment of a woman to the rank of Police Constable. They said that women were not 'proper persons' to perform such a role. Indeed, like all her peers, she did not even have the vote. By the end of the war, in 1918, the Home Secretary ordered the Metropolitan Police to recruit women as Police Officers. It was not until The Sex Disqualification Removal Act 1919 that women were legally permitted to become lawyers, top civil servants, etc.

In 1918, at the end of the First World War, she resigned her post. She had developed a persistent chest infection and five years later died from a self-induced overdose of morphine. The next year Margaret Thatcher, later to become Great Britain's first woman Prime Minister, was born in Grantham.

Dorothée Pullinger was born at the end of the 19th century, near the port of Dieppe in northern France, to her British father and French mother. When she was just 10 years old the family moved to the UK and eventually settled in Paisley, Scotland. Her father Thomas, a well-known car designer, began work for Arrol-Johnston motor engineers as their managing director. Dorothée also worked there as a draughtsperson.

At the outbreak of the First World War the factory ceased manufacturing cars and began to make aeroplanes. Dorothée went to Barrow-in-Furness to work as a supervisor in the all-female staffed Vickers munitions factory making high-explosive shells for the navy and the military with 7,000 workers. For her outstanding work in this role she was awarded an MBE.

After the war she returned to the Paisley factory, now called Galloway Motors Ltd, to become both a manager and a director.

The staff remained almost exclusively female and there were female apprentices too – whose apprenticeships were cut from five to three years because they were such good students. At her instigation the company designed and produced a car specifically for women. She believed that because there were so many women who had learned to drive as a result of their work in the war that there was an opening in the market for a car designed for women, by a woman and built by women. The Galloway 10/20 was launched. It was smaller, lighter and easier to control than its rivals and, it had much more storage and a new invention called a rear-view mirror. She actively promoted the car, acted as a sales agent for the company and even became a winning race driver. Unfortunately, because of the national financial crisis, the car was only made for a period of five years, from 1920–1925, and fewer than 2,000 were produced.

In 1919 she became one of the founders of The Women's Engineering Society and remained an active member for her whole life. Dorothée was later to marry and, together with her husband, formed a steam laundry company in Croydon which used newly imported American machinery; they soon had 17 branches. She worked as an advisor to the government during the Second World War and afterwards moved to Guernsey in the Channel Islands and set up another laundry business. She remained there until her death in 1986.

'Torches of Freedom'

The history of smoke inhalation, according to archaeological finds, seems to originate around 5,000 years ago in the South American Peru/Ecuador region and was probably associated with ceremonies and rituals and used as a hallucinogenic to induce trance like states bringing man closer to the spirits 'on the other side'. The Babylonians, Scythians, Chinese, early Greeks, and many others used cannabis and other herbs. Cloves and Eucalypts (Myrtle family) were certainly smoked by both men and women in pipes in India for medicinal purposes such as clearing the head, nose and chest when congested and the process was allocated the word 'dhumrapana' which means 'drinking smoke'. The plants of this genus are indigenous in China, Indonesia, Africa, the Middle East and parts of Europe so it is likely that the practice was widespread. Incense burning has been used in religious ceremonies worldwide for a very long time and continues today.

Jean Nicot (of nicotine fame) introduced the smoking of tobacco to France in around 1560. In Britain it was Sir John Hawkins (not Sir Francis Drake) and his crew of sailors who were the first try it and bring it back to us. For many it was to become a fashionable and sophisticated new experience much like tea, coffee and opium. But, in 1604, King James I wrote *A Counterblaste to Tobacco* and described it as 'loathsome to the eye, hateful to the nose, harmful to the brain and dangerous to the lungs' (so, a man way ahead of his time in that respect).

But demand grew and it was even credited with having health benefits during the Great Plague because it would fumigate and kill germs; indeed, Eton College made its consumption compulsory. A greater popularity for smoking created more demand for tobacco and that, in turn, created a greater demand for workers to grow the crop – for slaves. The more we smoked, the more we wanted to smoke and so the bowls on pipes which were originally quite tiny became larger and larger. Working class smoking was based on the workplace and the public houses where clay pipes were given away by the landlords. There are Hogarth-style images of women smoking clay pipes but there are scant records beyond that of the uptake by women in general at this time. Women smoking was associated with prostitutes, 'fallen women' and drunken hags.

Matthew Hilton, in his book *Smoking in British Culture 1800–2000* notes how for the upper classes a handmade pipe of character became a symbol of status, masculine and sophisticated – as pictured with Sir Arthur Conan Doyle and his fictional character 'Sherlock Holmes'. Smoking such a pipe or a cigar, was akin to enjoying a fine wine or brandy. Hand manufactured cigarettes were seen as much more passive and 'feminine'.

By the 1880s, W.D. & H.O. Wills imported the American 'Bonsack' machine which made cigarettes by their thousands on a production line. For the working class at least, smoking a clay pipe fell out of fashion, and cheaper and more readily available 'tailor-made' cigarettes introduced smoking to many young men as a rite of passage between being a child and a working man. Thus, in 1908 The Children Act banned children under 16 from buying tobacco products. In 1908 in New York they even passed a law prohibiting any woman from smoking in public. Men, meanwhile, smoked cigarettes, pipes and cigars – and took snuff.

The image of a Tommy (a British private soldier) in the First World War smoking a cigarette was an enduring one (this was repeated during the Second World War). During the years of the First World War, women who were performing the work roles of men began to smoke as part of their working day – just as their male counterparts would have done. It is not recorded what caused this change in women's social behaviour. Were the women under such stress as to need the effects of smoking, were they smoking to get a release from the monotony of work given by a smoke-break or, were they using the opportunity of being a 'surrogate male' to reflect a male's behaviour pattern – to make a political point?

By the mid-1920s the cigarette manufacturers had realised the potential for a substantial increase in the sales of their products if they could get smoking by women to become a socially acceptable practice. If successful, the female half of the adult population could potentially become their customers too – providing a theoretical increase of 100 per cent of their current sales. It was in America in 1929 that women were first directly targeted in an advertising campaign – and a very clever ploy was used. Cigarette smoking by women, they suggested, should be seen as a symbol of female emancipation – no longer the sole prerogative of the male. For women to openly smoke would break yet another gender taboo. Cigarettes were promoted as 'Torches of Freedom'; cigarettes were for feminists, supporters of equality, they were symbols of emancipation. The effects of the advertising soon spread across the world and women actresses were seen smoking in films and it was thought of as a sign of a strong, sexy yet feminine woman. The cigarette manufacturer Philip Morris even ran a series of lectures to teach women the etiquette of smoking. By 1935 20 per cent of women were smoking. Mass produced cigarettes (tailor-made as opposed to hand rolled) became aspirational luxury items throughout the world. Later in the first half of the 20th century, in Britain it became rather 'avant-garde' for upper class women to smoke 'tailor-made' cigarettes – of the fashionable brands only, of course – and usually with an ornate cigarette holder; silver and gold cigarette cases were also in vogue for both men and women of a certain social status. Women were not to be seen smoking in the street, that was too common. The working class man was also brand conscious and 'Craven A' were even targeted at working class women. By 1949 it was said that 81 per cent of men and 39 per cent of women smoked. Post this period the individual pipe regained some status with numerous middle-class men wishing to assume a certain gravitas and air of character; Harold Wilson was such a man and this type of behaviour was even parodied by Morecambe and Wise in some of their comedy sketches. Cigars remained upper class although cheroot size cigars were a more a middle or even working class style.

There had always been a vague link between smoking and poor health. As life expectancy increased the difference between smokers and non-smokers became more evident. In 1950 a report was published in the British Medical Journal making a direct correlation between smoking and lung cancer. In 1971 there was a voluntary agreement for smoking products to have health warnings. In 2007 the ban on smoking in enclosed public spaces was enacted.

Amy Johnson, a Yorkshire lass from Hull, graduated from Sheffield University with a BA in Economics and moved to London where she took up flying aeroplanes as a hobby. Soon, she qualified as a solo pilot and became the first woman to qualify as an aeronautical ground engineer. She then began a number of well-documented world-record flights, including being the first woman to fly solo to Australia, before joining the Air Transport Auxiliary at the beginning of the Second World War. She died in 1941, when her plane had to 'ditch' in the river Thames in London, whilst performing this role.

Hélène Delangle, a Frenchwoman, moved from her home in the countryside to live in Paris; she changed her name to Hellé Nice and used her good looks and body to pursue a career as a stripper – renowned for her dance act with white doves. As a result of a skiing accident, which damaged her leg, she gave up her stripping and began racing Bugatti cars. Her life became 'racy' in every possible way; she travelled the world racing cars and courting glory, disaster and men. She was known as 'The Bugatti Queen' and forever in the media. Later life was not kind to her; she died poor and alone.

Violette Morris was born in France at the end of the 19th century to a wealthy and influential family; the youngest of six, she spent much of her childhood in a convent. She was an unequalled athlete gaining Olympic Gold Medals and other awards and recognition in shot-put, discus, javelin, football, wrestling, boxing and weight lifting – to name but a few; her motto was along the lines of 'anything a man can do Violette can do'; she was a very heavy smoker who was also known for fist fighting and defeating men. Although she was a self-confessed bisexual who often wore men's clothes, she was married to a man for a period of 10 years. She spent the First World War as an ambulance driver and served at the battles of the Somme and Verdun. Subsequent to her wartime driving, she took up motor racing and was successful in this too. Her overt bisexual antics began to cause social and press stigma for her in Paris. Allegedly, because of the size and shape of racing cars of that era her large breasts got in the way – so, she had both breasts removed in an elective mastectomy; some believed it was more a statement of her sexuality. She had a motor parts business in Paris which she lost as a result of the Depression; she then made a living as a driving instructor. Life for her had become mundane. As the Nazi regime began to thrive she came to their notice; she was invited as a VIP to the 1936 Berlin Olympic Games. When war approached she was enlisted into the Gestapo and, once again, gained the status she believed she deserved; she became a spy, an informer and eventually a torturer. Because of her treason she was hated by the French; and, in 1944, whilst driving her car, she was ambushed, shot and killed by the Resistance as a traitor.

In **1968** women in the sewing machine department of the Ford Motor Company's Dagenham plant went on strike. They walked out when they heard that the pay rate for their job was to be down-graded and that they would be paid 15 per cent less than similarly skilled men at the same plant. Three weeks later and after the intervention of Barbara Castle, the Employment Secretary in Harold Wilson's Labour government, the matter had been resolved and they returned to work.

The following year, under the auspices of the trade unions, a National Joint Action Campaign Committee for Women's Equal Rights was formed to put pressure on industry and the government for women to receive equal pay to men for equal jobs. A rally was held in Trafalgar Square in 1969. As a direct result of the above actions the government began work on the Equal Pay Act which passed through parliament in 1970 and came into force in 1975.

Margaret Thatcher (1925–2013) was born Margaret Hilda Roberts in Grantham, Lincolnshire on 13th October 1925 to Alfred and Beatrice who had both been born and lived in that part of the country. They owned two grocery shops in the town and lived in a flat above the larger of them. Her father was a strict Wesleyan and a preacher at the local Methodist church; he was also an independent member of the town council and served as mayor from 1945–1946. She was educated at Grantham Girl's High School and then went up to Somerville College, Oxford where she studied Chemistry.

Whilst there she became the president of the University Conservative Association. She gained a second-class honours degree and from there worked in Colchester as a research chemist. She was adopted and then ran as the Conservative candidate for Dartford, Kent in the 1950 and 1951 general elections. She moved to Dartford, and began working there too, and it was at a dinner after her formal adoption as a candidate that she met a successful divorced businessman called Denis Thatcher. It was a safe Labour seat so she did not win but her campaign was noted and earned her respect.

In 1951 she married Denis Thatcher and was then supported by him as she studied Law; she qualified as a barrister, specializing in taxation law, in 1953. Later that same year she gave birth to twins – Carol and Mark.

In 1954 she contested the seat for Orpington and lost but in 1959 contested and won the safe Conservative seat for Finchley but in what was to be a closely run contest. By 1961, in Harold Macmillan's government, she became the Under Secretary for Pensions and National Insurance. The Conservatives then lost the 1964 and 1966 elections and she became a member of the shadow cabinet treasury team and then the opposition spokeswoman.

In 1970, under Ted Heath's leadership the Conservatives won the election and she was given the cabinet post of Secretary of State for Education and Science and was noted for the abolition of free school milk whilst in that role. In a television interview in 1973 she is quoted as saying: 'I don't think there will be a woman Prime Minister in my time'. In 1974 the Conservatives lost the election and she was subsequently elected as the Leader of the Opposition – the first woman to hold this post.

In May 1979 the Conservatives won the general election under her leadership and she was duly appointed as the first ever woman to be the Prime Minister. She was noted for having raised interest rates in a bid to control inflation, for curbing the power of the Trade Unions, for having a strong and confrontational strategy to try to control the problems in Northern Ireland, for quashing the miners' strike, for privatising the public transport system and selling off council houses. In April 1982 the Argentinians invaded the Falkland Islands; she sent our troops and by June the Argentinians had surrendered. In 1984 she survived an assassination attempt by the IRA at the Conservative conference in Brighton. During this time British manufacturing capacity had fallen by 25 per cent but the financial services sector was growing. She replaced the 'Rates', a tax related to property rental values, with a Community Charge based on a 'per capita' tax. It was known as 'the poll tax' and public reaction to it was so strong that there were public riots against it.

At this point there was strong pressure from within the Conservative party for her to stand down from her position as Prime Minister; she did eventually agree and on 28th November 1990 she left Downing Street.

In 1992 she was given a seat in the House of Lords as Baroness Thatcher of Kesteven. In her retirement she began writing her own history and published *The Downing Street Years* in 1993, *The Path to Power* in 1995 and in 2002 *Statecraft*. By now she was suffering episodes of small strokes which became worse after her husband, Denis, died in 2003. In 2005 she was given an 80th birthday party which was attended by the Queen. In 2007 a statue of her was erected in the House of Commons. In 2010 a party to celebrate her 85th birthday was held by David Cameron, the then Prime Minister, but she was so unwell that she was unable to attend. Over the next few years her health deteriorated and she had problems with her memory. On 8th April 2013, aged 87, she died.

Whatever you think about her beliefs, she was a trailblazer for women as far as political self-determination was concerned. Through persistence and self-belief she got to the top political position in Great Britain – not through being a member of the 'old school tie' brigade. Her decision, during the Falklands War, to order the sinking of the Argentinian warship the *General Belgrano* – against the advice of many of the men in her cabinet – shows her use of power and her dominance. Yet she chose not to appoint women around her; perhaps, she found men easier to manipulate than members of her own gender. Margaret Thatcher liked men and enjoyed their company but, said that she saw them as the weaker sex. These attitudes and strategies were all confirmed in her biography. She did not get the nickname 'The Iron Lady' for nothing and her style of control and governance was so distinctive that it became known as 'Thatcherism'.

Opportunity 2000 was launched by John Major in October 1991 as an equal opportunities initiative which was meant to increase women's representation in the world of work. The vision was for equality in the workplace, at all levels, to be achieved by the millennium.

There were initially over 150 major companies signed up to it with a total of more than five million employees which represented 23 per cent of the national workforce. Whilst numerous companies supported it in theory, less than 25 per cent took the required practical or financial steps for its inception; they encountered too much internal and external opposition. Those responsible for implementing it found apathy at every level, from the boardroom to the factory floor. Even the women in those participating organisations were reported to be unsupportive. Another well-intentioned scheme was failing. The decade passed and, by the millennium, the campaign's lack of success was significant. Had it been implemented, almost a quarter of the UK workforce would have had an equal male-female split. Twenty-five years after the idea's inception and it has been replaced by 'Opportunity Now'; whenever 'Now' is going to be.

Contraception has always been a freedom of immense portent for women. Since time began a constant and very serious problem for women has been unwanted pregnancy. Its prevention has just two aspects; female contraception and male contraception.

In ancient civilisations, women used to insert fruit based jellies post-coitally in an effort to destroy the sperm – which was neither very effective nor very safe. Women have also, for a very long time, used internally placed sponges to absorb the sperm. The withdrawal method and anal sex were the other, and frequently used, alternatives. These, and magic amulets, were about the only methods available to women – although there is some evidence that they were aware of, and there was probably use of, inter uterine devices (IUDs) which were often formed from silver rings.

For men, the traditional method for many centuries involved some very basic forms of sheath. It is believed that the Japanese used rigid horn sheaths whilst the Chinese used ones made from a fine cloth which had been soaked in a special preparation and tied on with a ribbon. Along with these they used sheaths made from animal intestines which were presumably more comfortable – or at least less uncomfortable – than the other methods. Both of these latter examples were methods which were to become popular worldwide until the mid-19th century. Whichever system of contraception was adopted, it was generally only the wealthy who could afford them.

In the 16th century there was an epidemic of syphilis and gonorrhoea in the French army and thus also in an enormous number of women; the diseases then spread across Europe. At that time such venereal diseases were usually fatal. As a result, the French troops wore either the fabric or animal tissue sheaths to protect themselves from catching or spreading these venereal diseases. Subsequently, the expression 'French Letter' was coined because they came enclosed in an envelope. The French word for a condom is, to this day, 'un preservatif ' – something to help preserve the wearer from disease rather than to lessen the likelihood of a pregnancy. Previously, the sheath had often been minimal and covering just the glans, there solely to catch the sperm; a sheath to protect against transmission of STDs had to be full length. Manufacturing animal-based sheaths became a growing and lucrative business. In 1666, an English government commission survey recorded a fall in the birth rate which they attributed to the popularisation of the sheath. Contraception has always been a prominent issue.

By the mid-19th century, and thanks to a Mr Charles Goodyear (of tyre fame) and his invention of the rubber vulcanisation process, a new and more efficient – though certainly not perfectly reliable – type of sheath was invented. These sheaths had to be made by hand using a glass former and involved some pretty potent chemicals in their manufacture. They remained expensive and thus the ordinary man could not afford the cost of several months' pay for just one – but, they were supposed to be washable and thus reusable. Being made from rubber they were assigned the common and enduring name of 'rubbers'.

This same innovation in rubber was, towards the end of the 19th century, used by a Dutch doctor in the invention of a contraceptive membrane to be inserted inside a woman's vagina and placed over her cervix; it was held in place with an integral sealing ring formed around a watch spring. His nationality led to it being known as the 'Dutch Cap'. Women had never liked the sheath because it could not be trusted and, they believed, neither could men be trusted to use one.

For them, the advent of the 'Dutch Cap', together with a new form of IUD, provided an almost perfect answer; they now stood a much greater chance of controlling the likelihood of becoming pregnant.

The First World War was another source of greatly increased venereal disease; some governments issued their soldiers with sheaths but, not the British. By the end of the war the American government had identified almost half a million soldiers as having a serious venereal disease.

It was not until the 1920s that latex was invented. It was a rubber derivative but was manufactured using water – not made with aggressive chemicals. Condoms could also now be easily mass produced and the price reduced such that they became much more affordable. World-wide, millions of condoms were soon being used every day.

By the 1960s there were two new developments in female contra-ception which were to help to revolutionise women's lives. Since the end of the war researchers had been working on a hormone based oral contraceptive which became known as 'the Pill'. It stopped egg production (ovulation) by the woman; no egg, no baby.

In 1961 the pill was made available in the UK and, generally, was well received. The pill was seen by some groups as a form of abortion and counter to their beliefs; that view is still held by some people today. The pill is alleged to be a major factor in the sexual freedoms of that era. However, they were initially only prescribed to married women over forty-five years old so that they would not have an unwanted pregnancy that late in life; it was some time afterwards that they were made available to all married women. It was not until 1974 that they could be legally prescribed for single women.

Historically, there had always been an unwritten promise between couples that if the woman became pregnant then the man would do the honourable thing and marry her; there were also 'shotgun marriages' when an unwilling male was pressured into the marriage by the woman's family.

As the pill became freely available to all women couples could co-habit without the fear of an unwanted pregnancy. Interestingly, the birth rate per capita did not, as expected, change from the rates before the Second World War. It became assumed by the man that if the woman was on the pill he did not need to use a condom. A negative side effect of this was that the prevalence of STIs increased. Overall though, all the physical and emotional traumas related to unwanted and too frequent pregnancies could be controlled by women themselves and this gave an enormous boost to their health and well-being. And, it was not just the bearing of the children that was so taxing and disruptive, it was the ongoing work involved with bringing up another unplanned child which took its toll.

There has been considerable work put into developing a male pill which would, ideally, not have the negative side effects which women taking the female contraceptive pill had been habitually subject to. However, the initial attempts have not produced infallible results and women do not want to have to trust a man's reliability in taking a contraceptive pill regularly to control their own likelihood of becoming pregnant. An emergency contraception which can be taken by women post coitally has also been available for some years.

A very sure method of contraception, which also relieves women from having to take the pill and to endure the associated side effects, is male sterilisation – vasectomy or, as it is commonly known 'the snip'. A female form of sterilisation is possible; it uses plugs to close off the fallopian tubes and is irreversible.

Abortion is, for most women, the last resort; and, it is also a controversial subject. In the UK, before the Abortion Act 1967, an abortion was an illegal act. Backstreet 'surgeries' were the only remedy for some desperate women. This was a form of procedure, together with radical potions, which has been practiced worldwide for millennia. Abortion, like contraception in general, has been variously banned and promoted by the governments of different countries and by various religions.

Records for the UK show that the current number of abortions relates to one in three women having an abortion before the age of 45. There are 180,000 operations each year of which 10,000 are on women resident in the Irish Republic – and a few other countries. In Scotland the number is also 10,000.

One in five pregnancies in the UK end in an abortion and most women seeking an abortion are aged between 20 and 24. Ninety-eight per cent of abortions are carried out within 20 weeks of conception. One third of these women have had an abortion before and only one in seven was in a long-term relationship. It appears that some women are casually accepting abortion as a form of contraception. A prerequisite of abortion in the UK is that two doctors must agree that it is necessary in accordance with the regulations of the legislation. Whilst the NHS is not necessarily obliged to perform these procedures the private clinics currently only perform about 25 per cent of them. Worldwide, it is estimated that one quarter of pregnancies are terminated by an abortion and

DAVID deVIRE

at least half of these are illegal 'backstreet' abortions performed by unqualified people.

70,000 women worldwide are said to die from the results of an abortion each year. In contrast, according to the World Health Organisation, in 2013 35 million people were living with AIDS worldwide and, 1.5 million people died of an AIDS-related illness worldwide. They do not give the figures for each gender separately.

The contents of this chapter highlight a number of people, organisations and events which have had an influence on the promotion of women's equality issues in the British Isles. It is a far from exhaustive list but outlines the linear and incremental nature of the progression of the women's movement. It clearly shows that one seemingly inconsequential action by an individual can motivate others and instigate further action – sometimes simultaneously, sometimes decades or even centuries apart. The time lapses between these events are random and usually determined by civil disquiet together with the appearance of strong and motivated individuals in circumstances permitting a level of social reorganisation. Overall change up to the mid-20th century appears to have been at an evolutionary rate interspersed with moments of revolutionary fervour; a reflection of the development of society as a whole over the same period. In the last 50 years there have been exponential technological advances in areas such as communications, transport, manufacturing and medicine which have been reflected in the daily lives of everyone and altered accepted social mores. For people at one end of the scale the pace of change is a bit too scary and destabilising whilst for the opposite end of the spectrum change is too slow and too insignificant.

CHAPTER 4
IN TWO MINDS

Men have larger brains than women in proportion to their body size – up to 10 per cent bigger. The female brain may have less mass but it has a better and faster networking system. Average brain size has been gradually increasing; in hominids, early forms of humans, the brain volume was just 500cc, nowadays the volume is around 1500cc. So, the brain size of humans has trebled; the average sized brain now weighs about three pounds (1.4 kgs).

Grey matter is in the outer layer of the cerebral cortex, the curly bit you see on the outside of brains in pictures and on representations of brains. It is actually a pinkish-grey in colour in a living brain. It contains nerve cells called neurons; these are interconnected by synapses which is how the nerve cells communicate with each other thus allowing them to collect and transfer information.

There are more of these internal synapse connections in male brains compared to those of females. The grey matter is, in effect, the processing centre and is spread over the surface area of the brain. Men have 6.5 times more grey matter than women. It has been suggested that this may be the reason behind the stereotype that men excel in processing the types of information necessary in maths and map reading.

In females there is a greater concentration of grey matter in their frontal lobes which is why head injury in this body area can have more severe repercussions for women. The physical shape of the brain in people with dyslexia is different from those without. The responsibility for this seems to lie with groups of neurons which clump together, almost like blood clots, and as a result cause numerous functional problems; we know that dyslexia is principally a male affliction.

White matter is mainly hidden from view deep inside the brain, the brain stem and the spinal cord. It is a network of inter-connecting tissues, linking the various parts of the brain's grey matter, thus allowing the transmission of information from one part of the brain to another. White matter is the networking system of the brain; it is concentrated in its core. Women have 10 times more white matter than men and thus their brains have more connections between each part of the brain than men do. The function of cross-linking information is used to support the widely held belief that women are better at tasks such as language skills, multi-tasking and empathy.

Counter to many pseudo-scientific claims, in tests specifically designed to assess the comparative intelligence of male and female brains the results show very little, if any, significant difference – regardless of the differences in size, physical structure or function. Research, across four different nations, by Professor James Flynn of Cambridge University shows that if men have a score of 100 then women fall in the range of 99.5 to 101.5. It seems to be that the brains of both genders produce virtually the same results – by using different parts of the brain and different processes to reach the same conclusion. Brain activity during this process is more localised in the male and more widely distributed in the female. It is, of course, quite easy to create tests which will highlight different outcomes for each gender thus reflecting their individual strengths and weaknesses but, such gender biased tests have limited value as true comparators.

All these tests have been carried out by numerous research groups across the world, using Functional MRI, Diffusion MRI and PET brain-scans, mainly on adults of between 21and 40 years old. And this, of itself, poses another major question. Which variations in brain structure and function can be attributed to innate and immutable gender differences and which may be attributed to external environmental influences on a brain during the lifetime of an individual; and, what might be the causes and effects of these influences?

When a child begins to grow there are around 100 billion nerve cells inside it. Initially they are not all interlinked or assigned specific tasks. It is the use of functions such as motor skills and language that create these pathways and determine their cross-linking, complexity and strength. A baby can be seen training itself as it picks things up, feeling form and texture, as it puts the things in its mouth and compares the sensations. These actions are creating an information bank and cross-referencing it; learning about soft and hard, textured and smooth. That's how it starts.

Research has shown that young people's brains are very 'plastic', that they have the potential to be moulded, formed, reformed, developed and strengthened by their ongoing life experiences; these are imposed by their parents and family, by their teachers, by their peers (as individuals and as groups) and by society as a whole. We often, unintentionally, reinforce stereotypes, create actions and thought patterns which reinforce or negate stereotypical gender roles. Each time a thought or action is reinforced it stimulates an appropriate brain function and thus a change, however small, in the structure of the appropriate part of the brain. It reinforces the brain's development and its internal connections. Telling a child that it is good at something – or not good at it, telling them that they look pretty – or not, causes a brain response.

We grow muscles as the result of weight bearing exercise; we become more agile by performing actions and movement. Exercise any part of the body and it will grow – sometimes in strength sometimes in dexterity – and if you keep repeating the exercise you will see physical changes occurring – from the flexibility and balance of a gymnast to the biceps of a weight lifter.

Exercise the brain in different ways and it will grow and become more efficient at performing that task or making those associations, thinking those thoughts or feeling those feelings. But the development of the brains of all humans are also influenced by genes and by hormones; we are complex physical, emotional, chemical, and even electronic beings. We are a jigsaw of often irreconcilable paradoxes.

In truth, whilst we may think that we know a lot about the workings of the human body and the brain, we struggle to understand some basic functions and inter-relationships let alone the subtle nuances, the relative complexities and the differences between one individual and another. Science is, in many instances, still groping in the dark, we are often best-guessing, creating hypotheses.

Originally it was thought that boys and girls brains would be physically identical to each other and therefore work in similar ways. If there were differences in any type of behaviour – particularly in social behaviour or learning behaviour – then the culprits would be somewhere in the child's environment. Alleged offenders included gender bias, bad parenting, poor teaching, food additives, refined sugar intake; the list was almost endless.

The advent of cheaper, non-invasive and more freely available brain scanning made it an economically viable exploratory tool for use by researchers into behaviour patterns and their associated brain activity. This research has begun to help us to understand so many things about the structure and function of the internal organs of our bodies. We can watch the function of the brain both at rest and when thinking – such as in problem-solving and using language skills. These areas of research have opened up the debate on the differences between male and female brains, how they are constructed, how they work and, the effects of these differences.

Initial research showed that whilst it is apparent that girls have proportionally smaller brains than boys, this appears to have no effect on their functionality whatsoever. Scans also show that some of our very young males have proportionally smaller sections of the brain, than would be normal for other boys and for girls, particularly in those areas dedicated to language, reading and the control of emotions. These differences are still quite visible in boys of junior school age. Meanwhile, most girls have what is considered a normal volume in these areas – and, they are naturally more resilient to any form of trauma during these growth stages. In males, almost all of their language functions are in the front left hemisphere of their brains whereas females use both hemispheres; and, these two areas have many interconnections between them, including a broad band of nerves called the corpus callosum, allowing one side of the brain to potentially act as a back-up system for the other. This would, in theory, allow the facility of cross-checking and therefore bolster the ability of girls in their language skills. In effect, like having your own inbuilt spell-checker and grammar tutor.

At 18 months of age girls have, on average, a vocabulary twice as large as that of boys and, further, the girls can also understand, if not use, almost twice as many more words than boys. Girls tend to remain ahead of boys by using more words; this stimulates areas of the brain which then increase in capacity, it also increases communication and promotes conversation; it develops inter-personal skills and the resultant relationships.

Females have the propensity to retain much greater, more intricate and more complex sets of emotional memories which can take up a large proportion of their available memory space at any given time and therefore this can leave little spare space for other things. Thus, compared to their male counterparts, women may sometimes appear to suffer an impaired memory or memory loss which, in turn, can lead to bouts of depression. Men, being more fact oriented rather than emotionally centred, use less of their available memory for such storage processes.

It had always been thought that brain development ended before puberty but now, thanks to recent research we can observe both the structure and function of the brain of a living person in real-time and its reaction to cognitive experiments.

This has shown researchers evidence that the brain is still in a growth stage right through the teens and into early adulthood. The part of the brain which controls decision making, planning, social cognition and interaction and which controls our behaviour or misbehaviour – the pre-frontal cortex – is the centre for this activity. It appears that we are born with numerous pre-installed and pre-connected nodules in the brain which can be used to interrelate different situations – actions and reactions. When they are first used they become active and begin to grow and inter-communicate; those parts which are not used eventually become dormant and, as such, disappear leaving only those which have been previously activated. These form a wiring loom which operates and controls our brain and thus our actions. The brain seems to have the ability to work a 'use it or lose it' policy.

So, a teenager's interactions with others around them is forming a developing pattern within their brain. The diametrically different reactions to parents and peers is the brain trying to connect and make some sense out of the teenager's environment. Peer pressure seems to have a strong, though not always positive, effect on these actions causing a teenager to be more of a risk taker when in the company of their peers, to be more outgoing and adventurous – ways of acting that they do not follow other than when with that peer group. In the company of parents or other forms of perceived disapproval or authority they behave differently, they become belligerent, almost confused; they are not sure how to behave. How the world and their peer group interacts with them, relative to each situation, has begun to form a pattern within the brain which can eventually become learned behaviour. That surly or misbehaving teenager that you see is not just being affected by a surge of disruptive hormones but is also trying to make sense of a tangle of random and often apparently illogical brain connections which frequently short-circuit. They see a situation or set of behaviours in another person, and subconsciously try to evaluate it and react appropriately for that set of circumstances. Their stronger peer pressure developed language and actions may well cause them to behave in a way which they can sense is inappropriate to another social situation and which then leaves them feeling insecure. We see teenagers pushing personal and social boundaries, daring each other to commit, hopefully small, acts of dissension from society's mores; they experiment with personal relationships, drinking alcohol, bravado or even petty acts of shoplifting. Hopefully, with the right guidance from the reactions of family and society they will form the best set of brain connections to allow them to develop appropriate words, actions and reactions; these are the life skills which will help them turn into useful citizens. Just like we did, they will grow out of being socially inept; it's just that now we have the knowledge – the inside story – of the processes their confused brains are going through in the journey to get there.

We have seen that boys' and girls' brains develop differently from each other as they mature. The hypothalamus, at the front of

THE TAIL OF THE TIGRESS

the brain, controls hunger, thirst, fight and flight, sexual arousal and desire. Initially it is identical in size between both sexes, that is, until the boys reach pubescence whereupon, for them, it more than doubles in size.

The advances in our understanding of how our body and mind work, as a result of the Human Genome Project, have identified the effects of different chromosome and gene variations; these have shown the gene's potential to be a contributory factor, as one of the causes of various modes of social (or antisocial) behaviour, of interpersonal relationships, of certain learning ability differences and also in language skills.

In 2003 the mapping of the human genome was completed thus finalising the blueprint of 23,000 genes; the complete 'recipe' for creating humans. The print-out for each individual looks like our own, very long, personal barcode; lots of bits are similar to other people's but no-one has exactly the same DNA code as another. A decade later and scientists have created genetically engineered mice that have, within the cells of their bodies, a human chromosome. It is, apparently, an experiment to test the possibility of curing disease by replacing faulty human chromosomes with perfect 'engineered' replicas – HACs (human artificial chromosomes). The National Cancer Institute in the USA says that they have, for the first time ever, made a totally synthetic human chromosome. It is believed to have been engineered from individual chemical components or 'building blocks' rather than from existing human tissue as had been done in previous research experiments.

It has recently been found that the genes within the human body are not finite in number nor in characteristic; they can be switched both on and off throughout our lives with consequent results. Genetic modification is not only possible but it can have dramatically beneficial effects. A new genetic adaptation of the herpes virus is now being used to kill cancer cells directly and also, at the same time, to promote the body's own immune system to locate and kill the cancerous cells too. It has already shown a very high cure-rate in skin cancers and has the potential to be modified to help to cure other cancers.

Humans, like all animals and plants, are made of cells, billions of cells. The core or brain of most of these cells is called the nucleus and lives towards the centre of that cell. Inside are chromosomes; humans have 46 chromosomes – arranged as 23 pairs – in each of those cells. Forty-four of those chromosomes are common in function to both males and females but the last pair are different in a male and a female; the female has two 'X' chromosomes and the male has one 'X' and one 'Y' chromosome. Chromosomes are the 'instruction manual' for how our bodies should be made and how they should function. Different creatures and plants have different numbers of chromosomes each carrying different 'instructions'. The number of chromosomes has nothing to do with intelligence. Whilst humans have 46 chromosomes, dogs have 78 and the crayfish has 200; the fruit fly has just four.

Genes are part of each chromosome, they come in pairs like chromosomes and both are made from DNA. We get half our genes and chromosomes from each of our parents – so, we are half of our mum and half of our dad; which bits we get from each parent seems to be a bit of a lottery.

To produce a female child there must be two 'X' chromosomes; to produce a male child there must be one 'X' chromosome and one 'Y' chromosome. Inside every egg produced by a woman is one 'X' chromosome. The other chromosome necessary for the fertilisation of the female egg and the subsequent formation of an embryo is produced by the male. Both the 'Y' chromosome and 'X' chromosome can be produced by the male and there is just one in each sperm. Thus, the one male sperm which fertilises the egg determines the gender of the embryo. If the male sperm contains an 'X' chromosome when it pierces the female egg containing an 'X' embryo there will be two 'X' chromosomes and therefore a female embryo will be created. If the male sperm contains a 'Y' chromosome when it pierces the female egg containing an 'X' embryo there will be one 'X' chromosome and one 'Y' chromosome and therefore a male embryo will be created. All girls have two 'X' chromosomes, all boys have one 'X' chromosome and one 'Y' chromosome; there are no other options.

Genes make proteins; we don't fully understand yet all the information about which gene makes which protein and why. Good genes make healthy creatures and plants; bad genes, ones which have somehow mutated, can cause us problems – most obviously with illness and disease. Some illnesses and diseases are thought to have a hereditary factor; some types of cancer can appear more frequently in one family as opposed to another or to be gender specific. Breast cancer is one such disease; interestingly, one in fifty people diagnosed with breast cancer is a man. Some bad genes can come from one of our parents and cause what are known as inherited diseases; some genes mutate in our own bodies in our own lifetimes. Gene therapy is a branch of medicine which is trying to repair or replace these faulty genes to allow us to have more healthy disease-free lives.

The female 'X' chromosome contains 1,098 genes; the male 'Y' chromosome contains 78 genes. All the other chromosomes have the same number of genes whether you are male or female. Therefore, females have 1,020 more genes than males; 1,020 more ways of producing proteins. The 'X' gene is proven to be the most powerful in disease protection; thus, females are genetically predisposed to have better health. According to the National Institute for Medical Research in the UK, the disproportionate level of genes between men and women is a significant factor in explaining many of the other differences between men and women too.

The male body tries to compensate for this difference in genes by using some of his own 'X' chromosomes in a different way but, as a result, has made his chromosome distribution weaker and unbalanced and thus males are more vulnerable to disease. Over 250 medical conditions in males, including autism and mental retardation, have been linked to this. On the positive side, the same chromosome and gene imbalances which cause medical susceptibility to disease can also create geniuses. Male and female IQ in humans may be broadly similar overall but in the male there is far greater variance at both of the extremes of intelligence; thus, compared to females, there are more male geniuses but also more male imbeciles.

Identical (mono-zygotic) twins are caused by one egg which has been fertilised by one sperm; the fertilised egg then decides to divide into two and thereby creates identical twins; we do not know why this happens. Identical twins are always the same gender; only one third of twins are identical. Non-identical or fraternal (di-zygotic) twins occur when two separate eggs are each fertilized by one of two different sperm at the same time and both develop over the same duration, the same gestation period. Because the two female eggs are fertilized by two different sperm they can both be either the same gender or different genders. The only certain way to evidence identical twins is by comparing DNA samples from each; identical twins will show 99.9 per cent similarity whereas non-identical twins will only show around 50 per cent similarity.

Differences between identical twins used to be thought of as caused by environmental influences; nurture as opposed to nature. Normally, there are two copies of each gene; each one originates from each of the parents. If a gene from one chromosome is missing it may indicate the potential for a health related risk; leukaemia is one such disease.

Identical girl twins show more subtle, individual differences between them than identical twin boys do. The twin girls both have the same genetic code but each uses it differently from the other; they have the same DNA, the same number of genes. Identical twin girls both get one 'X' chromosome from their mother and one 'X' chromosome from their father; the same chromosomes but with different genes inside each one.

As a tiny embryo, of less than 100 cells, it may make a random and inexplicable choice to deactivate one of the chromosomes. The cells then continue dividing, time and time again, as the embryo grows but some of the cells inside have been made inactive; the gene pattern of each of the twin girls is therefore slightly different, one from the other. This process is known as Lyonization Theory or 'X' Inactivation. We know that when this happens in mice and cats, as an indicator, the colour of their fur differs from one to the other.

One identical girl twin will be more similar to her mother and the other more similar to her father – depending on which cells have been switched off. Girls have two copies of their 'X' chromosomes therefore, girls have two copies of the 1,098 genes found in each 'X' chromosome, making a total of 2,196 genes; boys have just one set of 'X' chromosomes and one set of 'Y' chromosomes therefore, boys have one copy of the 1,098 'X' genes and one copy of the 78 'Y' genes making a total of 1,176 genes. All males have a deficit of 1,020 genes compared to females. Because genes make proteins, the chemical mix of them in an individual body will differ. Too little or too much of a particular protein can cause health problems. Your body can, as a result, get confused and cause auto-immune disorders because the body mistakenly believes it is being attacked. In girls, with two copies of their genes and thus two copies of their associated proteins they could, potentially, turn the inappropriate one off; the body's way of solving a latent health problem. Boys who have just one of each of these genes would have the risk of problems if a particular protein was turned off.

The recently discovered genetic differences which are found between twins can be of immense benefit to medical research when used in a 'reverse-engineering' context. If one twin suffers from a particular hereditary disease and the other does not it is possible to compare their unique gene sequences and find the one gene that the diseased twin has but which the non-diseased twin does not have (or vice versa); thus the link is made. A particular gene can be directly identified as a causal effect of a particular disease and therefore, in theory, if that gene could be eradicated in the next generation, then so could the likelihood of that disease be eradicated. Medical research using this line of theory is in its early stages but making a cause-effect link between genes and disease has huge implications. The body is an immensely complex system which we take for granted when things are going well but complain about when we do not get the results that we want. It has many parts, each interlinked; some appear more important than others but we cannot exist as healthy humans without them all functioning properly.

A German study 'Myopia and Education', reported in the US journal *Ophthalmology*, examined 4,685 people using eye tests and examinations, physical examinations, and questionnaires on individual lifestyle found that the higher the level of school and tertiary education the higher the incidence of myopic refraction. Over 60 per cent of graduates were short-sighted whereas the group who had not graduated from high school (after 13 years of full-time education) only 27 per cent suffered with short-sightedness. There are more female than male graduates. So, is reading bad for your eyesight – should brainy kids spend more time playing outside rather than reading books? Which is cause; which is effect? Perhaps the short-sighted among us, which means more females than males, just prefer to stay indoors reading?

The human body is a bit like a railway system – but very much more complex. We may tend to just think about our particular journey but for that to happen we do not just need a pair of rails and a train. We need a power source, a signalling system, main lines and branches off them, places to get on and get off, places to refuel, innumerable people to keep it running day and night including a team to repair things when they break down.

Part of our brain is called the hypothalamus; it has a number of important roles to play in the running of our bodies. It controls our heart rate and blood pressure, our appetite, digestion and thirst, our weight, our temperature and our sleep patterns. Through the pineal gland it is the link point between our nervous system and our endocrine system; through the pituitary gland it is the control centre of the whole endocrine system which causes other parts of the body to release, or stop releasing, hormones.

The endocrine system is made up of several other important glands. The adrenal gland releases adrenaline when you are stressed and controls the way your body uses energy; the pancreas controls your intake and use of sugar; the thyroid governs your metabolism; the thymus controls immunity in children; the parathyroid controls bone development; the ovaries produce the hormones oestrogen and progesterone in women and release their egg cells; the male testes produce the hormone testosterone and create sperm.

Hormones are powerful chemical messengers which hitch a ride around your body in your bloodstream on their way to various areas of tissues and to organs. They affect your growth and general physical development, your metabolism – the chemical changes in cells which allow them to maintain and grow, your moods, your energy levels, your reproductive cycles and potential and, of course, your sexual drive and function. Small amounts of certain hormones can cause big effects.

The female sex hormones, oestrogen and progesterone, and the male sex hormones, androgens – including testosterone – can all be found in both males and females. It is the quantities and ratios of these hormones which differ between each gender and also, to a much lesser extent, between each individual within those genders. Consequently, the distinctive cocktail of hormones carried by each person has its own particular effect on each of these unique humans.

Hormones are, in fact, chemicals which are manufactured in and released by the glands; their job is to tell cells what to do. They are the catalysts which cause other cells to behave in a particular way.

Testosterone is produced by both men and women; men produce around 10 times the amount of testosterone that women do. It is the main sex hormone in males and it is an anabolic steroid. When a boy's body begins to produce large amounts of testosterone for the first time it indicates the onset of puberty. Puberty in boys tends to occur at any time from the age of about 10 years old and upwards but it is more usual for it to start as they reach the beginning of their teen years; for some it may not start until they are in their mid-teens. This surge of testosterone will cause them to put on a growth spurt and become more muscular, for their voice to become deeper, for them to begin to develop facial, body and pubic hair, for their penis and testicles to become larger.

Testosterone is the sex drive for men. Such is the addictive power of all this testosterone rushing around a male body; it can easily overtake rational thinking. It is a natural drive for men to want to have sex and the fact that their ejaculation is such a sensational high reinforces this urge to repeat the experience of that pleasure as often as is both physically and socially possible. The level of testosterone in a man's body varies from hour to hour; it is highest first thing in the morning and at its lowest during the night. Its life-long potency builds until it reaches its highest levels of production during the years from around 20 until around 30, it then begins to slowly diminish – although many men still produce enough to continue to be sexually active (and fertile) well into their pensionable years.

It is not unusual for men's testosterone levels to fall well under the average for their age; this will usually first become apparent by a lack of sex drive or difficulty in getting or maintaining an erection; other signs can include enlarged and tender breasts, a loss of muscular strength and a low sperm count. This drop in the production of testosterone can usually be attributed to stress, poor diet, excess alcohol, illness, too much weight or even too much exercise; a sustained resumption of healthy living can usually resolve the problem. Levels of testosterone which are abnormally high are quite rare. Just to complicate things men also produce the female hormones oestrogen and progesterone; in normal circumstances they do not appear to have a great influence on men's bodies, however, in excess, particularly when exacerbated by ageing they can cause female-like attributes and a loss of libido.

When it comes to the physical effects of testosterone on the male body, there is a line of thought that male athletes, from a diverse range of sports, should refrain from having sex for the period immediately before a competitive event; that having sex will, in some way, deplete their reserves of energy. Opinion differs and always has done; Plato, around 400 BCE thought that athletes would be better by abstaining, 500 years later Pliny the Elder thought it a pointless diversion.

Mohammad Ali was probably the most high profile proponent of the abstention strategy – and he had a pretty successful sporting career. Interestingly, it seems that Olympic athletes are ignoring this advice – identified by sales of condoms in Olympic villages; indeed, as, according to *The Telegraph* and *Huffington Post* amongst others, the athletes complain that supplies of condoms at these venues have actually run out on more than one occasion. The benefits, or detriments, of abstention from sex is a standpoint which is relevant to all males at one level or another. We do know that abstention from sex for a male, for periods in excess of a couple of months, can cause the testes to dramatically reduce their production of testosterone and can cause the levels of testosterone in a male body to drop to those of a pre-pubescent boy.

Research has been done to see what the different physical effects are on the same groups of male athletes when they have had sex over various and varying periods and included having sex the night before the tests, and also with those same men when they have abstained from sex, and again, for various and varying periods of time. None of these tests have shown any significant physical benefits from abstaining from sex in preparation for participation a competitive sporting event.

These tests were carried out by researchers into sports medicine using scientific methodology and involved exercises as diverse as hand grip strength, treadmills and weights. The only really negative effects came if the athlete had sex a couple of hours before the tests. One of the problems with tests like these is that they are carried out on competitive young males who know that they are guinea pigs and under scrutiny and therefore want to prove themselves and show that they are both extremely virile and infallible. It's a boy thing.

The theory of the benefits of abstention from sex prior to competitive sport for women has not been propounded and therefore there do not appear to have been any scientific tests of the effects of any such abstention.

It has been suggested that the amount of energy a human body has is a bit like many other systems which rely on 'reserves'. If you use a lot of energy today and it is more than you would normally have available then you must rely on the extra energy being supplied either from what is left over from yesterday or borrow from what you will have tomorrow so, leaving you more tired tomorrow.

According to new research by the University of Montreal, in a fairly normal lovemaking session between two regular partners men use up 100 calories whilst women only use up less than 70 calories. What it does do, and what was an unexplored physiological experience in those tests, is to cause both participants to be happy, physically and emotionally satisfied and to remove all traces of aggression and competitiveness. A satisfying sexual experience with a regular partner can relax both parties, remove the stress of pre-match nerves, promote restful sleep and leave a feel-good factor. It is significant that research of this type has restricted itself to males. Is it not so much that having sex saps the strength but rather that it reduces the adrenalin inspired aggressive and competitive streak that so many successful athletes and sportsmen are renowned for? We do know that a satisfying love-making session releases endorphins in a woman's body and that they are nature's pain blockers.

It is interesting that research finds that men displaying the behaviour normally associated with lower levels of testosterone are frequently more valued by women; probably because they are considered to make better, more reliable, long-term partners or husbands. It is obvious that this cannot be an overt selection process; it is, perhaps, just that the behaviour of less testosterone-driven men is more attractive to women during courting and is more likely to lead to a less confrontational marital environment.

This appears to be a more modern phenomenon; in more primitive cultures having a male with higher testosterone induced behaviour indicated a better protector for a female and her offspring and, perhaps, a more fertile mate. Testosterone helps to make men stronger but it also adversely affects the immune system and thus the ability of men to survive illness is diminished. This is true in animals as well as in humans.

In men, their testosterone level does not appear to be proportional to either wealth or status; indeed, the inverse appears to be true. Those males with lots of testosterone tend to do jobs at the 'blue collar' end of the employment spectrum whereas those in the 'white collar' professions tend to have lower testosterone levels. Interestingly, it appears that, according to research from the Northwestern University, Chicago that women who have high status jobs or who make significant progress in the upper echelons of business, have higher levels of testosterone.

Testosterone in women also acts as the promoter of sex drive although women's bodies, in general, seem to need only around 10 per cent of the quantity of this addictive drug as men do. Some women do produce more testosterone than others and this, in combination with their female hormones, can cause extreme highs and lows of sexual desire depending on both the individual and the phase of their monthly cycle.

Girls with Congenital Adrenal Hyperplasia (CAH) will be likely to have been exposed to abnormally excessive levels of testosterone in the womb which, according to the Mayo Clinic, has the most obvious sign of abnormal genitalia looking more male than female. Their high level of testosterone almost predestines them to grow up as tom boys and to show more male behaviour characteristics. The testosterone alters the development of the brain. Because they can be seen as being 'different' by their peers, some become even more aggressive as a defence mechanism; the better positioned ones may just grow into adults who are drawn to more male lifestyles and tend to avoid motherhood.

Oestrogen and progesterone are considered to be female specific hormones although, as we have already learned, men do produce them too. In girls, they are the instigators of puberty and cause them to develop breasts, pubic hair and then the menarche. Thereafter, they work together in causing and regulating the monthly reproductive cycle and, eventually, the menopause.

Every month both of these female hormones cycle in turn – between a constant base-level of production which then increases and rises to a peak before falling away again. Oestrogen levels begin to rise from day one of the menstrual cycle stimulating the body to ripen an egg ready for its implantation in the newly developing lining of the womb. By day 14, having performed its task, the level of oestrogen returns to its base-level and is replaced, from day 15, by a rising level of progesterone which then nurtures the egg and prepares for possible fertilisation until day 23. It then returns to its base level too and, in the absence of pregnancy, a period happens and they both await a new cycle.

If the woman does become pregnant then both hormone levels rise and will stay at a high level throughout the pregnancy – they have a lot of important work to do. It is at the end of the pregnancy when the levels of both hormones drop from their sustained high levels to their previous base-level that the woman's body can feel a set of withdrawal type symptoms which manifest themselves in what we know as post-natal depression.

When the woman's body reaches the stage when it is no longer going to be able to reproduce, a time that we call the menopause, the levels of both of these hormones reduce dramatically and in the process can cause mayhem within the woman's body – and with her mind. In a perfect world all these natural hormones would work beneficially together inside the woman's body in a beautiful and mystical chemical ballet. But, that is not the way it is. Disruptions caused by lifestyle, diet and stress create adverse symptoms and can play havoc with a woman's body and with her emotions and in the process cause unpleasant physical and emotional side-effects. Add to the lifestyle influences the synthetic hormones and other chemicals women are likely to put in their own bodies – to regulate their periods, in the contraceptive pill and eventually in hormone replacement therapy – and a woman's body can be subject to decades of chemical abuse and the reactions they cause.

Structurally, the body's nervous system appears to be fairly similar in males and females. It is thought of as a system with two interdependent parts – the central nervous system (CNS) which is located in the brain and the spinal cord and, the peripheral nervous system which includes all the other nerves, fanning out through the rest of the body to its extremities, which are, in turn, connected back to some part of the CNS. Nerves pass information to the neurons in the brain and on across the synapses as electro-chemical pulses; these are called neurotransmitters. If you touch a hot surface with the tips of your fingers your nervous system will send a message back to your brain cells to tell them what you are doing and to assess if the temperature is too hot. It has been estimated that there are more neurones in one human body than there are humans in the world.

Adipose tissue – what we call fat – is a grouping of cells distributed around male and female bodies in different areas. These adipose tissue cells are thought to be generated by both male and female hormones. They can lie, almost dormant, until excess food and drink intake and a lack of exercise cause them to grow and multiply in proportion to the excesses imposed on the body.

In men they are mainly concentrated in the intra-abdominal cavity; excess fat in the stomach area is called 'android obesity' and, in men, is activated by a combination of excess calorie intake, lethargy and possibly by an associated testosterone change and is directly linked to an increased risk of Type 2 diabetes and to cardiovascular disease. The risks of enlarged stores of android adipose tissue and its associated health risks increase with age.

Adipose tissue cells in women's bodies are mainly concentrated in the femoral and gluteal areas – thighs and bums; in excess, it is known as gynoid obesity. Because of pregnancy, and on reaching the menopause, women become at risk of producing excess adipose tissue in the stomach area too – android obesity. There is a difference between male and female android adipose tissue distribution; in men it is stored in the upper area of the abdominal cavity whereas in women it is stored in the lower part of the abdominal cavity. Again, in women the incidence of excess adipose tissue is linked to ageing, lack of exercise and excessive calorie intake, and causes a higher risk of both Type 2 diabetes and coronary heart disease (CHD); the risk of the latter is 50 per cent higher in women than in men.

Cardiovascular heart disease may be thought to develop 7–10 years later in women than in men but it is still the major cause of death in women. The number of women affected has been rising over the last 25 years, particularly in the 35–55 year age group whereas the number of men affected has been falling. Smoking appears to have a more deleterious effect on women's health than on men's health, particularly in their mid-years. Identification, testing, diagnosis and subsequent treatment appears to be a slower process with women. As oestrogen levels fall at the beginning of the menopause systolic blood pressure increases (hypertension) with symptoms as diverse as chest pain, palpitations, headaches and hot flushes; these symptoms are frequently, by association, wrongly blamed on the menopause and thus no investigation of blood pressure irregularities is thought necessary. Hormones can be blamed for so much; their presence in the body is dictated by the brain and their effects within the body cause further changes in the brain.

From the early days of lying in their cots baby girls tend to look at faces whilst baby boys look, not so much at faces, but at things. It is known that baby girls begin to talk earlier and use more words than boys do; they subsequently show a more complex use of language. Four times more boys than girls grow up to develop some form of language problems – including use of the spoken word, reading and writing. This can be proven to be caused by neither coincidence nor by the child's environment but by the innate physical systems and structures found within the body of that particular individual. Research shows these types of differences can be identified in twins where one of them is female and the other male. Their physical attributes at birth were recorded and reflected known gender differences. To show absolute equality of opportunity it was ensured that both of the twins were brought up together in the same environment and that they were given similar life-chances. As they grew and developed, the effects of their innate gender-imposed physical differences became apparent in their learning outcomes.

Boys are more likely to derive pleasure when they are allowed to chase and fight and make noise; they don't take turns easily or play by the rules of fairness. Whilst they may have difficulties with reading and writing they are generally good at systematic and organisational thinking and are also better at maths. Boys are poor at developing social skills; they get told off more often – sometimes, seemingly, just as a pre-emptive strike.

Many boys do not want to (or find it difficult to) obey the rules of school or accept the academic ethos of learning; boys want to know 'why?' 'what is the point of learning this?' and excesses of this type of behaviour are now recognised by the NHS as a form of Oppositional Defiant Disorder (ODD) with its more severe form being Conduct Disorder. This behaviour of overtly challenging received wisdom, authority or the status quo alienates boys from authority and those controlling the system whilst girls, in general, acquiesce, try to learn and try to behave well. The difficulties the boys find in trying to learn, rather than being admitted to by the boys themselves and help sought, are hidden behind belligerence. No-one wants to admit to not understanding something; especially when you are a boy and the girls all seem to understand. In most schools teachers do not have the time or freedom to develop and use strategies to alleviate these life-restricting learning deficiencies.

Top groups of boys can and do excel – especially in maths and the sciences; in boys, the development of skills at different ages and at different speeds does help males to catch up a bit when they are older but nowadays they have to compete alongside the best girls – which wasn't always the case. It used to be that sustained efforts were employed to ensure that boys were given every chance to be educated up to a particular educational level. Girls were not thought worthy of education beyond a certain basic level; that it would be a pointless waste of time and effort when they were destined to become housewives and mothers.

Girls like people; they find reading people's faces and emotions more easy, they are more considerate and are much more likely to show empathy, they communicate more freely and more frequently, they tend to play by the rules (or manipulate them) – even when they don't like them, they have an innate sense of fairness, they are social and sociable, their language skills, reading and writing, are better. Their spatial skills are worse.

This is not to say that there aren't problem girls, of course there are. But, the statistics show – US National Library of Medicine & National Institute of Health (and others) state that boys present a higher prevalence of mental retardation and learning disabilities – that there are more problem boys than girls and that the boy's problems are generally very much worse. It's not necessarily that boys have become worse than they were before it's just that now society has begun to change, and females have been given and realised the opportunities for their own success, that they have taken and used them to their advantage; and, they have succeeded in excelling their male counterparts.

This is a great change from the days when girls were the victims of educational discrimination. Whilst being treated as though you almost did not exist was difficult to accept for bright girls it did, as a strange by-product, at least allow those girls who were finding learning a difficult process a place to safely hide their inadequacies away. Perhaps, it was the only benefit of the traditional lack of expectation of academic achievement in girls.

As they grow up more than one half of our babies are likely to have one or more of the following problems: attention deficit disorder (twice as common in boys), a learning disorder, behavioural problems or Asperger's syndrome (which is 10 times more prevalent in boys than girls); indeed, the victims of the vast majority of these types of problems are usually boys.

See that mixed group of 10 kids; well, at least five of them, and probably all boys, are having to struggle up a slippery slope to survive as part of the society they find themselves in. They develop coping strategies to protect themselves from shame and ridicule. They didn't ask for it, they don't deserve it, it just happened. A roll of the dice; and we all know that the dice are usually 'loaded'.

All male embryos show more effects as a result of a mother's stress during pregnancy. In a 20-year study on children from birth to 18 years old, boys were found to be more susceptible to illness, injury and death in infancy than were girls; at any age and at every age. It has also been suggested that because girls have two 'X' chromosomes (as opposed to boys who have one 'X' and one 'Y') and also more genes that this gives girls a 'back-up' system. If something goes wrong in one gene, they always have spares to fall back on. Girls are also far less exposed to the male hormone testosterone which seems to detrimentally affect brain development. Males also have greater rates of most chronic illnesses even though testosterone boosts physical strength. It seems the male immune system is less effective – as shown by hospital infections and survival rates; another thing that can be put down to the genetic chromosome difference.

Whilst females of any species have always had to be strong enough not only to survive their pregnancy and the birth of their young, they also have to be able to continue to rear their young for, in some cases, as much as several years and to teach the young females how to be good mothers; also, they are usually the providers of food and the omnipresent protectors of their brood. Their life is invested in their young.

The male, meanwhile, only needs to be strong enough to fight off rivals and thus to earn the right to mate; some stay around to protect their young. After breeding, having passed on their genes, it is far less important for the male to survive – let alone become old. Males of most species develop more slowly, tend to take more risks, get ill or injured more often and die younger. In humans, an overt sign of the slower physical development of males can be seen in the effect of the delays in the growth of connections in the part of the nervous system which signals a full bladder. Some young boys tend to be unable to stop bed-wetting until they are much older than their female counterparts.

Just as in the animal kingdom, males tend to reach sexual maturity later than females and then, given the opportunity, the males become more promiscuous.

Humans enjoy sex, it is not just used for procreation; and, apart from bonobos (pygmy chimpanzees) and, possibly, dolphins, humans are unique in this aspect of their lives. The bonobo can only be found living wild in war-torn Congo and are exposed to potential extinction because of man's activities. They live in large social groups, where most members display all the positive attributes of female humans and, these groups have sometimes been referred to as a 'gynocracy'. They enjoy bonding by kissing and cuddling. In these groups physical sexual activity between all members has become a source of both pleasure and of social cohesion. Sexual encounters are also used as a greeting and for conflict resolution. They all have frequent sex with each other, across the whole range of age and gender boundaries, purely for pleasure – except in the case of mothers and their adult sons (that helps to keep the gene pool as diverse as possible). Because the males will have penetrative sex with the very young it is good that the male penis is conical in shape – thus, he can control the level of penetration; sex is seen as an act of bonding not of aggression. The female has a very large clitoris, akin to the size of a tiny penis. Both males and females often have face to face sex and enjoy oral sex and masturbation with all other members of both genders; this is not a monogamous society.

As mammals, we have a part of the brain, the neocortex, which gives us high levels of (self) consciousness. We are able to anticipate and enjoy things which give us pleasure and as a result we repeat the experience so that we can get more pleasure. Neurotransmitters in the brain release chemicals which make us feel good. We anticipate and enjoy food and drink – even when not that hungry or thirsty and, we anticipate and enjoy sex for recreation – not just reproduction; we enjoy music and the arts. Most of the animal kingdom sees food and drink, and even copulation, as survival strategies. For them the act of sex may give pleasure – look at their faces and body language at orgasm – but its frequency is controlled by oestrus (the female coming into 'heat') and the chemical signs released indicating that she will be fertile but for a very short period of time only. Animals cannot afford the luxury of enjoying sex just for pleasure – it takes up too much energy and makes both of them vulnerable during the act of copulation. For example, members of the dog family can be locked together for at least half an hour during the mating ritual. In animals, the chemicals emitted during oestrus create a temporary change in the levels of the sex hormones for both males and females but, just for the duration of the mating season; afterwards, it's almost as though they become impotent until the next time the female is 'in-season' – and that is controlled by when she is pregnant and suckling her offspring and the associated chemical production in her body. Whilst the male being in close proximity can afford protection for the female and her brood, many females in the animal kingdom do not want the males to stay around anyway; the males are likely to want to mate with the young females and kill the young males – whom they see as competition.

In humans, finding a receptive partner albeit it for a 'one night stand' or for the beginnings of true romance, may be even less in our direct control than we first thought. It seems that it is not so much a case of physical attraction as chemical attraction. Drugs, powerful euphoria-inducing drugs; are supplied by our own bodies.

Sexual desire, or lust, is activated and promoted by high levels of testosterone and oestrogen. They are the chemical sponsors of sexual attraction – either for the powerful first stages of your new romantic relationship or, as the sex-drug instigators of your lust during that 'one night stand'. The more you want, the more you need, so the more you get. Then you want more, you need more, so your body gives you more. Beware of the effects of a drug overdose.

Attraction; if that 'love-struck' phase invades your very being, when you just cannot get that special someone off your mind, to the detriment of work, eating or sleep, then you have been doped by the trio of attraction drugs – dopamine, adrenaline and serotonin.

You are in the second stage of your romantic, sexual relationship. Dopamine gives you that lovely warm and glowing feeling of reward when you are in the company of that special someone or even just thinking about them. It activates the brain in exactly the same way that taking cocaine does. Adrenaline gets your heart racing, makes your hands (those hands that you so want to be held) hot and sweaty and makes that mouth (that mouth that you so want to say the right words, that mouth that you so want to be kissed) feel so very dry. Serotonin then drops making you obsessive, it gives you driven urges, it can take away your appetite and change your mood.

The drugs which help promote the final stage of your new, and hopefully stable, romantic relationship are oxytocin and vasopressin. Oxytocin makes you want to hug and kiss and cuddle. It is produced in quantity during that pleasure crescendo which is sexual orgasm. In a very recent study men with high levels of oxytocin were far less likely to seek another sexual experience.

Research by Bar-Ilan University, Israel found a direct correlation between high levels of oxytocin and bonding in, and longevity of, a relationship; further, it increased the incidence of 'mirroring' each other's behaviour and thought patterns.

Researchers have also observed men in a social context where there were numerous attractive women. The physical proximity of the men to the women, how close they chose to stand to the attractive women, was observed. The men were then given a puff of nasal spray containing oxytocin and their behaviour was continually monitored. Subsequent to being given the oxytocin, the men were noted to be standing noticeably further away from the attractive women; exactly the same women with whom they were standing in close proximity to in the earlier session. The conclusion is, that if women can keep their men sexually satisfied on a frequent basis, the men will have high levels of oxytocin in their bodies and therefore will be far less likely to feel the need to stray; something that many women have realised, at an intuitive level, for a long time. Better sex helps to create and sustain a better relationship which then has better sex; it forms a virtuous circle. Vasopressin is a chemical which, somehow, makes you want to commit, to be devoted to your partner; we don't know exactly how it works but we do know that if it is 'blocked' then there is little evidence of any kind of devotion or commitment behaviour.

The signs, symptoms and intense flush of a new sexual relationship shows a striking similarity to the chemistry of, and the signs and symptoms of, obsessive compulsive disorder (OCD), depression and seasonal adjusted disease (SAD). Anti-depressant drugs used in the treatment of these disorders can change the chemical ratios in the body and as a side-effect can kill romantic attraction and sexual desire.

When you make that special two-way link with someone it is the brain chemicals which will determine the outcome, not logic. That is why a blind date organised by friends or family is not often likely to succeed. They may have tried to match both of your preferences in looks, style, personality, physique and ages together with your jobs and your hobbies and all those other personal interests but, if there is no special magnetism, no chemical attraction between you both, then however nice the person who is the subject of their logical selection process, if you want a life-changing passionate liaison then it is destined to disappoint.

There needs to be that special chemistry for both of you; to ignite that spark, to kindle a burning passion for each other within your very souls. It needs to include that combination of special factors, when your eyes meet across a crowded room, including, according to research, 55 per cent the body language, 38 per cent the tone and style of the voice and just 7 per cent what that person actually says.

As you get just a little bit closer, it is your olfactory senses that will either attract or repel. At an almost subconscious level our noses can identify a potentially attractive mate; it's the pheromones. The male exudes a pheromone called androstadienone, which is also found excreted by the glands in the male's armpits and in his semen; it is his 'signature' scent and will be irresistible to the right woman. She will exude the pheromone called estratetraenol, which is also found in female urine, and this will be her aphrodisiac for him.

Science has known about pheromones and human sexual attraction for some time; initially it was at the theoretical level, the 'stuff of legend', but now they can be identified more clearly, although the causal links between the sex hormones such as testosterone and oestrogen and the pheromones is complicated and not fully understood; they also contain steroids. It is not clear if things like hay fever and smoking may affect a person's ability to identify pheromones. There is not just one universal sex pheromone; there is no one olfactory aphrodisiac. If there was, all those French parfumiers would have made it, bottled it and be selling it by the millions. Each gender has their own style of pheromone cocktail determined by their distinct gender-specific melange of hormones; and, within those parameters, each individual's own set of pheromones is as unique a formula to that one person as is their face.

In tests, babies have been shown to be aware of the scent of breast milk and will home in on where they believe the mother's nipple to be. They can also 'smell' the mood of their mother. Sweat recognition tests have found some people able to identify their own partners body scent, for heterosexuals to identify attractive odours from the opposite sex (and, perhaps, a mate capable of rearing better, stronger children) and for gay people to identify attractive same-sex sweat. Even the taste of the tears of a female partner could be sensed by, had an effect on, males; it did not induce empathy as expected but did lower the level of testosterone/sexual arousal in the male perhaps because he had believed that sex was unlikely.

Do pheromones contain traces of hormones, do hormones 'advertise' via pheromones; it is a subject which merits more research. Perhaps, 'sniffing out the right partner' may not be that far from the truth. But, in real-world situations, as opposed to in research, the olfactory perspective is just one of the subtle complexities of attraction. Every aspect of the five senses – vision, hearing, touch, smell and, eventually, taste will all play a contributory role; so too will the genes, DNA and a complex of social factors. And, of course, this means that each gender has their own attraction strategy. Sex can be fun, in the right circumstances; it can bring a lot of pleasure. Humans seem to be the only species which indulges in sexual activity for the pure joy of it, rather than indulging just for procreation. It all begins with that rite of passage that is puberty. Unfortunately, the instruction book containing the accumulation of appropriate information is not hidden somewhere in your gene bank ready and waiting to support you on the treacherous journey from childhood into adulthood. There is no manual outlining the impending physical changes or the emotional turmoil caused by the effects of a rush of powerful hormones through every cell of your body. You begin to seek an intimate knowledge of the opposite sex at both a physical and emotional level, you know that you are excited by them and want to get close to them but it is an alien feeling; and, to make things more difficult, that young person you want to get closer to is just as confused, traumatised, embarrassed and vulnerable as you. You do not know the appropriate social manners let alone the sexual etiquette. And how to cope with all this and relate to the rest of society in an appropriate and dignified manner – without looking like the gauche adolescent that you know you are. It is like trying to learn to tap-dance in a minefield.

It gets no easier when you are an adult.

CHAPTER 5
JUST KIDDING

I suppose the most appropriate place to start is at the beginning. Well, a beginning...

Bearing a child must rate as one of the most natural things in the world. Some women claim to know they are pregnant; but, more usually in the West the cessation of menstruation, followed by a home pregnancy test, and a subsequent visit to the appropriate medical professional will confirm the pregnancy (by detecting a hormone level in the urine).

Picture, if you will, a woman who has just become pregnant. She has already admitted a shoal of male sperm into her body and has chosen, this time, to allow just that special one the honour of fertilising her egg. Maybe the initiation of her pregnancy was a random chance of nature, that most romantic of conceptions. Perhaps she just stopped taking her contraceptive of choice; as, one would hope, a joint decision with her partner. Hopefully too, it's a wanted baby. Only she can decide to take the final steps to try to become pregnant; he cannot. These days you can even buy donor sperm on the Internet; and, who would ever know? Women are the ones who, ultimately, have the potential to control if and when they have children, and how many.

Whatever, this fertilized egg now nuzzles in the lining of the woman's womb and begins to grow. The remaining millions of discarded sperm lie dead or dying.

From this moment, for a period of about eight weeks, the mother carries and nurtures her embryo, as a baby's first stage is known. The gender of a new embryo is female; it is always female – because a baby's sexual and reproductive organs always are female during this stage. Is Mother Nature trying to tell us something, trying to make a point? Slowly the embryo begins to develop into a foetus. In the process of doing so, it begins to grow all the necessary limbs and organs to become a human baby. By 12 weeks it has developed so much that is now possible for medical science to determine the final gender of the foetus. The male hormones found in the 'Y' chromosome, including testosterone, cause the changes which erase the femaleness and creates the maleness. More male embryos are created at conception but fewer survive; the female embryo is more robust.

Amniocentesis is the medical procedure during which a sample of amniotic fluid is taken by inserting a long, hollow needle into the amniotic sac around the baby and withdrawing a small amount of amniotic fluid. This sample is then diagnosed under a microscope and can not only determine the sex of the baby but can also be used to screen for any foetal abnormalities.

The female foetus is about three weeks ahead of a boy's in skeletal formation; by the time of their birth girls are developmentally about four to six weeks ahead and by puberty girls are two years ahead. Baby boys generally have a greater body mass than girls and their birth, on average, takes one and a half hours longer. Apparently, all negative traits and outcomes are higher in boys; they are more vulnerable to disease, illness and accidents. Whereas, girls are more robust and healthy; girls cry less often and can be more readily pacified, particularly by touch. The development of human skin is promoted through the hormone oxytocin; the levels of oxytocin are 10 times greater in females than those levels found in males, yet although they have more oxytocin in their bodies the skin of all females, not just babies, is thinner and more receptive to touch and stimulation. Therefore oxytocin levels appear to be inversely proportional to the thickness of human skin.

A female embryo is said to carry six to seven million eggs; by the time that girl reaches puberty she will have less than half a million left. The ravages of just being alive and developing into a young adult causes the stock of eggs to diminish. Boys have no sperm when they are young; their bodies only begin to produce them as they reach puberty. Thus, all those random erections which a young boy will quite naturally have are all impotent.

For a total period of about nine months, the bond between the mother and her new offspring strengthens and grows in exaggerated proportion to her girth. Every sensation created in one stimulates a response in the other. What mother eats, feeds baby; if mother is sad or happy, stressed or relaxed, baby will know, will share the emotion. Baby moves, mother feels it. A mother converses with her unborn; plans an imaginary life together. The initial stages of an unspoken bond which, as they rightly say, 'wild horses' could not break.

The father – is somewhere else.

The child growing within the woman is an excellent device by which the behaviour of both parents can be modified; will be modified. Often, the mother will instinctively choose to ride the high horse of her virtue and eschew some, or all, of her once enjoyed vices including, perhaps, drinking alcohol, dancing, smoking, curries, nights out – and, indeed, anything involving loud noise, speed, exaggerated movement or any other real or perceived danger. Those girls-only shopping trips will, of course, continue to be seen as essential excursions.

And, whatever she decides is sauce for the goose, must be construed as a very reasonable choice of sauce for a caring gander too.

The larger the mother becomes the greater her inconvenience. The greater her inconvenience the greater will be the father's inconvenience. The prospective parents are being conditioned and their behaviour patterns are being continually modified by their unborn baby; for one of the parents in particular, more directly than for the other.

Impromptu social occasions – from going out for a meal or seeing a film – to a trip to the seaside in his two seater sports car or on his motorbike – will all become but faint memories. All suggested forays will, from now on, be subject to forethought and planning; and, they will all warrant a 'risk-assessment' to include the need for level access and the ready availability of toilets as being of paramount importance. And, for him, the proposed freedom of 'nights out with the boys' although not specifically defined as out of bounds when mentioned in mixed company will be, in practice, deemed as a lack of support (if not outright mutiny) behind closed doors.

Men do not understand the importance of ante-natal classes to some pregnant women; or, what effect their role could have on his life.

Anti-natal classes – that's what men hear; their first reaction. From childhood – in comics, books and films they learned what an anti-aircraft gun was, what an anti-tank mine was. So, it was all a bit confusing, these Anti or Ante classes. But, although correctly instructed, he still believes that he could successfully feign his interest and support, if not show actual enthusiasm.

The man's perceptions become shattered. He is innocent, unready, unprepared – a lamb to the slaughter; initial instinctively negative mental images soon become reinforced. A few women pressure their partners to attend the ante-natal classes, with the apparent intention of the man's subjugation. Allowing their male to be sacrificed to a classroom full of grotesquely pregnant women led by their scary 'mother superior' (or should it be, he thinks, 'superior mother'?). For men, the nicest interpretation would be – too similar to dog obedience training classes for comfort. Too scary, too intimidating; the sincerity – overbearing.

Father – wishes he were somewhere, anywhere, else.

It is easy to think that this does not apply to you. But, the social circumstances in which you were brought into this world and the manner in which you were raised determined substantial aspects of your personality for life. No matter that, as a young adult, you sense that you do not want to have children. Or, that you truly believe that the way you do or would, bring your children up would be different – as if somehow they would be solely influenced by your personal value system, remain unaffected by every other child and adult you or your child ever comes into contact with? Get real. Whatever happens, however determined you may be, your child will be the product of the society it finds itself in; not just a creation of your well-intentioned personal philosophy. Your financial situation and social status, for example, will take care of great chunks of your child's personal development. Unless, of course, you have your own personal 'desert island' from which the rest of the world will be excluded for a decade or more. And, the child which eventually arrives may well be different from the one that was anticipated and planned for – perhaps not in gender, but in both character and personal traits too.

So, do we know baby's gender? The great advantage of knowing is, in fact, twofold. For the mother her motivation can be more specifically directed; imagining and planning her child's intended future. The second is, or so it appears, that when baby clothes buying begins in earnest the 'right' colours and styles can be selected. Random elderly relations can buy the 'right' wool and get out the needles. And baby's new room, the cot, the wallpaper, the curtains, the mobile, the changing mat, the bath, the cuddly toy can all be organised. To many a dad's chagrin, even the pushchair will be bought on a mum's street-cred rating rather than its engineering quality or its cost.

Do not be fooled into thinking that baby girls are in some way more delicate, more vulnerable; the reverse is true. A girl baby's height, weight, teeth and bones all develop quicker than those of a boy. Baby girls are more independent, occupy, amuse and console themselves more readily and also develop motor-skills, coordination, language and inter-personal skills more easily. They grow up to be more resilient, show more immunity to illness and disease and are less prone to accidents.

The interaction between babies and adults is important. In an experiment, adults of mixed gender were confronted with babies of un-revealed gender who were dressed in identical unisex clothing; the adults were unable to assess if there were gender differences between the babies and thus treated them all similarly. Later, when they were introduced to the same babies, whose gender had now been identified by the colour of their clothing, it was noted that their treatment of the babies of one gender was very different from their treatment of the babies of the opposite gender. This confirmed the assumption that we display a learned behaviour when dealing with babies of different genders.

Compare and contrast (as they say in all good exam papers) the generalisations which best describe the bedrooms as created for little girls and boys:

- The kitsch pink Cinderella/Fairy Princess/My Little Pony theme – all lace and frills, softness and gentleness, co-ordinated pastel colours and soft textures – on walls, on curtains, the baby-mobile, rugs on the floor; leotard, tutu and ballet shoes in a corner, hanging hopefully…

- The 'action man', bold (football team?) colours, adventure theme, fort, soldiers marching around the wallpaper, toy cars and lorries with road-map rug; football shirt, shorts and boots in a corner, hanging hopefully…

Baby arrives; 'Isn't she pretty, got her mother's eyes', gently caressed and nurtured; bodily functions discreetly dispatched; all is swathed in decorum. Pink 'girlie' dress with matching hat and white tights.

Baby arrives; 'He's big, looks like Churchill; look at the size of those feet – you know what they say 'big feet, big…'. A less cosseting care; bodily functions a cause for hilarity. Decorum ignored. Blue and orange, a miniature boiler suit, hand knitted hat and bootees of dubious taste.

And off home in the car – bearing a sticker: 'Little Princess on board' (a treasure, to treasure) or 'Little Tyke on board' (beware, a potential problem).

Baby's arrival, often appearing like a screaming, blood-red and purple wrinkled prune, may not be what many parents will have been conditioned to expect their baby to look like. It can be a test for the nine-month bond that the mother has established with her baby; it is not unusual to have an overwhelming fear of knowing that you are now totally responsible for every need of this creature. For the father, it is like being involved in the screen-test for an alien film; and, he is so insignificant that the father's name does not even have to appear on the birth certificate. Oh, and regardless of whether it's a boy or a girl, don't forget to take a picture of them in their christening dress.

Nature is clever; even devious. A little parcel of joy, initially small enough to fit in a supermarket carrier bag and just as easy to carry around. Mother, designed and ready to dispense the ultimate hygienic, temperature controlled, nutrition. Just a few nappies required – and they are small, discreet and disposable nowadays. Life will not really be so different, just special.

And a father must be seen to be proud and protective of mother and child (including, of course, when he is out at work or otherwise deployed).

Everyone likes a small baby (allegedly). And, even anyone not actually wanting (or feigning) to be allowed a cuddle, appears to show uncharacteristically tolerant behaviour. Indeed, intolerance at any level towards baby or mother is greeted – especially by elderly great-grannies, those all-seeing matriarchs – with breath being sucked noisily through rattly false-teeth like geese hissing an initial warning; only to be swiftly followed by a verbal onslaught and backed up by aggressive physical gestures indicating the impending danger to the un-besotted onlooker. Negative reinforcement for negative behaviour.

Women have better hearing than men and are more aware of, and receptive to, the high sound frequencies produced by a crying baby; for the mother it is more likely to induce a positive reaction whereas for the male, the dominant reaction is to want to stop the noise. It is all a matter of aural pitch. New babies are likely to have an accent which is an amalgam of those of their parents and the area where brought up; part of this is the song of language heard in-utero plus, once born, the sounds from parents and others. It can restrict our ability to pronounce certain noises, certain words. That is why learning some new foreign language can appear particularly difficult for some cultures.

As baby grows it slowly trains Mother as its carer and keeper. Food and warmth (no, not too much) and baths and clean clothes and amusement – a baby can train parents, grandparents and siblings – indeed anyone – in a time, at a speed and to a level only dreamed of in the Royal Marines.

Father's less time-intense training by infant (even though reinforced by Mother) still makes him compliant, if a little bemused and preferably detached.

Growth demands more complex needs; now becoming too large to be easily carried, requiring sustenance more substantial than its mother's milk can supply – yet not ready for adult fare; crawling and unable to be left unattended for more than a mere moment. The bond between mother and child continues to grow almost visibly and is a glue both elastic and yet entirely unbreakable.

Now a vast range and complexity of absolutely essential kit must accompany mother and child wherever they travel together. If affordable, a capacious car will become a necessity. If unaffordable then the mother will have to struggle with less convenient arrangements and the father will be made to pay – one way or the other, he will pay.

If the trip is to Granny's (who loves her frequent babysitting duties) the needs will be slightly less. Granny, as they all seem to, will have already installed a full range of 'kit', enough to enable her to take up duties as a reserve home for the local playgroup. At this very moment, and as a result of a lifetime's training, Grandad's interest in the contents of his shed will increase. He will, nevertheless, have been instructed to be ready, at a moment's notice, to erect a swing, slide or indeed perform any other duties as required.

Father is at work. Overtime, like the potential for a promotion with its higher salary and longer hours, becomes a necessity both financially and for sanity.

Sometimes it feels to him like he is slave to an insatiable double-headed monster. He works harder so that he can supply its needs; but, then the bigger and stronger it grows and the more it needs; so, he works harder so that he can supply its needs; but, then the bigger and stronger it grows and the more it needs; so he works harder so that he can supply its needs but...

But there's always someone else – or so he is frequently told; a relative or a friend's husband or some mythological man down the street; someone who can apparently supply more things, better things, more easily.

But the journey has only just begun...

Mummy's little princess or Daddy's little girl; a fall, cuddles, there there. Guess who is encouraged to dance and sing, play dressing-up, dollies and tea parties.

Mummy's little boy or Daddy's little soldier; a fall, up you get and off you go, little man. Guess who has been given a ball, a toy car, a hammer, a drum.

This eternal pattern surely cannot pass unnoticed by any parent; indeed, by anyone. But, for most, it really doesn't matter; their baby is their baby; and perfect – exactly as it is. And so is their parenting.

From its very first days, baby will be introduced to other children; some will be of a similar age, most will be older; some will be family, some will not. For certain, most who sustain any interest at all will be girls. Boys, in general, just do not get babies; which is convenient because, after initial and perfunctory introductions, they are usually kept at arms-length or, better still, are totally ostracised.

Initially, at least, little girls are interested and compliant if not enthusiastic students of all areas of childcare; they become eager little helpers. Whether this is part of a universal strategic policy by mothers to begin the training of the next generation is difficult to say but, it is certain that these girls have all the advantages of the best seats in the house for changing mat duties, bathing and feeding.

When little boys are on the changing mat there frequently seems to be a need for comment on the little chap's equipment and bodily functions. Laying on your back, displaying absolutely everything and peeing in the air with half an erection and smelly poo – there's a recipe for hilarity; for so many females to be caught laughing, utterly helpless themselves as they cry tears of unbridled mirth. No wonder he cries; it's enough to scare any male. He's a nice easy target; with nowhere to hide from prying eyes and hands and baby wipes. The spectators and commentators are, unsurprisingly, always female – of all ages. After all, it helps to perpetuate the ability to discriminate and ridicule; and it reinforces negative gender stereotypes right across several generations at one go. Now that's just what we want – and so brave to take advantage of a vulnerable, helpless little chap. Still, at least everyone present gets to add another specimen to their mental catalogue of willies! And then, after all that humiliation, you can let him loose on the floor, totally naked, for an encore! How he tries to be brave and act nonchalantly. Being a mum isn't always this much fun you know.

When little girls are on the changing mat the rules change completely. Her body was built to hide everything whenever possible; that's the way it is and that's the way it will be. No-one will say anything detrimental and all will try to avert their eyes from this little angel's body in an almost reverential way. Peeing is ignored and just dealt with, and poo treated as though it were a treasure which smells of roses. Nothing is seen, therefore, nothing is obscene. And, if you are male – do not go anywhere near the vicinity of that changing mat under any circumstances or say anything whatsoever to anyone, do not even have eye contact with anyone present – unless you want to be ostracised and branded as some kind of pervert for the rest of your days. After all, you are only her Daddy!

And that is the scene at one of the most important initiation ceremonies for each little girl. This ritual happens several times a day for months on end. It's a rite of passage for little girls. Let's hope that she doesn't too readily make the connection between the baby boy on the mat and Daddy – whom she adores and controls in equal measure.

Children do not own or control anything, including their bodies; they are like refugees. Most of your home is like a transit camp to them. They just pass through it, stopping occasionally; everything there is yours, they do not own it or control it in any way; you do. Their bedroom is the nearest thing that they will have to anything like the sanctuary they so need. That will be all the territory they have for probably as long as two decades; and, it's leased to them – as they will be frequently reminded in their teenage years. And, they may well have to share it. It is your responsibility as an adult to strive to give them a comfortable and welcoming place of refuge; somewhere, anywhere – even if, for a little one, it is just a corner or a cupboard. If you are able to, but do not, then not only is shame upon you but, you will live to reap the vengeance and wrath of that child when they become a teenager for never having done so. You have been warned; do not ignore this warning!

Little boys seemingly have a need for a bedroom with bold colours, perhaps the colours of a football team or rugby team, and cars and buses and lorries and tractors and Bob the Builder – even if Daddy is incapable of putting up a flat-pack unit for them to be displayed on. A rug with roads on is a must for planning their escape route. And a special place to store all those interesting finds and bits of broken toys. Do not subject him to soft colours or textures which may offer too much comfort, it will only corrupt his true nature.

Little girls are unable to survive their childhood without suffering from some form of severe psychological trauma if they have not been given the opportunity to be immersed in pink; a liberal use of all shades of pink; and, of course, frills, lots of frills. Pink must appear on walls, curtains, carpets and bedding. And somewhere to secrete away all those personal childhood mementos and priceless collectables. Clothes without pink and /or frills are simply too dreadful to even contemplate having in one's bedroom. If she is given them but chooses something else she will have been treated properly, with due respect.

If children are not given these things for their bedrooms then, when they visit new friends' houses and see that their friends have them, they will feel impoverished and may be ostracised by that individual and risk becoming totally socially isolated by their entire peer group. They will then not want these new friends to visit them in their house because it would become apparent that they are in some way inadequate.

At best, at the very best, your child will attract sympathy for being subjugated by parents who are absolute uncaring morons and who show no signs of love or even empathy for the needs of their child. Your child's friends will tell their own parents of this horrendous evil and, like it or not, those parents will not be allowed contact with you, the offending parents, until there has been seen to be radical change. Now you will be the victim of your own inadequacies.

Also, please remember that bedrooms need updating and modernising as the child grows older. For boys, Bob the Builder will have to succumb to a Star Wars invasion and Formula One; eventually the bottom of the wardrobe and under the bed will become caches for pictures of naked women. Thankfully, with girls, it's clothes, and more clothes and accessories and pictures of members (in its nicest meaning) of boy bands.

Tradition has it that little boys need to be given access to the great outdoors, or at least a garden, so that they can 'let off steam'; thereby they will become vaguely human until the next head of steam needs to be released – and so on... They will doubtless have been given a ball and made to take it with them – so, as that boy, you try to do something to amuse yourself with this ball. If you are really lucky there may be someone else or a dog to play with; this will inevitably involve much shouting and chasing and getting dirty. Steam vented, the boy will be allowed back into the house (once clean) on condition that he now plays quietly with his cars etc. Boys, and the men they grow up to be, generally feel less concerned about conforming to social stereotypes and are more happy to be identified as an individual, as a character and thus, do not have the same social pressures to conform as girls and women do.

Meanwhile, little girls are much too delicate to go outside unless the weather is good and anyway their pretty clothes may become dirty or torn. So, they stay indoors and sing, and dance, and play with dolls, and dressing-up, and try putting on make-up, and help Mummy cooking in the kitchen. It's such a busy life being a young lady. But, girls and women will spend a lifetime under pressure to conform to social stereotypes, of wanting or trying to be pretty or beautiful, desirable in both looks and behaviour. Having your ears pierced can become a rite of passage for many babies and young girls. Because there are already strong established social roles for girls and women, and pressure to conform, girls soon identify the role that they believe they should be playing. This happens regardless of the family having either a male or female at its head.

From now on, until 11 years old, they will be subjected to the social whirl of play group, then pre-school or nursery; next reception class and eventually in 'proper school' through infants and up to the top of the juniors. There will be uniforms to buy and outgrow, and pens and pencils and pencil cases and school bags to put them all in, and so many other things. People to meet, friends to make.

Not by chance are those who teach, manage, act as support staff or as carers in our primary education system almost exclusively female. It is true that there are a token number of men (who, to get appointed in the first place, must display female-biased empathy, attributes and tendencies – rather than being too overtly masculine) who actually teach – and who usually manage to escape the classroom and disappear into administration, organisation and management.

The approach of making the physical environment at school as alluring and child-friendly as possible – without turning it into a theme park, works well. These surroundings create an ambience which allows mothers to feel safe leaving their child there; and, more importantly, safe in the knowledge that after years spent caring for and training their child they can hand over the reins to more females thus perpetuating the appropriate style of indoctrination and therefore protecting the child from any prolonged exposure to males and the corrosion that male testosterone fuelled bias can cause.

The atmosphere at primary level schools has been created to be as sympathetic, interesting and stimulating as possible. This allows the children to morph from play into a more structured environment and most seem to enjoy so very much of it. But, you can't please all the people all of the time.

For lots of boys, school is a social structure that causes difficulties. The rules, the expected behaviour, trying to learn such apparently meaningless stuff and in an almost incomprehensible written language, poor dexterity meaning struggling with pens and pencils to form letters and words that all seem so obtuse yet so similar. Friendship can be alright but there is always someone who you don't like trying to make you do something, trying to dominate. So, you retaliate; you are so frustrated by it all. You don't have the words to express how utterly lost and inadequate you feel; your weaknesses get covered and hidden by bravado and you become another belligerent and troublesome boy. Your strengths have little value in a school environment. So, you are always being told off – sometimes, just in case you were thinking about being naughty. And all the teachers are women who you think don't like boys or worse still men who act like women – and how do you deal with them, and the girls keep getting everything right and everyone says how good they are. Don't worry, lad, there are only an absolute minimum of 11 years of compulsory full-time education ahead of you; by the end of that they should have rubbed your nose into the fact that you don't fit in and can't do anything right. You'd get less for murder; and you wouldn't get all this negative reinforcement all day, five days a week.

Some boys do, of course, fit in and perform well. But, the school curriculum and environment is not best suited to a large proportion of the population. The school system, as we know it now, is just the evolution of an antiquated system structured to encourage a nucleus of well-bred, if not always intelligent, well-motivated and therefore well behaved young men to stride through to university and the privileged professions in the life beyond. And that description is no longer going to apply to many of us.

In general, boys seem naturally drawn towards toys and hobbies based around action and noise. Even if just a spectator rather than a participant, they tend to be drawn to weapons, combat, tanks and battleships, fighter planes, helicopters, cars, lorries, tractors and, indeed, any type of machine or mechanical device. Too many structured toys or similar controlled stimulations can retard free-play, imagination and invention, activities which can increase self-reliance and self-determination. They are not so attracted by dolls, dressing-up and tea parties. Boys are competitive rather than communicative.

All children will have birthdays and thereby the question of parties arises. The same basic rules appear to prevail from the pre-school days onward into early puberty. Please note that the role of the father is, like him, discreetly, but very deliberately, excluded from children's parties.

For a girl it is important that things are done 'just so'. Printed invitations with RSVP are a must. Colour, co-ordination and good taste at the venue are of paramount importance. Anything which glitters, sparkles or twinkles is good, as are feathery things. Food should be not only be pleasing to the eye and taste fabulous but, must also be made from low-fat organic produce. This will especially appeal to the attendant mothers (for whom a little white wine must be on offer). The dress code should encourage opulence and make-up should always be encouraged, though not made obligatory. Pastel coloured tissues must be freely available for both physical and emotional upsets which are certain to occur. A range of dance music is a must (and karaoke a popular addition), as are numerous mirrors at the right height – for both the children and their mothers. Only the boys who attend the same ballet classes as the girls may be invited – although certainly not encouraged to attend. Party bags will not be made from brown paper or gaudy plastic or contain anything one would not wish to receive oneself or, especially, anything like something received in a party bag from any guest's party. Please note that the above is a bare minimum and will be amended year on year until it naturally flows into the school leaver's ball phase at about age 15 to 16 years which will act as a rehearsal for the subsequent wedding reception. Anything less than this will be a social stigma which will traumatise a girl for her entire life. For girls from age 13 years and upwards – a warning – mother beware both of girls disappearing and young men in their late teens climbing over the garden fence.

For a boy, should he be accepting of the concept of a party, this is a much easier thing to organise. Invitations should be by word of mouth – but don't spread the word; everyone wants to get rid of a boy for an afternoon/early evening. Fripperies and frivolities will have no appeal. Parents are not encouraged to attend unless it's fathers taking on duties as bouncers. Do not attempt, in the name of equality – or indeed for any other reason, to invite any girls even including accredited tom boys. Large quantities of vulgar, chemical-laden food should be supplied, to be consumed by equally vulgar (and when older, chemical-laden) friends who will do unspeakable things to each other and to any small creatures they are allowed access to. No music more melodic than heavy metal should be played. The back of the garden shed will suffice as toilet facilities. The party bag should contain large lurid sweets and as many noisy, garish and rude items as can be found. This recipe will generally work well – though with differing levels of vulgarity – for boys with an age range from age two to age 11. Thereafter, cider, cigarettes and soft porn can be discreetly added to the above menu as demand requires but are not intended to replace any item on it. However, many boys will not want to have or be seen at a party, under any circumstances; most particularly as they get older. Therefore, in the case of older boys leaving a bag containing crisps, cider, fags and a lighter by the back door will usually be an acceptable alternative (minimum suggested age 12 years). Forcing a birthday party on a boy can cause permanent social dislocation within his peer group.

Fathers tend to expect boys to deal with and sort out their own problems even if it means some form of discomfort for the boy in the process of doing so; behaviour to develop self-reliance and as a survival strategy. Boys are brought up to deal with small personal accidents – like falling – and are allowed to be assertive and even aggressive in their endeavours to protect themselves or their things. If boys succeed in some endeavour they are usually told that it is because of their ability and efforts and thus they begin to believe success to be a natural consequence of effort. They are not taught how to behave well in social situations or expected to do so; not in the same way that girls are.

Whatever he may say to the contrary, a male generally has a pretty positive long-term relationship with that most masculine part of his body and is really unlikely to insult it. There are so many words for the male sexual organ, so many euphemisms; and yet few of them, if any, are even slightly gentle or romantic. From birth, it seems that little boys are described as having a 'little willy' or 'Wee Willie Winkie' or some play on words of a very similar nature. Usually with the size as part of the descriptor; who says size doesn't matter and that it is men themselves who are obsessed by penile size. If your own mother has been reading rhymes and making a reference to the size of your 'wee willy' – however surreptitiously, since your very birth, what chance do you stand of countering this conditioning as you grow up?

Young boys frequently seem to be encouraged to run around naked and in places and situations where little girls certainly would not be allowed to. It does not matter if it is in the safety of his home or in the garden or someone else's home and garden, in the park or at the beach or wherever; you will frequently see little boys running about and playing – wearing nothing but a sun-hat and a smile. As he plays, it jiggles and swings around; how can he possibly be expected to forget its existence. Because it is positioned right in the front on the outside it cannot be ignored. It is totally and completely exposed; and it pees frequently as if to remind him of its existence; it also pees in whatever random direction or spray pattern it likes; it can stand up or disappear, seemingly at will; and, in general, it seems that it has a mind and life-force all of its own.

Thus, to its owner, it is an ever fascinating plaything which, he will very soon find out, if played with in a certain manner, can be both very comforting and very stimulating. Whilst this preoccupation is not actively encouraged it is usually not greatly discouraged either – unless 'present company' would be likely to be offended. Given the opportunity and lack of risk of being caught, some inquisitive little girls can seem very fascinated with his plaything too.

Another interesting thing happens when you are very little – this warm, squidgy, smelly stuff seems to appear from almost nowhere. You may be sitting there or having a lie down – just minding your own business (excuse the pun) – it's almost as though it creeps up on you from behind. That is, until you investigate and find out exactly where it does come from. That place can make some really funny noises too and usually it feels really good when this happens. However, the pleasure and relief are soon forgotten as the consequences then become an irritation.

However, society has decided that as they get older little boys must try to learn some etiquette. In the male toilets little boys are expected to stand in line, abreast, shoulder to shoulder, and pee in company; looking for all the world as if they are hostages waiting to be shot in the back. Once they begin to mature they have to understand some of the basic rules; they must learn that as an adult it is an absolute no-no to ever look at the 'equipment' of another male whilst you are in the toilets or in the changing-rooms. Throughout life, and given the opportunity, peeing in the great outdoors, unregulated and unfettered can, most males find, be bliss.

Putting drugs into your body is crazy – welcome to the world of testosterone! In boys, puberty can be both an embarrassment and an adventure; and, the subsequent self-conscious quest for information on sexual matters and relationships is a million times worse. That hormone, testosterone, is flooding through your body and changing its very structure and function; it is creating drives and desires that you have no control over, no understanding of. When it comes to puberty, if you are lucky enough to have had an older brother or cousin or close friend or someone else in the family who is enlightened, you may be given some idea what to expect. The more usual scenario involves hurtful teasing from peers and adults alike regarding puberty, followed by a smorgasbord of misinformation on relationships with the opposite sex, their anatomy and the techniques necessary; and all this espoused by those whose information is itself based on an accumulation of ignorance and errors.

To have hair beginning to grow from your chin is a pleasant indicator that you are becoming a man; to find it sprouting from under your arms and then from around your willy too is a bit of an unexpected thing. And, it is quite a surprise when that little thing, that has been just hanging there and allowing you to play at hosepipes when you go for a pee, has taken on a life of its own.

Unexpectedly, your willy has begun to grow greatly and, frequently for no apparent reason, you feel a tremor in your groin as within moments 'Little Willy' has gone stiff – as stiff as a stiff thing; and you have no idea why or if it is normal. Are you ill; is it about to explode; what is going to happen to the rest of your body; why does it feel so good; who can you, dare you, ask? A crackly, quaking, wavering, breaking voice can fill your heart with embarrassment and is a bad enough thing to keep happening in public at the most unexpected moments – but erections? Everyone in the world can see that erectile bulge in the groin area, see it showing distinctly through your trousers, watch you squirming with embarrassment.

The boyish allergy to washing is soon to be replaced by a new campaign of cleanliness, an eternal triangle – of attempting to shave without causing rashes or drawing blood (the beginnings of a lifetime tyranny), zit squeezing and indiscriminately applying hair and body products in almost industrial quantities. In defiance, every pore of your body seems to have started putting out its own unpleasant odours, which is not the confidence booster that you could do with at that stage of your life. Oh, for a non-judgemental mentor to guide you through this maze.

Unlike girls, boys do not seem to warrant any forewarning of the effects of impending puberty or, any subsequent instruction in the etiquette of male grooming let alone dress-sense, they have no hierarchy of supportive elders. How can men, on becoming an adult, be expected to teach a boy about something that they had no training for themselves?

Regardless of the lack of any parental guidelines boys keenly adopt one particular aspect of puberty, their new and special hobby of masturbation, with a missionary-like zeal; any lack of expertise being made up for by an excess of enthusiasm. That is, and will be for some years, the sum total of sexual experience for boys – apart from the occasional bout of co-experimentation. The prominent position of the male genitalia has always given them a high profile in the life of any male; but, for pre-pubescent boys to be suddenly confronted with the stimulating, if sometimes embarrassing, antics of his penis is a temptation to great to be ignored. It is destined to develop into a lifelong obsession.

It remains, however, quite disconcerting to have spontaneous erections occurring; erections at a time and in a place, outside of your control. Being sent to see Granny and getting an immediate erection is rather a mixed message – one that is unfairly imposed upon unsuspecting boys.

At senior school, boys are expected to strip off naked and act casually yet confidently in large totally open changing rooms full of other naked and half-naked boys. (This scenario will continue through his entire life be it in swimming pools, gyms and armed forces medicals etc.) They will then have to wander through the changing room, with a towel loosely wrapped around their middle, whilst saying some sort of prayer to the 'penis god' asking it not to give him an erection – not here, not now. They will then have to drop the towel, walk into the long narrow shower area, and stand nonchalantly under one of the numerous shower heads being stimulated by the rivulets of water sensuously tracing over their bodies. They are standing there close to, in front of and, embarrassingly, sometimes actually being jostled and caused to inadvertently touch, other boys – each of whom is experiencing the same predicament. Even the act of rubbing soap on this, now quivering, body is too much and a dash is made to grab your towel and seek some form of dignity in a dark corner of the changing room.

Circumcision is evident. The loss of the foreskin has an optical foreshortening effect. And as we have all learned, size apparently matters. So, ridicule is rife. Sadly, at that age, boys are unaware of the surveys which show that, in general, non-circumcised men get 'excited' much more quickly and thus have less staying-power – the matter is really not up for discussion in a boys shower block! But your religion certainly is.

And, here's yet another thing primed for embarrassment. Research shows that erect penises fall into a particular and fairly predictable set of length and girth ranges; but, and here is the really cruel bit, the size of a flaccid penis is absolutely no indicator of the size of the same one when it is erect. And, in its differing flaccid states the size of any one penis can vary immensely too. A bit of a lucky-dip if you were selecting a contender for 'biggest willy of the week' from a group of unknown flaccid penises!

Now, given the propensity for the penis to do exactly what it wants when it wants, and whenever possible to completely embarrass its owner and possibly ostracise them from their peer group, every male knows that he can almost guarantee to start get some kind of erection in the least appropriate of situations. Like being strapped to an unexploded bomb with the time-clock ticking, it has a potential to affect the psyche of its owner for his entire life.

As boys get older they have all the problems and benefits of puberty to discover and contend with. One boy can now sing alto if not baritone, has a bush of pubic hair, can be deemed to be shaving perhaps a couple of times a week and has a penis which has, rather pleasingly, grown. Meanwhile, his poor self-conscious and embarrassed classmate still sings soprano (but with the occasional crackle); on a cold day he feels like he needs a magnifying glass and a pair of tweezers to find his pride and joy; and, if given the right frock and make-up, could be taken for a virginal girl. If there is a divine maker, they think, it has to be a woman, and perverted at that; who else would subject a young boy to such enduring humiliation?

And, on that school trip to, perhaps, an art gallery or museum everyone can see the statues, and some paintings, showing the male genitalia recreated in splendid detail on everyone from cherubs, to gods, to demons whilst on the images of the females her maternal breasts may be revealed but the pubis, if not completely hidden by a swathe of strategically positioned fabric, is smoothed into a featureless mound. Stereotypes reinforced by the establishment in a bastion of knowledge and beauty.

Just as it will be for their whole adult life, boys do not have the learned behaviour skills to allow them to talk constructively to other males about anything personal – except on rare occasions and with especially supportive individuals – particularly about those subjects relating to intimate personal relationships, sex or emotions; most cannot dance, and the vast majority cannot converse meaningfully with females. The few that have transcended this mystical barrier have a golden opportunity with the opposite sex.

All that most teenage boys can talk about, in conversations with their peers and with girls of a similar age, is to boast and brag about what they might like to think they could or would have done in some imagined sexual, dominant or aggressive encounter. As their testosterone level rises so exaggeration increases in exponential leaps – so too does its narrator's ridiculousness. And, their undeveloped sense of humour is just not funny. Lucky are the boys who do not have the confidence or stupidity, to join in these grotesque and embarrassing masquerades.

Conversations with adults seem to evolve into a world of grunts, shrugs and bowed heads, whilst avoiding eye contact. Food, but only of their particular liking, is consumed by boys almost continuously yet hunger is rarely conquered; and their clothes are no sooner bought than grown out of. Hearing is apparently badly affected by puberty as their music, such as it may be described, seems to always be on full volume. And, now possessed of an attention span of minutes, they are permanently bored.

As men, they will evolve; they may tend, initially, to be focused on the physical attributes of their desired female, the sexual allure and the potential for them to realise their own sexual fantasies. They will misguidedly think that the physical attributes which they believe other men would be impressed by in them (or intimidated by in a conflict) such as penile size, a muscular or athletic body, money or power, would also impress their desired female. These things may form a shallow and passing form of attraction for some females but those women looking for a deeper more meaningful and committed relationship want a real man, a multifaceted man, a man with a sympathetic character, one compatible with their own personality.

These adolescent boys are in a transitional drug induced state, victims of an overdose of testosterone, living in a land of constantly changing perspectives in a body that appears to belong to someone else, trying to make sense out of the irrational. They are gauche, they are victims of that twilight zone somewhere between the innocence of childhood and the autonomy of manhood. They are awaiting their launch into the adult male world anticipating money in their pockets and the freedoms it will bring, of pubs and clubs and motorbikes and cars. But, in truth, what they will actually get is a lifetime of slavery, working in a boring unfulfilling job to provide for an all-consuming, apparently ungrateful, family, they will have to provide the money to pay the rent or the mortgage and then, weighed down by their ever expanding waistline and the effects of their malfunctioning heart they will be consumed by a tyranny of illness and of disease and of physical injury and of mental stress, until their early death beckons. Not an adult, not a child; the male teenager lives a half-life in the half-light, innocently anticipating the imagined adventures of adulthood.

Little girls, and nakedness; well, given the summer garden/beach scenario and they will be wearing, *de rigueur* a bikini; and both parts of a bikini at that. A tiny scale replica of an adult woman's fashion bikini. It must be obvious to everyone, the necessity of hiding her nipples from the sight and scrutiny of the world. After all, they are so different from those of the naked little boys of the same age who are also running around – aren't they? And those bikini bottoms. Please tell me it is a fashion statement not some form of psychological chastity belt that this poor child is being conditioned to be constricted by for her whole life?

A female's sexual organs are mostly hidden from view; unlike men, women do not usually give pet names to them or refer to them in a humorous way (or expect or allow another to do so).

A little girl standing totally naked shows absolutely nothing to the world but her innocent, natural beauty. Compared to the outer fold of her 'modesty' obese babies will have large and prominent creases all over their bodies – including at the tops of their legs. And whether she is small or not so small, you can see little inappropriate of a young girl. What is your problem, mums?

We all like to find things out, to solve life's mysteries. Were a young boy so inclined, he would need to be hiding down the appropriate worm hole in the lawn (and equipped with his Sherlock Holmes magnifying glass and a torch kit too) at exactly the same time that a naked young girl did the splits. And, of course, a little boy would be so inclined. If you have a secret, everyone wants to discover it; whereas if you flaunt it (as boys are frequently encouraged to do) no-one will be very interested.

Nowadays, those twinkling lights that shine in the eyes of our children and which are the very representations of the innocence of childhood seem to begin to fade so quickly, whilst the children are so young. Children are seemingly metamorphosing into small adults too quickly, before their time.

Should children be taught in detail about the geography and function of their own genitals and those of the opposite gender, including both their pleasure and reproductive potentials? If so, at what age; should it be formal or informal; should it be taught in ongoing stages; should it have a 'practical' element; should boys and girls be taught together or in gender groups; who should be the teachers for each gender and what would be their social and criminal position? David Niven, the actor, related being taken, in his early teens, to spend time with a woman whose major role was to instruct him, at a totally practical level, in such things as the etiquette and process of male-female sexual relationships. He said that it stood him in good stead and was not only to his advantage but to that of all the young women he had his early relationships with.

The social context and consequences of young children being exposed on a regular basis to overt sexuality, both in general and more worryingly directed specifically at their particular age group, is disturbing. The usual routes by which they are exposed are via television, video clips (especially for music) and the Internet – thanks to the likes of Madonna, Lady Gaga and so many others, little girls are innocently singing and dancing to songs with lyrics like 'You can use my body' whist trying to emulate the provocative moves and dress code of their idols.

Parents are now able to buy young children, and almost exclusively little girls, clothes which would have been thought provocative and inappropriate for a teenager only a decade or two ago. At a purely personal level, I find it disturbing that parents would not only allow but also encourage and assist prepubescent girls in putting on make-up and wearing these provocative clothes outside the home (here, we are not talking about little girls playing games together in the bedroom, with the dressing-up box and mummy's lipstick).

There is also the seemingly premature, yet no-longer infrequent, physical development with girls reaching puberty whilst still at junior school. Their young bodies are reaching a level of sexual maturity which their minds and emotions lag behind. This development has been attributed to things as diverse as better nutrition and healthcare and to the hormones given to animals, to promote the development of more meat on each carcase, leaching into watercourses and eventually being drunk as chemical laden water by humans.

I do not think that it would be possible, even if thought desirable, to stop and/or eradicate both the social and the natural processes causing this nascent maturation process. Therefore perhaps society's only option is to find some sort of coping strategy.

From the delightful innocence, energy and self-belief of a pre-pubescent – as seen it the top years of junior schools – children find themselves travelling along the bumpy road towards puberty and adolescence. In girls, oestrogen causes her to grow breasts and larger hips, to feel sexual desire, to be able to enjoy sexual pleasures and to seek for these drives to be satisfied. This is where nature's drives clash with parents' sensibilities.

A growth spurt in the legs of young girls is usually an indicator that the hormones are beginning to course around their bodies which will be confirmed by the rite of passage which is their first period; following this, the growth will be in the torso with the enlargement of the breasts, hips and thighs being the obvious priority. Most girls will only grow another 6cm in height after the onset of puberty; by 14, the spine has stopped growing and the hips are ready for childbirth.

During puberty, steroids and hormones are produced by the body and their release promotes not only increases in the growth of particular areas of male and female bodies, it sparks off sensuality and sexuality and also a growth in the size of the brain and, as a consequence, its function. Young people try to question more of their once accepted values, they try to understand the inter-relationships between things, actions and reactions, rights and responsibilities; wisdoms they once blindly accepted, they challenge – thus adolescents can be 'difficult' to live with while they come to terms with the physical and mental processes of adolescence.

Teenagers look at the media and advertising and see what they think that society expects of them at that stage of their lives. They soon work out the rewards implied for looking a particular way or acting a particular way. They also learn what to expect if you have an unattractive body or personality or outlook. It is little wonder that teenagers are so insecure – with radical changes to their bodies, their ways of thinking, their sexual drives and desires, their fears, their social standing. Insecurities and mood-swings appear, body and lifestyle change, priorities are altered, freedoms sought. And, just as they are getting to grips with their new young-adult status they start thinking about leaving home and learning yet another lifestyle. Sadly, of late, economic pressures have determined that this is a transition which has to be deferred by a few years.

Historically, information, for the luckier girls, was through older girls at school or older sisters or cousins or perhaps, forward thinking aunts; they were given some access to information but it was incredibly random and basic and, sadly, also frequently incorrect. A pack of sanitary towels complete with its little booklet seems to have been fairly standard issue and this was occasionally accompanied by a very rudimentary pamphlet on the mechanics of the most basic sexual acts for girls about to get married. Nowadays, thankfully, there has been a revolution in attitudes towards women, their sexual anatomy and function, and to their sexuality.

As these freedoms have increased and more liberal attitudes to sex and relationships been relaxed, so children are being taught at school, as part of the educational curriculum (as opposed to the alternative 'playground curriculum'). They learn about their own bodies and the bodies of their opposite sex, both externally and internally.

They are also given some insight into the connections between romance, sex, emotions and relationships. They are taught about and how to use condoms and about other types of contraception, about creating babies and the responsibility that it brings and also about sexually transmitted diseases, how to avoid them, how to prevent them and how to recognise them.

When it comes to puberty the experience for girls is, perhaps not unexpectedly, very different from that of boys. Initially, the most significant difference is that puberty and all its effects will not come as a surprise to a girl. Indeed many girls are, although with some trepidation, looking forward to their first steps towards womanhood.

Oestrogen starts to make its presence felt at an often quite tender age; it can happen at any age from as young as seven up to about 17. Mothers, ever watchful, say that there is sometimes a distinct and often not pleasant scent emitted by little girls' bodies which starts, with the beginnings of puberty, to become quite noticeable and, for that transitional period of time, can become a not very attractive odour. And, soon after, the first signs of the buds of her breasts appear. That first bra is such a significant and long anticipated rite of passage. The smooth contour of a young breast just highlights the svelte shape of the female form. The pubic hair may be a sign of a move towards adulthood but is not seen, by most girls, as in any way beneficial to the look of her perfect body. And hair under the arms – bizarre; what is that all about. She is already very well aware of adult females spending time and money, not to mention discomfort, removing hair from their armpits, legs and their bodies. Why are you given body hair if you have got to spend so much time shaving it off; it seems so unfair.

For girls, it seems that the beginnings of puberty are the key to a new more adult lifestyle; a very significant step. The price that little girls pay to be enrolled into womanhood is high. The first surges of this chemical cocktail, which includes the hormones oestrogen, progesterone and even testosterone, may well induce stomach ache and cramps and, for the first time in her life, menstrual bleeding. It may be that her natural bodily functions are signalling a progression from childhood into womanhood and engendering a certain feeling of pride but it also makes her feel vulnerable, makes her feel unclean. The necessity of being prepared for her period, at a practical level, and all which that entails changes the need for a handbag into an essential practical companion rather than a purely aesthetic accessory.

Thankfully all the significant women in a girl's life, and all her female peer group, know what is happening and become members of her support network. A change in the style of her clothes and make-up reflect the change in her status; she can now begin to adopt the more sophisticated and alluring fashions of her coming teenage years and shed the innocent clothing of her childhood. Now, more earnestly, she is taught the essentials of the daily rituals of cosmetics application, making the best of your hair and dressing to be noticed – for all the right reasons. These become distinct indicators of her new social position, as if exchanged in some trade off – girlhood for womanhood – or at least the first steps in that direction, the beginning of that special apprenticeship. Amongst her own peer group a new pecking order is being created, puberty is forming a hierarchy based on the knowledge gained from experience. One by one, and for some, in a frustratingly slow transition, little girls become little women. The things and ways of childhood are put aside and replaced by the alluring sophistication of impending womanhood. Skipping on the pavement is exchanged for sashaying down the street.

But let us not imagine for one moment that this transition is all sweetness and light. The mood swings and sullen behaviour that parents would once have thought inconceivable of their little princess are now commonplace. Rudeness, inflicted on a defence-less father, hits hard. Long sessions spent in the bathroom disrupt family life. Self-imposed solitary confinement in her room, except for the compassionate visits of her once happy-go-lucky childhood girlfriend – now, perhaps, a monosyllabic Goth. Ever-changing diets, damagingly loud and repetitive music. 'You are NOT going out in THAT!' conversations, shouting out her demands or not talking at all.

Girls have traditionally not had the same sort of relationship with their genitalia that boys have. In her everyday life, its bodily position hides it completely from a girl's direct line of sight, whether she is standing still or moving about a little. In the same sort of position but with the benefit of a mirror, there is nothing but a crease of skin to see. When she urinates she feels the sensation and sees the resultant flow but, no more.

In contrast, a boy has his willy immediately in his line of sight whatever his stance; he also feels direct sensation in it when he moves – whether he is naked or wearing clothes; it can easily be touched or stimulated either accidentally or intentionally. He has to hold it and watch it when he is urinating, an event which, of course, happens many times each day. Is it surprising that males have a close relationship with their genitalia and enjoy masturbation?

For previous generations, most girls had learned not to ask questions about anything of a sexual nature of their parents' or indeed of anyone of their parents' generation (and certainly not of the older generation). Therefore puberty was often unexpected and unexplained, a dark and scary rite of passage that they frequently had to negotiate alone or without much in the way of physical or emotional support; and, their own sexuality was totally unacknowledged. Hence, they had seldom discovered anything worthwhile beforehand, if at all. Indeed many had been totally denied the existence of, let alone ownership of, their own sexuality; and having been so controlled since their early childhood they had not ever taken the opportunity to fully investigated the geography of their own bodies let alone pose those 'which bit does what' type of questions. And, of course, they felt unable to ask and knew that they had no-where to find out.

'Nice girls' used to be taught not to unnecessarily touch themselves and certainly not to inspect themselves – with or without a mirror. The only snippets of information elicited by them were how incredibly painful sex would be at first, how it was only the man who got any enjoyment out of it; that they were likely to have a baby and that giving birth would hurt a hundred times more than losing their virginity; and that raising their children would doubtless ruin their bodies and their lives or be a lifelong pleasure – depending on the source of information.

Once married, it was their duty and responsibility as a wife to be receptive to all their husband's needs; and to bear and care for 'his' children. They had practically no physical or emotional self-knowledge; their knowledge of men was based purely on, and proportional to, their exposure to the bodies and habits of male family members of all ages, plus the few other males they may have been allowed contact with in their everyday lives.

A woman's genitalia were put there to allow her to pee and, when married, for her husband to find comfort and stimulation there. It was unseemly for a woman to feel other than just contentment and connection with her husband during sex; she was certainly not to expect to feel the same sort of sexual arousal and satisfaction that he did. It was also there for the delivery of her baby from her womb into the world and that meant dealing with her menstrual discharge, in as discreet a manner as possible, was a monthly challenge.

After a lifetime of being exposed to this distorted perspective is it any wonder that many women strove to suppress their mostly unfounded fears whilst trying to deny the existence of their own sexuality and knowingly attempting to smother its undeniable potency. This insane diversion of these natural human impulses, through the practice of intergenerational ignorance and fear, has often been the root cause of a life-devouring lack of fulfilment. Perpetuated ignorance and misinformation. That so many women believed that they became the unwitting victims of an involuntary self-imposed frigidity as a result of this indoctrination is quite unbelievable. And this was part of the 'dowry' handed down to one generation by the previous generation.

As a result of these types of strategy, most girls used to grow into womanhood not understanding the geography of their own genitalia let alone being aware of existence of their own clitoris, G-spot or other erogenous zones.

By the middle of the 20th century things were beginning to move in a more positive direction. Sexuality in both men and women, even if couched in suggestion rather than in action, was becoming more overt in print, films and music. The manufacturing methods for condoms made them cheaper, more comfortable and more reliable; and even unmarried mothers and unwanted pregnancies were, very, very slowly being accepted with less inhumane attitudes.

The results of a survey of adult women found a distinct split between the majority, who had been brought up having been instructed never to touch or investigate 'down there' and had obeyed, and the second group who had been taught about their bodies or had experimented and self-examined at some level. The larger group felt they had remained ignorant of most of the detail and function of their own anatomy (up to the beginning of puberty and even beyond) and also the nature and power of their emotional and sexual drives. They remained unknowing right until their first scary teenage or young adult sexual experience which had, at best, engendered a very distorted and reserved attitude to their own and other people's sexuality. They were ignorant of how to bring about their own pleasure, a rapture they barely knew women could achieve, let alone to be able to teach their partner how to arouse and satisfy their sexual desire. Meanwhile, the women from the second group had, because of parental attitudes, been given information either directly or indirectly; they had felt empowered to investigate their own bodies and to learn how to pleasure themselves – without shame or stigma – and were subsequently able to show their partner what they needed. Some remembered this self-awareness developing from as young as when they were toddlers or pre-school age; others older, as prepubescents. They reported that they now enjoy a relaxed and fulfilling relationship with their own and other people's bodies.

Thankfully, modern women have transcended these barriers. Many, of all ages, are now encouraged to self-inspect, to know the geography of their own bodies and to know how to stimulate themselves to orgasm. Female masturbation is good; there are all sorts of sex toys out there specifically designed and manufactured for women to enjoy sexual stimulation and orgasm. If you can't know your own body, if you can't give yourself an orgasm, how are you going to teach your partner what is good for you? There are books and Internet websites that will direct them to the appropriate information. Enlightened mothers are no longer stopping young girls from touching themselves, exploring themselves, it is a natural thing to do and can only bring long-term benefits; they are now encouraging their daughters to know their own bodies, to enjoy their own bodies.

An interesting, apparently random event recently happened during a routine scan of a pregnant young woman in America. As well as the mother, her partner and the technician were present. Very soon, over 20 qualified medical staff came to witness what was happening. The baby, in-utero, was a girl; this was already known. What they all saw was this small baby beginning to manually pleasure herself over a protracted period of time and culminate in a body tensing orgasmic climax. They were all mutually in agreement with what they had seen and agreed that there could be no other logical explanation for it. Needless to say, none had ever seen anything like it before. It is a significant discovery. If nothing else it helps to reinforce what a perfectly innocent and natural thing female masturbation is.

Pre-adolescent girls, just like post-adolescent women, will feel a growing drive to experience the joys of physical attraction and may well follow-up on those feelings when they find themselves in an environment in which they feel physically and emotionally safe. Both these females, although at different ages and stages of maturity, are sexual beings with all the urges this can produce; both are able to enjoy sexual pleasures, can masturbate and reach orgasm. The girls can, and probably will (given the opportunity) seek out playmates, of either or both genders, with whom they feel they can enjoy physical intimacies and experience sexually derived pleasure at some level. The motive for this is not necessarily immediate sexual gratification but is a form of experimentation, of learning about their potential, even though the acts themselves may have some form of sexual nature. The biggest difference between the situations of the females of different ages is the testosterone which drives the woman's sexual desire to copulate, and her ability to bear children, which is not present in the pre-pubescent girl.

Teenage pregnancy has been the norm for millennia – even though, mainly because of nutrition, puberty started later than it does nowadays. The reasoning seemed to be that as soon as a girl's body showed signs of being ready to breed, that is what should happen. Diet and the hard life she had led also caused women to become barren at a younger age. Thus, the period of a woman's life when she was best able to bear children was shorter than today and many women spent much of their adult life pregnant. Over a hundred years ago, with no reliable or affordable mode of contraception, females had a baby, on average, every two years. Infant mortality was common; only 50 per cent of babies reached five years old. Mothers frequently died as a result of childbirth; only 50 per cent of women lived long enough to reach the menopause. Modern medical and social advances have radically altered this situation.

Traditionally, sexual energy, sexual desire could only be perceived as good if it was experienced (but very discreetly) by a married woman with her husband. Casual sex, multiple and /or female partners or any sexual display or experience outside marriage was seen as a sign of sexual social rebellion. For a man, whilst his girlfriend could be of dubious sexual morality, his wife must be virginal.

The innocent joys of childhood with groups of young pre-pubescent girls dressing-up and putting on their mother's make-up, singing and dancing in a faux provocative way becomes exchanged for an overt sexually explicit courtship display with all its inherent risks. Adolescent girls sometimes appear to not realise the effect their proximity, let alone their naturally alluring body language, causes to adolescent boys with their pulsating, testosterone engorged bodies and their out of control brains; but, then again, perhaps they do, perhaps they enjoy every tantalising minute that they can hold power over their admirers. Most females, of whatever age, seem to either know instinctively, or have been taught, the potency of their powers of attraction and seduction.

A girl's imagination can create romantically alluring idols from music and screen icons and even males she has seen locally. She dreams about tender, romantic liaisons with imaginary suitors in minute detail, then she lets her fantasies strengthen and her thoughts stray to more lingering, tantalising, sensual scenarios. Her mind is preparing her for what she dreams her real-life romances will be like and that, in turn, prepares her body for the complex sensations she needs in order to become sexually aroused. She is learning how she wants to behave, how she wants to be seen, how she will portray herself, as the perfect romantic partner for her new beau.

But sadly her illusions will, one day, one way or the other, be shattered; her romantic dreams will have to remain unfulfilled, her imaginary relationships will become distorted by reality. Boys do not go through any similar romantic process, though not because society does not promote the concept of the ideal of a loving mutually supportive and satisfying relationship. And this is the reason; male bodies are testosterone driven and, boys are not instructed in the ways of the world as far as how to conduct a romantic relationship is concerned, not taught how to try to behave in a way that will appeal to a girl. Their biological drive is sexual, not romantic; their mission is to ejaculate and to do so with the least possible diversionary behaviour. And those basic differences between male and female perspectives on inter-personal relationships – which are each driven by the individual's brain and their sex hormones – are the root cause of all gender based incompatibility. Good mutually satisfying sex, and the physical and emotional relationship it should be based on can be the glue which hold a relationship between two people together. Selfish, demanding self-gratification drives a wedge between two people. Women give sex to get love; men give love to get sex.

As she matures, she needs to go out and be seen by the right people in the right places; it's going out and staying out till too late that causes the problems at home. And boys, well, young men; with cars and motorbikes ready to whisk innocent daughters away from the protection of ever loving parents. Exuberance and singing and dancing – then, floods of tears and the end of the world.

Somehow, both men and women find boys erratic, driven behaviour less complex, more explicable, easier to deal with, less enduring. Whereas with girls, their fathers are mystified, find extreme difficulty in rationalising how their little girl changed so; the mood swings from elation to abject depression. Whilst the mothers are, if not always tolerant of their behaviour, always indulgent of it; they understand, because they have been there, done that. The strength of the sisterhood transcends its generations.

And, what might await an adolescent girl in her adulthood? Time once spent in innocent play is substituted for play of a different kind; for claiming her place as an attractive, fashionable, self-assured woman within her own female peer group. Meanwhile, enjoying coyly toying with the erupting emotions of males, playing them like a fisher-woman catching that special fish amongst a shoal of other fish, hooking that chosen prey with just her deceptively simple, delicate tackle, reeling him in a bit and then letting him out a bit until all his energies are spent and she can, when she chooses, land him. And then, at her bidding and to her timetable, she and her beau will be together, she will soon toss away her career, get married and have babies. How 'new woman' of you to do exactly what your mother did and what her mother did – and what most women do, and have chosen to do, since time began. Women's bodies are stretched by pregnancy and by birth. The distortion of a woman's body makes sex less desirable, less physically stimulating for her man and thus less stimulating for the woman too – who is only infrequently stimulated purely by physical penetration alone. Psychologically, she feels less alluring, more 'dirty and deformed' by her physical labours and he gets less physical stimulation from being inside her or performing oral sex on her. A wedge is slowly being driven between them. Sleepless nights from responding to a baby's unceasing needs, the subsequent weight gain. Cellulite and varicose veins and, as the era of childbearing comes to an end, the rigours of the menopause begin. Your hormones will guide you and constrict you throughout a lifetime of disillusionment, of abject servitude to your loved ones, of disappointing relationships, of shattered dreams until your once potentially reproductive body begins to shut down and in doing so tortures you with all the indignities of a massive chemical hormone imbalance as gravity takes your ever expanding bodily features and heads south with them. Subjugated by a combination of Mother Nature and the Brutish Sex, a sad and unjust finale to a once potent life force.

CHAPTER 6
LITTLE THINGS

When it comes to an individual's own gender-related perspective and their relationship to the way they are brought up, it becomes obvious that the way we, both as parents and as a society, raise our children can have dramatic effects on the way they subsequently live their own lives and, as a consequence, how they interrelate in social situations for the duration of that life.

The value systems of all children are instilled by each and every one of the adults and other children they come into contact with. These encounters, however brief and superficial or long-term and intimate, affect behaviour at all levels. A child who has not seen, or been party to, a secure and loving environment when growing up is as surely undernourished as if they had not received enough food. The effects will stay with them all their lives; it will affect all of their relationships; it will affect how they bring up their own children. Traditionally women have always brought up children so, theoretically, their upbringing will have the greatest influence on a child.

From their birth, we bring up boys and girls differently from each other; sometimes intentionally sometimes unintentionally. The different ways we react to boys and girls is partly a reflection of our own upbringing and partly because of our adult life experiences. Even if we decided to make efforts to try to treat our boys and girls in a similar way to each other they would still be subject to the influences of our own childhood; our personal decision to pursue gender-neutral discrimination for our own children would have been as a result of our own gender-biased life experiences. Gender bias is, and has always been, a part of the structure of society.

Children are being brought up in a world full of individuals, some of whom will have similar values to us and some people who have values which are the extreme opposite of ours; most people's values will fall somewhere in-between. The members of the children's peer groups will also have been subject to both positive and negative influences; sometimes subtle, sometimes overt, but all such influences are beyond our control. And, as they grow, children will be influenced by all types and levels of media too; from story books and comics to music, films, television and the Internet. Life, as we all currently experience it, is not value-free, it is gender-biased and it is a patriarchy.

Babies, of necessity, start their lives as emotional manipulators; if they want attention they use their ability to cause a fuss until they achieve the desired result. As they grow they must learn that other people also have needs, which are different from theirs; this is an early form of socialising and although initially they may not understand, it is a skill which they must learn. Girls, much more easily than boys, learn the ability to appreciate the existence of, and the ability to empathise with, the needs of others; boys, in general, lack this social grace. It appears to be an hereditary gender difference.

A study in America looked at the ways in which boys and girls, of nine years old, related to their peers. The boys stayed purely task focused and did not did not seem to feel the need to share information about themselves with the other boys. The girls, in comparison, shared more personal information. Subsequent to the group interaction, it was found that the boys were quite indifferent about the other boys whilst the girls had created mutually appreciative bonds. Often, girls will not want to interact socially with another girl (or boy) who has 'upset' her; in adolescence, the moods swings caused by puberty redefine and reinforce all these rules.

Research by the University of California and the University of Akron seems to reinforce some of our gender biased images of children's behaviour. A group of young children were each given a glass of lemonade but, the lemonade had been adulterated by adding salt to it. The immediate reaction of the boys was to pull faces and make noises; after just a taste they wouldn't touch it again. The girls did not make a fuss and some in the group even tried to keep drinking it. When the girls were questioned about their reactions they admitted that they really didn't like it at all but that they did not want to offend the adults. Another group of children were given 'disappointing' presents containing just some socks and a pencil and once again their reactions were split by gender with the boys being dissatisfied and the girls trying to make positive remarks. The lemonade experiment was repeated with a mixed gender group of adults and had the same results. For me, the unanswered question from this interesting research is: is this learned behaviour – a form of social conditioning with a gender bias or something much more basic?

When little girls play in groups they tend to do so by a system of negotiation, compromise and personal rapport. Girls tend to gather into little groups which are mutually supportive; they constantly communicate with each other to ensure the well-being of both the individuals and the group. Little girls frequently have someone who is their 'best friend'. Girls are taught to suppress anger and aggression – certainly in comparison to boys. They have to learn to internalise these feelings and the result of this process is that they can harbour negative feelings about themselves, have a lower self-esteem. How these emotions are dealt with by the adults around them will have a profound effect on the long-term outcomes for girls.

Education Scotland's 'Journey to Excellence – Gender in Education' appears to have summed up the basic difference between boys and girls in education in the one sentence 'boys are more hierarchical whilst girls are more collaborative'. The project, in fact, was wide ranging; it actually covered a large range of aspects of education and at differing levels. It reinforces the commonly held belief that boys do not appear to be able to easily appreciate the concept of a mutually supportive inter-personal relationship. When compared to girls, they do not put the same value on the idea or the practice of having a 'best friend' and of working to promote that bond. Boys, when in groups of their peers, tend to try to either become dominant or to find ways to accept their own domination. They instinctively feel the need to create a 'pecking order', rather than a support group, and in doing so become isolated from each other by real or imagined interpersonal barriers.

Whatever their personal circumstances, children need good role models. They need a range of mentors of different genders, different ages and of different 'styles' of adults of each gender, to enable them to build a picture of how people are and thus how society is. Children who are raised in a home with two parents will have a different upbringing, and thus a different perspective, from a child brought up in a one parent family; just as a child brought up as an only child will have a different upbringing from one brought up with several siblings. They will each have been exposed to identifiably different upbringings. One is not better (or less good) than the other – they are just different. Many of us are no longer part of an extended family or of a 'village' community; we do not have elders whose experience and wisdom we can revere. We may well lack exposure to positive gender role models and experiences of marital harmony; moral, spiritual and religious frameworks are also often missing and relationships with the older generation have been replaced by a melange of familial sepia images and half-forgotten memories.

Knowing that you are loved and cared for is a basic animal need. Research at McGill University which used experiments with rats shows that those females who lick their offspring much more frequently, and give them more care in general, have offspring which are much less stressed. Indeed, there is a similar effect even if the baby rats are handled and stroked by their human carers – so it seems to be the experience received rather than who is administering it. This result is subsequently multiplied by each generation; thus, the offspring of 'high-licking' rats licked their own offspring more and these young were even more relaxed than their parents. Ad infinitum. This conclusion is not just the result of observation of behavioural patterns but can be confirmed by differences between the anatomy of the brains of 'high licking' and 'low licking' rats. In humans, these results can be shown to be similar; women who show a closer and more caring relationship with their offspring result in those offspring having lower stress levels. Knowing that we are loved not only lowers our stress levels it alters the structure and function of our brains; it forms a virtuous infinite loop.

We have to accept that, like it or not, society is changing; statistics report that over 50 per cent of couples divorce within five years of their marriage. The same statistics do not record what the numbers are for those who don't get married and subsequently split-up. There are twice as many young men aged between 25–35 years who are living alone compared to women, although the figures are rather skewed by all the single women living with their children as one-parent families being recorded, technically, as not living alone. Over the age of 65, there are more older women than men – because the men die younger. There are more pensioners than there are young people under 16 (ONS). Sometimes in families the mother can find that the father has become an unnecessary complication to her already stressed lifestyle and a problem which she wants to rid herself of. As a result, such men initially become ostracised, then shunned, and finally isolated and invisible; these men have become unwanted encumbrances. But, his income is wanted; it is seen by the mother as a rightful source of her income. Withholding or avoiding payment of maintenance and child-support gives back to the man the feeling of power denied to them by their partner, it is not a tactic intended to hurt the children, it is a by-product of the man's strategy to gain revenge for his perceived humiliation by his partner.

Those men who want to offer support and maintain some form of contact with their children can find themselves tied up and gagged by a strongly female-biased legal system. The Social Security and other state support and legal systems will always try to ensure a reasonable level of financial and practical help for a mother and her children. This is a safety net, which has only been in place in recent decades and which continues to grow in its championing of women and their children. The laws which enact these systems have been voted for by Parliament, the majority of whose members are male. An example of the power of female social and lobby groups.

Before the benefits of the social welfare system, the only refuge for women in this position would have been from their own families, charity or the arduous life and degrading humiliation of the poor house. The support given by the state to women and their children has instigated a new order; one where even an honourable man's protection and support has become devalued, less relevant. The traditional, positive, male attributes have become a currency which has depreciated. Society's practical, financial and legal support systems favour women and their children and as an unintentional consequence are making a woman's need for the male no longer a necessity; having a man's company is fast becoming a lifestyle choice – like having a cat or a dog just for companionship. Hanna Rosin has even written a whole book about this situation; it is called *The End of Men*. Thus, there is a potential for men to be seen by women as becoming almost superfluous. So, where will the children who are brought up in such circumstances get their everyday male role-model cues from; are they necessary any more?

Both our imperfect gender roles should always have been, historically, different but interdependent facets of a parental relationship; nowadays one has rather less value than the other. One man and one woman make, on average, 2.4 children who may subsequently be raised by one woman. Therefore the effects, positive or negative, of their relationship are multiplied by a factor of 2.4. It is easy for divorced or separated male parents to become estranged from their children. Pressure comes from those mothers not wanting contact with the previous husband/partner, and from new families; physical distance is often put between the father and his children, a reflection of the parent's emotional distance from each other. Thus, perhaps, the reason that cohabitation is on the increase but, these relationships do not last as long as marriages; and, according to the ONS, children who are brought up by lone-parents have worse mental and physical health, are less likely to have stable relationships or employment, will earn less and are more likely to go to prison. We invest much in selecting the right car or the right home yet, are often happy to drift into and out of our relationships in a casual manner; what we choose to invest in them reflects their importance to us.

More and more people are living in units with just one adult; therefore, it appears that people don't like or trust other people. The implication of this is that society is producing too many people who are not able to live with another adult; we are becoming a mutually incompatible nation. The only reason that we have the ability to do this is on such a scale is because the State supports people living as single adults through the social and housing benefits system which is directly funded by our taxes. Because there are more one-adult units we need more homes; double the number of homes than if we were to be sharing with another adult. The number of homes is finite; more people wanting one of a small number of homes. More demand on a static supply means prices for rents rise; thus, more people have to rely even more on Housing Benefit to supplement their housing costs; as a consequence, taxes are increased.

In general, adult males tend to be more physical than women when they play with their children; it is a reflection of the way the men were brought up, by fathers who had spent little time with children and had no other way of communicating with them. Showing emotional as well as a more gentle physical closeness to children was not in their repertoire. Some children can find this type of play exciting, an adventure, whereas others may feel vulnerable or frightened. As a generalisation, boys are more likely to respond positively to such play whereas girls may feel less secure; thus, we reinforce stereotypical gender behaviour.

Most women who become successful in business have a clear memory of their relationship with their father; of him promoting their self-sufficiency and trying to make them think and behave as strong individuals. They remember their father as a strong spirited, independent, intelligent person who also revealed to them a caring facet to their nature.

Fathers tend to try to protect their daughters from practical problems and their real or potential effects; they do try to support them when the girls are being emotional too but, men tend not to be so good at dealing with sensitive situations. Compromise is a necessary strategy for father and daughter relationships. Girls can develop a learned behaviour of 'helplessness'; because they know that appearing vulnerable will cause someone else (usually a male) to sort out their problems. This type of behaviour is not common in girl-only schools. Girls are protected, socially, from getting themselves into potentially dangerous situations and are dissuaded from being dominant, aggressive or overtly angry;

thus, they do not learn strategies which would allow them to deal with such situations and such feelings. Fear can be used as a positive impulse – used as a warning of impending danger; but, being 'paralysed' by fear makes people vulnerable. Overcoming small and less significant fears, perhaps of a new experience or situation, can be a first step to learning to cope with fear, it can be empowering.

Participating in gymnastics displays or horse-riding gymkhanas, playing a musical instrument in public or reading poetry to an audience are all valid means for girls to experience limited levels of fear in a controlled environment and can help them to develop more self-confidence and strategies for conquering greater fears.

The U.S. Stanford Center report 'Gender Differences in Children's Achievement-Related Beliefs and Emotional Responses to Success and Failure' finds significant gender based differences in self-belief between boys and girls. For girls, their successes are often attributed to something external rather than always being directly proportional to their own efforts or skills, failure was attributed to being not good enough; they may feel that they succeeded because other competitors were less able or that the exam questions were easy. They can grow up feeling undeserving of their own achievements, of being the beneficiaries of fate. Whereas boys are much more likely to attribute success to their own excellent ability and failure to bad luck. Some toys that are specifically targeted at girls, which are depicted in their various forms in the advertising media, are not always promoting positive role models; the manufacturers are striving to sell their product and make money, they are not in business to promote the beneficial development of children. Dolls of exaggerated fashion-model proportions and style have now been around for almost 50 years. These dolls are impossibly proportioned – unnaturally slim, with unnaturally long legs, an unnaturally small waist combined with an unnaturally large bust; she is usually dressed in high heels and short skirts in an effort to emphasise her unnatural proportions. For many little girls they have become imaginary role-models of a style of femininity which they may believe is real and that they should aspire to. Many adults will buy these dolls for their daughters yet at the same time acknowledge that they are actually symbols of unhealthy and unattainable extremes which are based on a distorted image – perhaps, of a male fantasy of female perfection.

Little girls, in particular, like fairy stories; with their handsome male heroes, their moral and just outcomes, they make good reading material for little princesses; hopefully these types of dolls are just fanciful extensions of these mythological characters. Some parents make a conscious decision not to buy one for their daughter but, you can be sure that one way or another she will soon get to play with one if not come into possession of her own doll by one means or another. Nowadays, you can at least dress these dolls up as a pilot or a policewoman or an explorer or some other unisex role. Somehow, you have to trust that your parenting is sufficient; you will never be able to control every experience in your little girl's life. Nor, would it be good if you could.

As part of their training, little girls are encouraged to try 'dressing-up' in different clothes thus experiencing different styles, colours, combinations, fabrics and textures. This is reinforced by the little girl's awareness of adult women doing the same sorts of things with their own wardrobes – talking about and experimenting with different colours, styles, combinations. They are also given an introduction to wearing make-up and jewellery. Boys who begin to take more than a cursory interest in dressing-up, colour or pattern were once thought of as having inappropriate 'gay' tendencies – which was seen as a bad thing; nowadays such prejudicial attitudes are rare.

The fashion and cosmetics industries are guilty of promoting stereotypical beauty values which are based on a false premise. Images of undernourished women, hair-brushed and air-brushed, wearing unviable costumes whilst posing unnaturally are turned into inordinately expensive caricatures of someone's artificial concept of what female beauty should look like. Why has the natural beauty of women become not good enough, why should it be so undervalued? Just because the fashion and cosmetics industries and all their associated 'hangers on' have found a way of exploiting the natural vulnerability of women in the pursuit of corporate profit and, in the process, robbing these women of their money and their self-worth. Their powerful advertising campaigns are guilty of having reset our natural value systems. One company, at least, is reflecting the concerns of many women. Unilever, the beauty and skincare manufacturer that produces the Dove range of products, has launched their 'Self-Esteem Project' and are trying to promote the status of 'real' women and discourage girls and young women from pursuing unrealistic perspectives in relation to their own appearance, to their self-image.

Whatever happened to the diverse images of female beauty such as depicted in Greek statues and works of artists through the ages – such as Rubens depictions of women; as they show us, the fashion for the ideal proportions of women has both changed and been manipulated over centuries. Are we losing sight of reality; is natural feminine beauty not perfect enough? The faces and bodies of normal 'everyday' woman have often specifically been excluded from modern advertising campaigns on the grounds that they are not sufficiently attractive to the public, because it is believed that they will not promote the appropriate image for the brand which in turn will not promote high enough sales of their products. These media advertising campaigns can make women feel insecure and undervalued; surely it is time for realistic advertising, promoting clothes and other products which will be valuable assets to all real women. But, things are changing; the opinions of women regarding the use of skinny fashion models is one high profile campaign which has caught the media's attention – particularly as France, one of the bastions of fashion, has now made it illegal for models who are considered too skinny to be able to parade on the catwalk.

If you are a successful woman in any type of really high profile role or business, and you are attractive, you are sure to get some media attention. If you are thought of as being plain or ordinary, but equally successful in your chosen role, your image will not be so readily sought – with a few notable exceptions; as women who are treated in a way that says 'look, even a woman who is not beautiful can sometimes make a success of herself'. It is a strategy which is degrading to all women. A result of this is that, frequently, good looking, well dressed people are treated as though they are more clever, more personable, more successful; values based solely on their looks. For some women their natural good looks can become a currency which they can exploit. They may not have the intelligence, personality or the business acumen to succeed in other spheres, but they will achieve some form of financial reward for their beauty – which is a gift of nature – even if those benefits are bought by being attractive to, and often marrying, a wealthy man. If a woman has brains, beauty and personality the world can become her oyster – because men value physical beauty very highly.

Should such blatant, wealth-generating behaviour be considered in the same way as prostitution or is beauty, like intelligence or sporting ability, just another natural human trait to be exploited for financial gain? The fashion and beauty industries are joined by the sex industry in selling a distorted perspective of female beauty for profit.

But, as we all know, such women are a rarity, a phenomenon that the vast majority of women will never be able to emulate. Meanwhile, normal women are made to feel insecure because the media has shown them images of an ideal woman, a look which is unattainable for them. As a result, women spend their hard earned cash to buy products, clothes and services which they are led to believe will transform them. Their insecurities are intentionally exploited by the fashion and beauty industries; these companies make a fortune selling make-up, clothes, accessories and body-transforming interventions to the very women they have made feel vulnerable.

According to the 'World Economic Forum – Global Gender Gap' report, the world average salary for a woman is $11,000 and for a man it is $20,500; they say that on extrapolation of existing trends it will take another 118 years for there to be parity. Given these statistics, when it comes to men's grooming products and fragrances they lag way behind those of women. Men account for only 11 per cent of global sales of beauty products with Asia and Latin America being the current areas of growth – according to the website of market research firm Euromonitor.

When women feel that their bodies, their personalities and their other attributes are undervalued they undervalue themselves, they feel unworthy, unlovable; they have a negative body image, a negative self-image, and this can lead to a downward spiral culminating in various forms of eating disorders, drink or drugs abuse, depression and, in extreme cases, even suicide. These feelings of being unable to fulfil some artificial concept of beauty and therefore of being unworthy of love or, even of being despised or ridiculed, are now being experienced by young pre-pubescent girls; these are children who should be unaware of such vacuous expectations.

The media creates and exploits gender stereotypes in television and radio programmes, in newspapers and magazines, through content and through advertising; and, someone of authority, someone holding the purse-strings, has to 'sign-off ' these items. Even government information films are similarly influenced. There were two 'Blood in Pee' information advertisements which were shown on television during the autumn of 2013 in the UK; one was directed at women, the other was directed at men. The campaign was aimed at promoting visits to GPs by people who have found their urine tinted red – to check if it has been caused by blood contamination – and for them to be able to find out the cause and get treatment. The male version of the advert was based on film footage of working-class men appearing to be standing and peeing. It showed shots of them taken from behind or in a three-quarter rear view, peeing whilst standing in various styles of toilet cubicles with the doors open and in one a shot of several men standing in line-abreast at a bank of urinals. The toilets, it appeared, were situated in different types of male work environments; they included a shot of an old railway arch which had a general ambience of being dirty and 'down at heel'. The men were whistling in an apparently nonchalant manner; there was no dialogue whatsoever; the soundtrack was realistic of such a situation. What they were doing was completely unambiguous. The female version of the advertisement, in contrast, showed women talking about discoloured pee being the effects of just red wine or perhaps an infection. They were filmed in different scenarios – whilst having a cup of coffee together, whilst at work, and whilst chatting on the top deck of a bus; their conversations merely alluded to one of them having found something different about the colour of their pee. The actual reference to it formed part of the conversation and was very casual and almost fleeting, there were no scenes of toilets; none of the footage showed anything which could in any way have been construed as being even suggestive of a woman actually peeing. The government reinforcing negative gender stereotypes is not a problem if it is only applied to the male gender, it seems.

The women were depicted as chatty, intelligent, social people to be found in various positive environments; their male equivalents were silent, uncommunicative beings inhabiting the shadowy corners of a world of darkness and despair.

What chance do we, as individuals within society, stand if not only the media but government too has decided on what our gender-biased stereotypes should look like. Perhaps the current differences in the distribution of males and females in the workplace and in society in general reflects a more open and fluid state than we might at first acknowledge. We are different mentally, physically and emotionally; we have different needs at different times in our lives and react differently to similar stimuli.

Perhaps the way society is presently structured is a reflection of the current situation and thus appropriate at this stage of this new and evolving fluidity. If equal opportunity, as opposed to equality, is the goal then this would be a more easily achievable objective but, it would have to be a two way process. Equality of opportunity would not necessarily equate to an equal outcome.

When women were deliberately excluded from education and the professions by men they wanted inclusion; they now have it. Men have rarely sought inclusion to the world of women. Research has shown that the life satisfaction of women who achieve high levels of reward in business, the professions and politics is inverse to their level of rewards and responsibility – exactly the opposite of what the researchers expected. In other words, the more money power and influence women got the less satisfied they were with the entirety of their whole-life package. We should concentrate on creating a lifestyle which suits our physical and emotional needs rather than trying to live a life that we have seen in the media or which we believe that society expects of us; don't do something just because you can, do it because it feels right for you at that stage in your life and don't rule out changes as your life morphs from one phase to another.

Business wants women workers, they have a better work ethic than their male counterparts. The current problem is working out a system which is sympathetic to women's needs without disadvantaging the level of corporate financial returns. But, is this, potentially, a price too high to pay for the advantages won? Perhaps some men will not want to change the system because it acts as a filter, a way to keep women out of positions of control. The more aggressive and life-consuming the style of any commercial enterprise the less they will attract or retain female staff. Top jobs can be greedy of your life; and, women value their social and familial relationships more highly than men.

According to the Federation of Small Businesses a total of 15.6 million people are employed by SMEs – that represents 60 per cent of all private sector employees. And, according to 'Women in Enterprise' (RBS Group 2013) 17 per cent of business owners are women. Therefore, most businesses are small businesses; anyone who has ever run a small business will tell you that it is not possible – either practically or financially – to sustain such a model for female employees. And, the situation is little better for large companies too. There is always a cost-benefit analysis to be made and shareholders expect the best return possible on their investment; they are not social engineers, and most are not philanthropists either. The compassionate acceptance of the importance of a work-life balance is at odds with the historic structure and function of business, commerce, manufacturing and government. At present society does not have a means for allowing this to happen let alone the motivation to actively promote it.

Girls and women may get incentivized to enter traditionally male spheres of work but there are no similar incentives for men to enter the female world of work. Surely any form of quota – gender biased job quotas for instance, are sexual discrimination and therefore illegal. Women are not forced to take employment in particular areas of work or to leave at a particular age – these are their own choices. Governments have spent large amounts of money on high profile schemes to help girls into science and maths based courses but no high profile, media promotions for helping boys develop in the languages, communication and interpersonal skills areas. The problems that boys have with language, social skills and behaviour can be readily confirmed by looking at the results of research but how much is spent, as a result, on helping these boys to use their best endeavours in a productive way rather than as a quasi-apprenticeship to a life of low achievement or even crime? Successful multi-millionaire businesswomen could, either individually or together, choose to set up companies where these pro-female values are not only supported but are promoted; but they don't. Their companies will often buy the cheapest materials and employ the cheapest labour from wherever in the world suits their needs – regardless of the political regime or women's rights in that country – just to make the largest profit margin possible for their shareholders and for themselves.

In truth, the world of work for the vast majority of men and women is equally mundane and not well paid. These are not the headline-grabbing 'movers and shakers' who inhabit the media savvy world and who are intent on transforming society. They are just very nice, very ordinary people trying to have as pleasant a life as possible with their family and friends and doing as little harm as possible to the rest of the world in the process. They would like life to be better for them and theirs but are fully aware of their lack of potency to change 'the system' or indeed, to have any influence on the system. Their lives change by evolution not by revolution.

Human nature, that's what spoils most good ideas.

CHAPTER 7
CAT WOMAN

Man is fatally attracted by feline ways. Woman is a proud and powerful tigress. At one time she is soft and sensual as she struts that slinky, seductive, mesmerising walk; at another, she is a gentle caring, protective mother; and yet, also within that same beautiful creature are secreted lethal fangs and talons capable of inflicting lifelong scars on her victim whether at play or, in anger, of bleeding a man to death at will, of devouring his very being. Red of tooth and claw. She is a stunning and magnetic creature; a deeply dangerous temptress. She is the secretive ruler of life's jungle, a creature of legend. Almost magical.

Female kittens are cute. Fluffy bundles of fun with large alluring eyes, displaying endless innocent playful antics in bouts of hypnotic behaviour, agile of movement, wrapped in a soft coat of many colours – those are the things which first attracted him to her. Then, they were both young and naïve – just playmates; they grew up sharing each other's worlds. When he was inattentive she commanded his attention in whatever manner amused her and she always got results. But, when he tried to approach her she might choose to acquiesce or, to walk away out of reach, with determined steps, aloof, detached. Equally, she may turn on him flattening her ears to her head, swishing her tail and hissing loudly – an unmistakable and unavoidable warning of an imminent pain-inducing attack. From his innocent and totally bemused perspective it appears an absolutely unprovoked act of aggression in response to his attempt to be close to her – however clumsy.

Sometimes, she would seek to seduce him; at first coy and cautious then approaching him and directly rubbing herself against him, nuzzling, burying her head in the warmth of his body, seeking his attention and purring loudly, rolling over on her back making herself vulnerable and pleading to be caressed, immersed in that moment of intense pleasure.

At her whim, and without any obvious signal, needle-sharp teeth and claws are unsheathed from the hidden depths of her soft body and used to inflict pain on him – sometimes in a playful, teasing, tantalising game then, without warning, a vicious pain inducing, blood-letting attack; the more he tries to escape the deeper the claws and fangs are thrust. Signs and signals sent by her behaviour may be obvious to another feline but to him they all remain a mystery. He is confused; he has unwittingly become her prey, her victim.

If, eventually, the complications of their mismatched relationship outweigh the benefits gained, he knows that he can easily free himself of the problem. Once he has decided to reject her she can be discarded so easily, thrown out onto the street without ceremony, without notice, left to fend for herself. Cruelly she is abandoned, left in isolation, left to face her demons, left to her fate, cowering in dark and dangerous places, left to drown in the bottomless lake of her own tears. When he feels so drawn, there are plenty more felines out there waiting to tempt him. And, kittens are always so much more appealing than some ageing battle-worn, flea-bitten, frumpy, grumpy, older feline.

Man, get away, escape; his logical mind says she's too unpredictable, too dangerous, too aloof – too tantalising. Her very being is a language he cannot comprehend; he does not know how to satisfy her needs. Everyone knows a dog makes a reliable, uncomplicated, undemanding lifelong companion; forget about cats says that small voice deep inside him.

Do not underestimate the powers of survival of this feline. If threatened or made to feel vulnerable, she is quite capable of raising her hackles, baring her teeth and claws in readiness, and fearlessly mounting a counter-attack of terrifying ferocity. Equally, she may choose to merge into the shadows, apparently disappearing yet still stalking her assailant, assessing his weaknesses, preparing for her moment of revenge. If badly hurt, she may slink off into the protection of the deep and dark undergrowth until she is healed, re-energised. A tigress is tough, she is likely to live almost twice as long as her mate. When ready, she will re-appear – that beautiful, powerful, alluring creature; she is the omnipotent queen of all she surveys, the true ruler of life's jungle.

The parts of the male brain, in heterosexual men, which react to immediate gratification stimuli like alcohol, leisure drugs and money react in exactly the same way to sexually arousing images of females. The general similarity between the overall shape of women's breasts and of their buttocks is no coincidence; from any perspective their combined roundness and softness signals a sexually mature female; the actual size and shape of them are, statistically, not particularly relevant and their relative appeal merely denotes the personal preferences on the part of the male. Puberty is the initiator of these attributes. The sight of breasts and a small waist below which is a larger bottom is one of the most important indicators which tells a male that the female has reached reproductive maturity. Women know, only too well, the powerful signals their bodies send to men and will stand and walk in a manner to show off their attributes and thus their readiness for mating.

Monique Roffey (a 50-year-old author with a self-confessed history of 'experimenting') in her book *House of Ashes*, deals with society's expectations for young men. She has said that when it comes to sexuality men's needs are so completely different from those of women. She believes most men don't get enough of what they want; that men ideally want to get sex as often as the drive takes them and, with as many different women as possible. A monogamous lifestyle limits the sexual fulfilment of Mr Average. Meanwhile, most women expect 'vanilla' heterosexual monogamy from their man. Hence, a relationship potentially lacking in harmony.

All human babies are born with proportionally shorter legs than they will have as adults, which slowly grow in length until the pre-adolescent growth spurt initiated by the hormones of puberty. There is a sudden and disproportionate extension in the length of the legs of pubescent girls; and their legs act like a direction indicator, causing the male eye to be drawn to their meeting point and thus the final target of his sexual desire. Women, and even quite young girls are very aware of the allure of, and signals given by, showing a leg. Thus schoolgirls who, against both parents and teachers wishes, roll up the waistband of their skirts so that they are shorter and thus show more of her leg are doing just this. High heels have a similar effect and also cause the body posture to alter in a most alluring way. Women may deny dressing to attract men; but research does not bear this out. Interestingly, the amount of feminine 'flaunting' varies during the menstrual cycle with its peak being around the time of ovulation.

Following research by Michael J. Cunningham, published as 'Journal of Personality and Social Psychology 1986', the University of Regensburg, Bavaria developed tests into the significance of 'babyfaceness'. It has been known for some time that young women with proportions which mimic those of young girls are, generally, found more attractive, particularly to men. Bridgette Bardot, as a young woman, is often cited in this context. The researchers used real photos of young women and of similar looking young girls and, using computer graphics, morphed or warped the proportions of them together in differing percentages. For instance, 90 per cent young woman, 10 per cent young girl in 10 per cent increments up to a 50-50 image. The more childlike the image the more it was liked; only 10 per cent of people preferred the original picture of the young woman.

Thus, the most popular image was that of a woman who does not, could not, exist. I have not been able to ascertain the number, gender or profile of the group who viewed the photos. There is some evidence that men are generally attracted to a female face which mimics the proportions of those of young girls and the most popular faces, in blind tests where the men were given no indication of the ages of the faces they were seeing, were those with the proportions of girls aged between 12 and 14. Some cosmetic surgeons even use 'templates' of similarly proportioned faces when trying to bring youth and desirability to more mature faces. The larger 'doe' eyes of baby-blue may particularly appeal to many males including those of

Caucasian descent whereas very dark eyes may tend to have a greater draw for some other cultures; and, for both, a smaller 'button' nose. When it comes to lips, researchers have made the link between the size, shape, colour and structure of a woman's lips and her labia. Similarities do not end with their looks; they both engorge when sexually stimulated, as do the facial cheeks and the cheeks of the buttocks. Since as early as the times of the Pharaohs women have enhanced their lips with lipstick and worn earrings to draw the eye to the wearer's face.

So, we know from extensive research what most attracts a man at a purely physical and lustful level; we also know that women deport themselves in a manner which emphasises these purely sexual signals, for whatever reason, and wear cosmetics and clothes which emphasise the effect. It would be futile to deny the strength of the sexual stimulus received by a man from a woman displaying in this way; and women know it.

In the end it is women, the apparently weaker sex, who are controlling the apparently stronger sex by the use of sex, apparently. It is an ongoing war of attrition.

Porn is mainly created for a male audience as a stimulator for their masturbation. The male roles are usually dominant and the females submissive; the woman is frequently portrayed as being under some form of duress. Perhaps surprisingly, the women 'performers' are usually paid a lot more money than the men are. Porn is said to be addictive and dangerous; speed in a car can also be addictive and dangerous. Just as no-one makes you speed in a car, so no-one is forced to watch porn. In porn pictures and movies the women are rarely forced to perform. Selling sex is seen by many as objectifying women – but, what about the well-paid women providing the 'service'; aren't a few canny women exploiting a male weakness and their own physical beauty and allure to create a healthy income? There are a large number of female sex workers of all descriptions who are more than happy to get rich whilst exploiting their bodies to stimulate men. The one big thing they all ask for is protection; not just health protection but, much more importantly, protection from violence and exploitation. Whatever you may think about men and women having some form of sex-based financial relation-ship it has been thus ever since history has been recorded. Don't forget all those others living on the fringe, like beauty queens and super-models. Who is it that forces them to rent out their bodies, to do this glamorous highly paid, high profile job? And, don't think that not performing sexual acts is not selling sexuality; the one thing a prostitute will not do is to kiss their client – it is an act which is much too intimate, not like having sex.

Women have a multitude of designs of dildos and vibrators readily available to them and that is socially acceptable; men have 'pleasure receptacles' sometimes known by the generic term 'Flesh-lights' but whereas the women's sexual toys are acceptable and even empowering, any form of male equivalent is seen as rather 'seedy'.

Everything you see, hear or read – on the Internet, in films or books – has its origin in the mind of another human. And, this work has had to be approved by other humans as being 'fit for human consumption'. If what you come across is what has come out of the mind of one of a group of people and has passed the tests of another for its suitability to be consumed by the public; this then makes you wonder what else is hidden in the darkest corners of the human mind and which has not yet been revealed. And, thus, the strength of the Internet porn industry is built on these drives, these preferences. Nearly 100 per cent of the content of these sites is of women and the comparatively few sites of men are, almost exclusively, those aimed at the male gay community.

Male sexual orgasm is a like a drug-induced high; and the drug-like substance responsible is testosterone. When men are function-ing at a more cerebral level they do understand that the woman who is the object of their immediate and lustful sexual gratification is likely to be very different from those whom they encounter in their real-life relationships. It is the juxtaposition between fantasy and reality. In their everyday lives men are primarily governed by visual stimuli, by a woman's body-language, the way she looks and the way she dresses; but, their social programming causes these male sexual drives to be modified by adding the attributes of per-sonality, humour, intelligence and that special and unfathomable 'connection' in the selection of their ideal partner. That is, in the end, what really matters; a meaningful multi-dimensional relationship with someone you are inextricably drawn to. What may disappoint some women is that because visual stimulus is so fundamental to a male's attraction to his mate, a woman who does not bother about her appearance will be seen by a man as someone who does not bother about him, someone who is not sexually attracted to him and he will therefore become less attracted to her. It may sound shallow but men just cannot help it; it is fundamental to their being that they are visually attracted to and by their mate. Sorry, ladies!

But, on a more positive note, a lot of women say how wonderful it is to get their hair, face and nails done and to put on a posh frock; it changes everything about the way you feel about yourself and the way the world sees and thus treats you. Good hairdressers have appointment books full for weeks ahead, beauty salons are every-where, spa weekends with the girls are fun, and even departmental stores give free beauty treatments. So perhaps it's not such a strange thing after all?

But, don't take it too far or become too self-obsessed as no-one wants to go out with someone who believes that they are the most beautiful, most gorgeous; most interesting and captivating creature in the world, do they? There is a fine line between being beautifully groomed and being utterly vain. Narcissism makes the most nat-urally beautiful creatures ugly. To some women, the world should learn to revolve around them. This new world would be pink; because they see it through rose-tinted spectacles or the rosé wine in the bottom of their glass.

If a woman is known as a spinster it has unwelcome connota-tions; if a male is called a bachelor it has positive connotations. There are numerous very negative words used to describe a woman, in comparison to the number used for men, words such as slag, slat-tern, hag, tart, witch, bitch, MILF, wench, bimbo, yummy-mummy, prick-teaser, battle-axe, virago, frump, chick, harridan, arm-candy, bird, floozy, Essex-girl, blonde, WAG, cougar, bike, whore, ice-maiden, pussy, old-bag, minger, babe, broad, gold-digger. This list is not exhaustive; nor, are these words exclusively used by men when speaking about women; it is not unheard of for one female to call another by one of these names. A male-equivalent list would be much shorter. It's not that men do not feel emotions it is that they do not allow their reactions to emotional stimuli to be seen by others. Neurologists at Mindlab, researchers of consumer behaviour, say that men can be more sensitive than women – it's just that they are better at keeping it under control, hidden. Mindlab created an experiment with 15 mothers and 15 fathers who, whilst their subconscious responses were being electronically monitored, were shown a series of four videos. The videos explored the emotions of 'blissful', 'funny', 'exciting', and 'heart-warming'. For the first three of these videos the gender specific responses were only marginally different – with the men showing a slightly higher level of emotional response – but, not great enough to be statistically significant. When the final video was shown the response from the men was twice as strong as that of the women. Neuropsychologist Dr David Lewis, a director of Mindlab and lecturer at the University of Sussex said that stereotypes are reinforced by media images and social interactions, that we like information which reinforces our own prejudices.

Whilst men tend to exaggerate about things women tend to exaggerate about emotions. This can have the effect of seemingly adding drama to her life – perhaps a reflection of women being the most avid viewers of soap operas (70 per cent female to 30 per cent male). With certain events in their own lives both exaggerated and frequently repeated for effect women can sometimes end up believing their own stories. Women have fantasies in the same way that men do, there are two basic differences though; firstly women's fantasies are not as frequently sexual, and secondly, they are kept more covert, more discreet.

Women's sexual requirements of a male partner have historically been fairly simple; she just wanted a strong healthy mate to produce equally strong and healthy offspring and to be the provider of food and protection. This fitted well with the standard role of the archetypal male of our forefathers. Women still seem to like a strong masculine face, a full head of hair, a broad chest with muscular shoulders and arms, narrow hips and a small tight bum – and a hint of gentleness and vulnerability. Historically, if the male came along with a largish stomach it at least showed his ability to provide plenty of food; that body-image is no longer alluring to most western women however, it remains a positive asset in some parts of the world. Since female equality has given women the power, like Oliver Twist she wants more; she has now added further criteria – she wants someone with a softer emotional side as well. Regardless of the current surge in gender equality, women are still initially drawn to the positive physical attributes of a hunter, particularly when seeking a 'fling'; in a long-term relationship they want to add the more caring attributes, a good personality, a sense of humour and sensitivity, he should be intelligent and, ideally, have a good body too. It's not much to ask, is it? Traditionally, each gender has looked to the other for the opposite physical and emotional attributes to their own. Opposites attract.

But, when it comes to close encounters of the sexual kind, men should never forget about the courtship ritual of the Praying Mantis; the female of the species will, during copulation, devour the male alive – starting with the head; the decapitated male body continues the process of mating even whilst he is being eaten alive. Now, if the male of the human species could be made of chocolate...

When a man is asked about himself by a woman, not just his job and his interests but about his upbringing, his opinions and, eventually, his feelings and emotions he may well be willing to talk – if he is sensing that he is in a secure and comfortable situation; take your time, wait for the appropriate moment and, you may get a lot more than you expected. The reason is simple and it is not a gender vanity issue. It is that when males are together such personal-level conversations are extremely unlikely to even be approached let alone fulfilled. Talking to a woman is a unique opportunity for his innermost thoughts, feelings and emotions to be given any value. Do not expect a man to easily 'open up'; it is an alien and a potentially vulnerable situation for him, he will feel gauche; the language of feelings and emotions are new to him. If it does not happen as and when it suits you do not get exasperated with him; take your time, take tiny steps, let his self-confidence and confidence in you develop. It is a bit like trying to get a wild animal to feed out of your hand. When he has, eventually, learned the nature and value of such trust then he will also be learning how to be in a better position to reciprocate.

If a man gives a woman a recipe book by a famous chef as a present it will, generally, be graciously accepted by her and is thus seen by both parties as being fine (unless, of course, she is known to be unable to cook). If a woman gives a man a DIY book it will, generally, be taken by him as being a sarcastic 'dig' at his inability to perform such tasks to her satisfaction.

Many little girls are still being brought up believing that it is their role to be 'sugar and spice and all things nice'; that they must be life's self-sacrificing placaters and mediators and as a result often lose control of their own self-worth. In reality, they want to be able to act as individuals with feelings and opinions of equal value to those of boys but their upbringing makes them feel that they should always take a passive role. The meaning of the word hysteria historically relates directly to a negative and irrational female behaviour pattern; it is linked to the word hysterectomy which was thought by the Greeks to describe an ailment in which the womb could move about inside the female body and damage other organs and that it was responsible for all sorts of inexplicable ailments and erratic behaviours in women.

From early childhood onwards it can be seen that females tend to compete with other females rather than with males. Where males tend to be physically aggressive and dominant in their search for control and status, females use methods which are less overt – they use various types and levels of social exclusion – which, though they are less dramatic interventions than those of males, are just as effective on other females; but, they are strategies which would be lost on most males. Women generally live longer and healthier lives than men and are less likely to attempt suicide. They are communicative social beings with an empathy which is lacking in males.

Research by James Haar, Distinguished Professor of the University of North Carolina has shown a direct link between positive social interaction and bonding and benefits in well-being, longevity and positive mental health. Women's nature is one of the reasons that women live longer and healthier lives.

There are far fewer girls than boys who show signs of dyslexia. Research reported in the US National Library of Medicine's 'Gender Ratios for Reading Difficulties' found that in a study of 1,133 pairs of twins the ratio varied from 2:1 to 15:1 boys to girls, with the average around 6:1. Comparison studies fail to identify the precise and statistically significant indicators of the causes of the differences in outcomes between boys and girls. However, it does seem that whilst having some difficulties with reading and writing, girls verbal language skills are quite fully developed and far in advance of equivalent boys.

Jobs-wise, women with dyslexia can succeed, even at university, and frequently find employment in the caring professions as, perhaps, a primary teacher, social worker or health worker. The structure of the female brain, in having more regions and interconnections dedicated to solely to language, may well be the saviour for these women. Men, lacking these advantages, can often find that achieving good grades in academia is a greater struggle. Women use their interpersonal skills to their advantage whilst men with dyslexia who succeed often end up in occupations related to 'things' rather than 'people', perhaps working as a tradesman, an artisan, an engineer, a designer or a computer expert. The difference in the choice of jobs means that, unintentionally, women can find themselves in lower paid jobs whilst the occupations that men gravitate towards may tend to be those which are, in general, higher paid.

The Russell Group, an association of Britain's top 24 universities, has just three of its universities with more male than female students and several professional organisations have identified the lack of new male graduates as a cause for concern. Meanwhile, the majority of the unemployed are men.

Women can excel in the educational arena; they are awarded more and better degrees than their male counterparts. The OECD (Organisation for Economic Cooperation & Development) collated the statistics for universities in 34 countries and found that in almost three quarters of the countries more women than men graduated. UNESCO (United Nations Educational, Scientific and Cultural Organisation) in their survey found the same sort of bias in countries as diverse as Brazil, Central America, the Caribbean, the Gulf States and Asia; not however, in Africa. Of course degrees do not equal jobs, let alone top jobs.

From the UN Statistic Division we find that, in the Middle East, there are more women than men attending university. Their examples show that in Lebanon 54 per cent of university students are women but women only make up 26 per cent of the workforce; in Qatar 63 per cent of university students are women but women make up just 12 per cent of the workforce. According to research by Dima Dabbous-Sensenig, Director for the Institute of Women's Studies in the Arab World at the Lebanese American University, whilst women have begun to do well at university they are under-represented in both the workforce and in politics. Many women, she says, go to university to find good, educated, intelligent husbands or to fill their time before getting married. Attending university is seen by many women as an opportunity for this otherwise controlled group to be free to socialise; the majority get married after graduating. Men often do not go to university because they need to earn a living as soon as possible and, also for this same reason, there are fewer men than women on Master's degree courses. Girls and boys upbringing is very different from their counterparts in the west and this reflects into their higher education.

Meanwhile, in UK, there are 13 medical 'Royal Colleges' representing their members who between them practice in each and every speciality in medicine. Of those 13 colleges seven have a woman as President. According to 'Inside Higher Education', in universities, women as academic tutors frequently have a high number of female students with negative feelings regarding their studies and their future than those female students with male tutors. Which is cause and which is effect, is it related to their representation as role models; do these female mentors actually attract these more vulnerable students or do the tutors just speak a greater truth, woman to woman, tell it as it is, not hold back on informing other women of the negative aspects of their prospects, whilst male tutors tend to have a more positive approach. The profession of being a women tutor is frequently seen by female students as a bit 'sad' for having dedicated their whole life to their professions to the exclusion of a more diverse range of life experiences; female students, as a consequence, are rarely willing to pay this price to emulate them. For these female students their tutor's lifestyle is seen as a mismatch in the work-life-home lifestyle balance and, therefore, they seek something they believe will be more interesting and more fulfilling. With male students, their restricted future lifestyle options are seen as the price men have to pay for being successful in their careers.

Educated women, in the period between the two World Wars, used to be thought successful if they reached the level of being a man's secretary, perhaps it was seen as some form of honour because it was a job done by men in Dickens's era. Many women do succeed in the traditionally male dominated higher echelons of business but very few choose to make it a full-time, life-long commitment. Women in top jobs are often seen by other women, and not unreasonably can see themselves, as being martyrs to the cause of feminism. But, a successful woman is not necessarily a feminist. Nevertheless, these women are frequently interviewed and their opinions sought; they are feted as mentors for younger women who aspire to emulate them. They can also be used as evidence of the lack of male bias in the world of work; sometimes the beneficiaries of, sometimes the victims of, the media PR machine.

The 'glass ceiling' retains its status in legend rather than reality as more and more women crash through it. Has anyone ever heard of the term 'a glass ceiling' in the context of any blue-collar or any other non top-level managerial situation; women are always welcome on the factory floor or the building site. Anyway, such attempts at elevation of professional position are just as relevant to men as they are to women; it's just that men do not have any excuse for their own poor achievement, whilst women could 'call-foul'. Perhaps, the glass ceiling is more of a one-way mirror; where male achievers look down at the shiny mirrored side and admire their own glow of superiority in the reflection (or, maybe, look up the skirts of the few women standing alongside them) whilst women look up from below and observe, unseen; do women see right through the concept of the 'glass ceiling'? Like a child in front of a sweet shop window, some women aspire to have the things they think they want from the other side; when, in reality, if they were to be able to get everything they think that they would want – it would still not satisfy them. Each time a woman does break through the glass ceiling she should be aware that she will be expected to clean up the mess that she will have made in doing so.

The wage gap myth has been discredited by numerous academics and their institutional researchers for years. But, the female publicity machine does not want to listen – why let the truth spoil their sensation seeking headlines? Yes, say the independent and unbiased researchers, there is a pay difference but when the level of professional role, expertise, salary structure and hours worked are taken into account any differences are too close to call. A nurse and a brain surgeon will not be paid the same – whoever is doing each job; it just so happens that, at the moment, the male is more likely to be the surgeon, the higher paid job. And, there are many very obvious reasons why it is currently this way – mainly related to a woman's chosen home-centred caring role.

Dr Joanna Williams is a lecturer in Higher Education at the University of Kent, for the Enhancement of Learning and Teaching Unit. She has also written books including *Higher Education: Why Learning Can't Be Bought* and *Academic Freedom in an Age of Conformity: Confronting the Fear of Knowledge*. As the Education Editor for *Spiked* the on-line magazine she wrote a lengthy and wide ranging article titled 'The Pay Gap is Dead' for their issue on 15th February 2016. In this article she says that the government figures of a 20 per cent gender pay gap are misleading and that the figure has been reached through combining part-time and full-time earning without taking into account either the age or the employment sector. She goes on to say: 'When we compare how much women and men are paid for doing the same job for the same number of hours each week there is no pay gap. Not only is it illegal to pay men more, such a pay gap makes no economic sense. If bosses could really get away with paying women so much less (for performing exactly the same job for the same number of hours) why would anyone ever employ men?' and 'Today, women in their twenties earn more than men of the same age – not just like-for-like but also on average. This means that irrespective of job type or hours worked young women are likely to take home higher wages. For women under the age of 40 and working full-time the pay gap is negligible'. The government Equalities Minister, Nicky Morgan, is on record as having said: 'We've virtually eliminated the gap for full-time workers under 40 and the gap for over 40s is shrinking too.' A contributory factor is that as 'high earners' retire (traditionally men of older age) the pay gap reduces.

It would be true to say that both genders would have real and illusionary barriers to their ascent depending on their individual circumstances. But, in reality, few jobs are at that level. Real equality would infer women doing all the jobs which men currently perform on an equal basis. Women would doubtless say, at this point, that they want equality of opportunity. What this means, in simple language, is that they want to have an equal chance of being considered for the top jobs or indeed any that they might aspire to but not every job – they do not want to share everything. Is the world of the male as attractive in reality as it appears to women or do they just want to 'cherry pick' the roles that attract them and avoid those seen as less appealing? How many women have tried to enrol on a mechanics course and been turned down on a gender basis? How many women put their names down to be sewerage workers? Long ago men left the door to emancipation open to women but the women have refused to leave the security of their own domination; the female perspective of Utopia is neither fair nor realistic.

The life of a kibbutz is supposed to offer an idealistic world of work based on equality but in reality females gravitate to the jobs that appeal to them – in childcare and communication whereas males end up doing the more physically demanding jobs. After years of trying to make life exactly equal for males and females the kibbutz system had to acknowledge that males and females are different and gravitate to the roles they feel most comfortable with.

Perhaps, there is a totally different way of looking at employment and its rewards; pay could be linked to your effort in relationship with your ability. Thus, if you have an IQ of 80 and perform a job with a required IQ of 75 you are working nearly flat out but if you have an IQ of 135 and work at a job which requires an IQ of 115 you are merely cruising. Our society needs to divert some of our most free-thinking brains to looking for ways to overcome the potential disharmony that every form of inequality can bring. Or, is it that we can only cope with life if things are kept simple, if people, like things, are put in readily identifiable little boxes.

The reason that women do not enter business in the same way as men is more to do with their aspirations than their academic qualifications. In 1958, UK university degrees were awarded to 7,700 males but only 3,360 females. Historically, females were under represented in all UK universities; by 1992 they were equal; in 2005 there were 10 per cent more women than men being awarded degrees. That is the highest percentage for any country in the OECD. In 2006, 107,000 degrees were awarded to men but 144,755 were awarded to women. According to the Higher Education Statistics Agency the number of women starting a degree course outnumbered men in 112 out of 180 subjects, three were equal in number and 65 had more men. Overall there are 67,000 more women now on degree courses (ACAS).The academic pendulum has now swung in favour of women. Therefore, with almost 50 per cent more female graduates than male graduates why are there not a similar percentage of women in posts in industry?

On 22nd September 2015 the *Daily Mail* published an article, in collaboration with the job-search engine adzuna.co.uk, outlining the correlation between university degree subjects studied and the average salaries which were subsequently earned. The top five best paid degree subjects were:

- Civil Engineering   £45k
- Engineering   £43k
- Computer Science   £42k
- Mechanical Engineering   £40k
- Mathematics   £40k

All of these university degree courses are dominated by males. The top five worst paid degree subjects were:

- Hospitality and Tourism   £20k
- Business Studies   £21k
- Sports Science   £21k
- Photography   £25k
- Health & Social Care   £25k

Apart from Sports Science, all of these degree courses are dominated by women.

The basic discussion seems to be: could women, with the same sort of training, perform the vast majority of jobs currently done by males? Yes, definitely. Women do not consistently apply for jobs and/or training schemes in equal numbers to men; why not, when they are better educated and there are so many skills shortages? Are women alleging that they are persistently turned down on a gender basis for men's jobs and training courses; if so, where is the evidence? Do women really want to go to work at 7am and return at 7pm; if so, why don't they? Who will look after the children – a child-minder; could the child-minder be a male? Could more men be capable of performing the same sorts of roles as women; child-rearing and care, shopping and cooking; housework? Why not exchange roles, men generally aren't as happy as women are either in the workplace or with their domestic and social roles. Hence, the suicide rate in 2013 for males was 4,858 whereas the rate for females was less than a third at just 1,375. In women, the rate was pretty similar across the age range. In men, the rate of suicide rose in a steep curve from the age of 25 years to a height in middle age and then dropped off towards retirement age – but, of course, by this time men are dying much more frequently than women anyway. As a general rule, you don't kill yourself if you are happy with your life – the statistics define the gender differences.

Female values and life-skills, which were once discounted as being of low value in the world of business, are now being acknowledged to have a very positive worth. These are values which have erstwhile eluded men. Women are, in the work market, more willing to trade pay and status for flexibility. Women may baulk against being paid less pro rata but currently find that it is a price that they have no option but to accept. Perhaps, the inherent fairness and predictability of the Civil Service is one of the reasons that over 50 per cent of all civil servants are women. Whilst women may be able to multi-task and communicate, men can have a single-minded attitude to performing tasks which is derived from a lack of sensibility for other people, for other things, and is outwardly self-centred. Men relate to the 'winner takes all' attitude in the world of work; women tend to look for cooperation and fairness. Until recent equality legislation, car insurance premiums for males were higher than for females – because more men drove more miles and therefore had more accidents. Men, if they live long enough, have to wait until they are older to get their pensions; and then men go and die younger. Women, traditionally, get their pensions younger and then live longer than men, look at the gender bias in the clientele at homes for the elderly; men have a rarity value.

Women flourish in Law, Accountancy, Medicine, Pharmacy, Veterinary, Biology, Nursery, Social Services; all professions with a need for people skills, caring, nurturing; they are clean, high social status occupations. They are not jobs with extreme hours nor are they jobs with extreme financial rewards. Many more women work in shops, offices and factories in much less glamorous jobs than the high profile occupations portrayed by the media when discussing gender issues.

In business, women highly value the ability to take time away from their occupational undertakings, as and when they feel it necessary, in favour of their family commitments and responsibilities and for other social needs. Traditionally this has been the reason that women reach a particular level in their chosen profession and get no further – the plateau effect. The usual reason for their career to take a lower priority is the decision to start a family and, although many women may believe that they will return to work straight after the birth, the reality of the situation is that the strength of the bond with their baby and the enormity of its needs, change the value systems for these new mothers. Women may want to return to work later on but will, ideally, need to be able to adapt their working hours such that they are only willing to be available at certain times of the day and, even then, only during school term-time, provided that the child never needs time off for illness and there are no unscheduled school closures; all this is because they have to fit in with the needs of their school age children. As the children grow the work-family balance can tilt in one direction or the other. During term-time there can be school nativities, plays, sports days; ballet and violin lessons and other performances to attend, then someone needs to be available all day during the school holidays. Once the children have 'flown the nest' their time-consuming needs are often replaced by duties caring for ageing parents and, eventually, by the arrival of grandchildren too. Most women would ideally want a totally flexible work-life balance to suit their ever changing needs. It is the nature of their caring role which most women's life choices are constricted by.

So, how does this fit in with being a member of the workforce in manufacturing? With production lines needing task-trained operatives it would be possible to lose certain workers and substitute them with another similarly trained operative reasonably easily and without disrupting the continuity of the manufacturing process. In some companies the shift patterns are intentionally organised to synchronise with school hours and holidays – but many of these sorts of production-line jobs are being lost to automation or to out-sourcing the work to other countries where material and labour costs are cheaper. But these are not the types of jobs that are the subject of a high profile feminist media campaign.

A similar strategy may be made to function for a shop assistant or a waitress or even a teacher or a hospital based nurse, but how do you have a pilot, a vet or a doctor or a solicitor or a line manager or a director of a board who is, often at short notice, sometimes there and sometimes not? How do you allocate a schedule of work and its responsibilities, how do you ensure a continuity of service. Clients will not be tolerant of a dislocated level of personal service or place orders in a fashion sympathetic to the needs of a certain marginal sector of the management team; they want what they want when they want it. And a company, however large, cannot carry enough spare capacity to blend the highs and lows of order density to allow for a minority of staff who want a flexible work-life balance – let alone numerous people in differing stages of the same process. And what if men began deciding that they would like a flexible life-work balance too. The current structure of business and industry does not, currently, allow for such fluidity of personnel and companies trying to do so may well find business is going elsewhere. It is a difficult enough strategy for large corporations; an impossible one for SMEs. These are the very reasons that entrepreneur business women do not promote equal numbers of male and female employees throughout every level of their workforce, they know it cannot work; they are in business to make money not to subsidise social experiments.

Women in work can sometimes display the symptoms of 'Imposter Syndrome'; it is a form of fear, where people feel as though they should not really be in their current position of power or authority, a position which they have actually achieved through merit, as though they are some sort of fraud or imposter and therefore don't deserve it. And, it's almost always women who have these thoughts. Men, generally, think that they are better than they really are, that they deserve promotion or better pay and will ask for it. That is one reason that men earn more than women when doing the same jobs; men ask for pay increases, women tend not to. Women tend to try harder, prepare more, do more research; not just because it is their nature but also in an effort not to be found as wanting, of being unworthy in some way. Thus, the by-product of this unfounded vulnerability makes them all the more dedicated workers and is actually the cause of them being offered promotion or more responsibility. But then they feel unworthy of the promotion; often they will make an excuse not to accept it, they can feel it a responsibility too far; sometimes they will actually leave their job to avoid the pressures. Male employers do not readily identify this problem and as a result can lose some of their best workers. This pressure, real or self-imposed, can lead to depression (depression is the most common mental health problem in women, affecting an estimated 10 per cent of the adult female population) and is frequently the cause of women leaving the world of work for a more caring, and less artificially stressful lifestyle. Therefore the world of business loses these intelligent and hard working women because of their innate lack of self-confidence.

If a well-educated woman decides to divert from a high status job and become a stay-at-home mother was the investment in her education wasted? In fact, it will be her children who, during their upbringing and their relationship with their educated mother, will benefit directly from both her education and life skills; society will therefore directly benefit from better brought up and more roundly educated children. However, would a girl child growing up in such an environment really appreciate it for what it is; or, will she think that by just staying at home and emulating her mother's domestic role she will not need higher education and will she therefore not feel motivated to reach the higher echelons of education and business as a career woman. Would a boy child's perspective see the domestic lifestyle of his mother as the ultimate female role? Is either situation right?

For some women the strength of love they feel for their first baby can be an overwhelming emotion. It is not uncommon for a woman who has one child, which she dearly loves, to become pregnant and as a result have a very real pressure imposed by this second joyful event. She finds herself struggling with her own conscience. She has already given her every drop of maternal love to her first-born; where can she possibly find all the extra love she so wants to give to her next child? But, there is no reason to be concerned; nature provides. Even the apocryphal stories of women lifting heavy loads off trapped children must have some element of truth behind them. A mother's love is a potent force of nature.

Is it even necessary for a mother to spend her lifetime caring for her child at both a practical and emotional level? From a medical perspective, breastfeeding has many benefits; mother's milk is best. But, beyond that stage, how important is it that a mother is always in attendance? A baby needs love and care without doubt but who supplies that need is more ambiguous; were that not so, surrogacy, adoption and fostering would not work. Perhaps it is that a baby, once nourished by breastfeeding could be cared for by another;

the mother-child relationship would then be dominated by an emotional bond rather than by a practical need. During the school years, a parent's support at events such as school plays or sports days and the like is important; like other children, they are empowered by such overt approval. In their teens, children frequently try not to be seen associating with their parents but still gain strength from a secure home environment.

Historically, children have often been brought up with one of two extreme models; either, being alongside their parent at home or whilst the parent is performing their working role or, being looked after for much of the time by a relative or other carer. Perhaps, in the end, it is not the quantity of time spent parenting which is most important rather, it is the quality of time; it's the quality of that bond, the quality of that enduring relationship, which matters most. Are financial rewards and social status, and a caring, nurturing lifestyle, mutually exclusive; is inner satisfaction more important than monetary reward or kudos? It is a practical dichotomy. Because your financial situation demands that you must be a working parent it does not, of itself, infer a lesser quality of loving child-parent relationship.

Many women have the option, from an early stage, to treat their adult life like a 'pick and mix' counter. A little bit of this, a little bit of that – oops, I don't like the taste of that – I'll throw that away and have something else instead. Men have been seen as being the providers; it is an ongoing full-time role; bills come in every month so a pay-cheque needs to come in every month and, men do not usually have the biological refuge of opting for a home-based parenting role.

Women tend to make a 'life-plan' from an early age which, whilst it may include going to university and then into the world of work, usually culminates in having children and her role as a mother. To draw a woman away from this maternal role requires a very strong pull. The thought of having to leave for work just as the children are starting to wake and returning when they are already asleep in bed is really not such an appealing thing for any mother. However, as an alternative to being a working mum, what happens to the role of a full-time mother when the children grow up and leave home and the woman is still too young to 'retire'? Not being able to cope with living without one's child(ren) when they grow up and leave home is about the loss and the need of the parent. They then move close to the grandchildren as a substitute, a need to feel useful and have a purpose in life.

If the world of work were to be organised, if not controlled, by women, could flexible working and the pull of domestic situations requiring her to be at home become accepted? As an interim stage, could certain women be working in business in an organisational role at management level and acting as a conduit or interface with the males of a higher rank and able to negotiate a company strategy conducive to the resolution of the needs of both the woman and the company? The 'comfort' level of all staff is crucial to a well-run company – and all staff have different 'comfort levels' to be considered. Should women at work be expected to behave as though they do not have a family and its distractions in an effort to be treated more equally in the promotion stakes? Would such a strategy require government sponsorship and ongoing financial support?

Alternatively, is it not possible to get satisfaction from playing your role within an organisation without having to strive to be the boss with all its stress, politics and endless meetings? In the end, all organisations are pyramids with just one person exposed at the top who is supported by a complex, complementary and interlocking structure of individuals – each one special in their own way and, in truth, none more so than another. It is the reward system, the salary structure, which draws most people up the promotional ladder, although a few sad individuals long for the power above all else; rarely is it the search for job satisfaction. All jobs have an element of tedium. What if the salary structure were to be reversed so that the more power, status and authority the lower the income; the more tedious, dirty and demeaning the work the higher the salary. Is the nurturing of an employment based ambition, held by so many of both genders, just a clever management ruse to bolster the ego of being the boss? The ultimate Pyramid Selling con trick!

Women, by nature, tend not to be risk takers, they are risk averse. If being a mother, carer, and housewife had the elevated status it truly deserves and if there was financial security too, would any great number women seek to be active in the world of work?

Given a generous and bountiful benefactor, what lifestyle changes, if any, would you choose to implement. What percentage of either gender would feel motivated to continue to spend their time and energy on developing a business life? The evidence seems to show men who have been brought up in a wealthy family and privately educated continue the stereotype by seeking the status which they believe to be in business or politics rather than to use their advantages to develop the social, emotional and spiritual facets of their lives. Meanwhile, many females who begin by pursuing a traditionally male career path seem to realise very quickly that they have been pursuing someone else's expectations and find their male oriented work life irrelevant to their inner needs; they then gravitate to more caring roles.

The poorer the national environment the greater the proportion of women seeking success in traditionally male roles and taking degree level qualifications. Whether they are subsequently allowed to pursue a career in their chosen area of study is a reflection of the structure of the country they are living in. The Indian subcontinent appears to have very positive outcomes for such women whereas the Arab states appear less supportive of independent women.

Thus, educational discrimination is not necessarily the cause of an alleged lack of equality of employment opportunity. In countries with all the opportunities of a more equal society, women do not always pursue and thereafter make the most of all the opportunities which are open to them. In poorer countries, with a willing and open culture, it is the qualifications not the gender which are the determinates of upward mobility in the commercial sector.

In the world of work, females, without specifically trying, get the same amount done as their male counterparts in less time and without the jostling for position within the company; they appear to support each other rather than compete with each other. Perhaps women are not actually pushed out of the way so that men can clamber past them on the ladder of promotion but, rather that they step aside, choose to opt out of what soon appears to them to be a seemingly valueless subterfuge; they opt for more attractive options. You don't know if you will like something unless you have tried it and many women try it and look at others climbing this promotion ladder and decide that the rewards are not worth the effort. To be able to do something, at both a physical and technical level and to have the opportunity to do so, does not necessarily mean that you will like it.

Women's natural choices are very valid; why should anyone try to push them into a 'male' role which, whilst they could do it, they are not attracted to. Being a mother, a carer should be given a higher status. Saying that someone should be reaching for a male role as 'better' or 'more important' devalues the nurturing roles and is destructive of a strong female role model.

Currently men may, in general, get paid more than women. The vast majority of people still live in units involving couples where males and females have different perceptions of financial priorities. For most couples the costs associated with just trying to live from day to day absorb almost all their pay each week without leaving much spending in the way of luxuries. If men do bring home more money than women there is little evidence of them spending proportionally larger amounts of their salaries solely on their own personal whims, leaving their partner as a needy 'poor relation' and the family impoverished. We each give ourselves 'treats' to make the mundanity of life less painful but it is not common that one gender suffers as the result of the other's outlandish spending.

To men it seems that women talk almost all the time. In their primal stages women needed to keep in constant contact with their children and other women and their children too. It was a matter of safety, knowing that everyone was still present and that they were well – that the safety and security of both individuals and the group as a whole, had not been breached. It allowed the children to get used to the voice of their carers and to recognise the meanings of the different intonations of voice; those which are a comfort and reassurance and those which are warning signs. Meanwhile, a man who was out hunting his prey or dealing with an enemy would need to spend most of his time as silent as possible, unseen and unheard.

The chance of a male dying as the result of an accident when hunting or in skirmishes or battles was high and the loss of her partner presented a substantial risk for his mate and their offspring. To act as a type of insurance against the consequences of that, women needed to create bonds with the other females so that there would be some sort of support network to help her and her family survive. .

Thus, brain scans of both men and women find the parts of their brains relevant to such tasks are more developed. In modern times it has been shown that women use at least twice the number of words compared to a man. The structures of their sentences are more complex and they use a greater vocabulary. The greater the quantity and quality of conversation generated by a woman the greater her feeling of liking and trust for that person. Women do not like talking to people they do not feel safe with; and silence is used by women as a punishment. For men, a woman's silence is frequently seen as a blessed relief from what he feels is her constant verbal assault.

It is important for men to realise that a woman should be allowed to talk, without his interruptions (although the occasional supportive word or gesture is appreciated), and that she is just going through a purgative process of 'airing' the currently important contents of her mind. There is absolutely no need for him to try to put forward his ideas or solutions. It is a cathartic process for her in exactly the same way that he wants to just sit quietly and uninterrupted sometimes. We just function in different ways; one is not superior to the other, just more appropriate for that person at that time and it is the duty of each partner to make the other person comfortable and secure in that time and not to see it as a reason for confrontation. For women this is a coping strategy that works, it helps them to alleviate the signs and symptoms of stress; it must work, because women live the best part of a decade longer than their spouses. And, much longer than single men.

A woman's ability to multi-task and her superior use of language means that she can be thinking about several things during a conversation and as a result she can stitch together sentences relating to different subjects in the same dialogue. In a simple example, she can be talking to her friend about a recent happening at the office and intersperse it with a conversation with her children about them getting out of their school clothes, turning off the TV and getting on with their homework. To a man each dialogue is a unique unit referring to just one subject matter. He uses direct speech and he says what he means and expects to get an answer in the same manner. It is not intended to be dominating or confrontational; it is seen as plain speaking by men but not always so by women.

But, he can do nothing else.

Women, whether in conversation with other women or indeed men – hint, drop innuendos, use indirect speech which allows for more flexible interpretation. It is seen as non-aggressive, non-confrontational and has built-in 'escape routes'.

Given the chance, women tend to enjoy spending 'free money' on meetings with friends for coffee and cakes, clothes, make-up, jewellery and accessories, and, of course, hair and beauty treatments. Women feel the need to keep abreast of the latest fashion trends knowing that doing otherwise could cause them to feel socially embarrassed. In the 1600s Venetian prostitutes wore red platform shoes as a sign of their 'profession' whilst at the same time, during the reign of Louis 14th (the Sun King) in France, high red shoes and wigs were a very positive fashion statement at court. Same shoes – different countries – potential fashion disaster. According to recent research, the average spending by British females during their lifetime is staggering; £500,000 on clothes, £100,000 on cosmetics, £40,000 on hair and £24,000 on age-reducing products and procedures. And, think of all those creatures who may have had to suffer or die in an effort to make women feel more glamorous. These are all costs that women can easily keep hidden because they are frequently bought when the men are not around and they are generally not noticed by their men.

Meanwhile, men spend their 'free money' on beer and snacks, sports related expenses, 'boys-toys', computers and technology (some of which have benefits for the whole household); and, finally, on clothes. They spend considerably less than half the amount women do. Women will be aware of each purchase because men are not good at keeping things hidden or secret.

Three-quarters of all fiction published is bought by and read by women and tends to be of a wide and varied scope but within certain parameters; women do not like violence and prefer romance and historical novels, they also buy numerous magazines on subjects such as fashion and home-making. Women are the authors of most books on human relationships and are also the readers of them; the books describe the problems that women have and show a deep understanding of them whilst suggesting strategies for dealing with the reader's predicaments. In magazines, women like to read their horoscopes and the sections from 'agony aunts'; but, have you ever heard of 'agony uncles'? How did *Fifty Shades of Grey* get written by a woman for women, how did it get such a worldwide readership? It runs counter to what we are led to believe is a women's true nature. How is it that a female author was happy to write against the alleged ethos of women and create what has been described as a Mills & Boon style book but with a spanking good plot. What does it say about the true psyche of both the author and her inside knowledge of what really turns-on women?

Men, meanwhile, seem to have narrower interests and buy fewer books and magazines and tend to be more specific in their interests such as spy thrillers, westerns and sci-fi books and, also computer, car and motor-cycle magazines. Nowadays, porn is sourced on-line rather more often than from the top shelf of a specialist shop.

Reproduction is the evolutionary *raison d'être* of all human females and controlling it was to be the Holy Grail. The advent of 'the Pill' was probably the greatest giver of sexual freedom to the contemporary generation; and, since then, it has filtered down into the following generations. Initially, the pill was only available to married women with children in an effort to stop them having any more. Single women were not, at that time, eligible for the pill; it was seen as a recreational freedom too far. This situation was to soon change as the pill became cheaper to manufacture and its social benefits more widely accepted. But, only a couple of decades or so later the beginnings of Aids curtailed much of that sexual freedom. Fertile women have if so desired, and always have had, the excuse for refuge from male sexual attention for one week in every four;

not an ideal curtailment of sexual activity from a male perspective.

Traditionally, sex was the strongest, and most valuable, currency that women had; it had a scarcity value. Now as women become more open to sexual relationships and therefore sex is more easily available to men, its value is decreasing. It is no longer the rare and precious commodity it once was. Both sexes become more promiscuous and men less likely to commit. This creates an even greater single-mindedness in men whilst women are left to find other 'diversions'. Prostitutes hire out their bodies by the hour; they don't sell their minds and souls too! The values of the vast majority of women are more discriminating than men; women aren't just attracted to, don't just marry, the richest or most handsome male they can possibly get but, the nicest person, the one they like best.

Women with more social power are less likely to 'accept' becoming victims – in any situation. When women are put in behavioural tests to assess aggression they tend to be less aggressive than their male counterparts – until they are in a situation where their gender and identity cannot be identified; they are then just as vicious and vindictive as the males. Interestingly more female suicide bombers are successful in their missions than their male counterparts; is this a reflection of their steely determination or just their ability to conceal more explosives more easily? A recent study was inconclusive – because there weren't many perpetrators left to survey!

Women's bodies are usually at their best in their late teens and early twenties; from the moment that women become pregnant their bodies begin a series of irreversible physical changes. These changes are caused first by growing and carrying a baby and then by the physical trauma on the body of giving birth – either naturally or by having a caesarean; these events tend to cause permanent detrimental changes. All totally natural, of course, but for some women, those who are particularly 'body conscious', the physical changes can cause negative psychological attitudes towards their bodies. This is exacerbated by the body's natural ageing process whereby, over time, tissues and muscles begin to lose their tone and elasticity. The psychological effects are just as life-changing too.

Because women's bodies 'run down' to the menopause, and in the process cause a lowered libido, they can find men's still powerful sexual drives to be unacceptable pressure.

The modern female usually begins menstruating, and thus is fertile, from about 10–12 years old (although some do so both earlier and later); and, can continue to be fertile until about 50 years old when the menopause begins. Thus a female human has a potential breeding life of around 40 years. The female human is generally thought to be most fertile from the late teens to the late twenties. Women are born with one to two million eggs in their ovaries but only use about 400 per lifetime. Pregnancy in both young girls and older women has the potential for complications for both mother and child. Each month there will be a few days when an egg is inside a woman is ready to be fertilised and has the potential to become a foetus and thus develop into a baby human being. The mating process requires that a fertile female must be impregnated by a fertile male for her egg to be penetrated by one of his sperm.

The male human usually reaches puberty a couple of years later than the female but can remain fertile and able to produce viable sperm for his whole life. There is no male equivalent to the menopause. The male is also thought to be most fertile from his late teens until late twenties. Early or later in life, fatherhood has no directly detrimental effects on or consequences for, the male.

Research by the Open University (Sperm Counts, June 2005) says that, whilst quality and quantity can vary widely, men are able to produce up to a maximum of between 100 –300 million sperm per millilitre of ejaculate with the average ejaculate volume of just over 2.75 millilitres (but with a maximum of about five millilitres after long periods of abstinence) thus a theoretical maximum of 1.5 billion sperm in one ejaculation. One average ejaculation is just over half a teaspoon in total volume.

The reality is, however, that these maximums are mathematical possibilities not actual occurrences. Many sperm are slow swimmers, deformed, disoriented or even dead. But, for most men, there are still millions of healthy and potent sperm delivered at each ejaculation. The number of potent sperm per millilitre of ejaculate has diminished in the last 50 years – even allowing for the more accurate modern methods of counting them. In 1940 the average count was 113 million/ml; in 1990 it was just 66 million/ml. It continues to decrease. There is 37.5 MB of 'information' in one sperm thus 15.875 TB in one ejaculation (Genome Reference Consortium).

According to Europa, the official website of the European Union, the current population of the EU is around 500 million of which 51.2 per cent are female; thus, there are about 256 million females of all ages in Europe of which about 100 million are of child-bearing age. Therefore, it follows that there are potentially more than enough viable sperm in just one male ejaculation to impregnate every fertile woman in Europe.

A woman unable to bear children can apparently carry a lifelong grief for babies that she never conceived. One in six women in the UK has problems conceiving and frequently have to resort to surrogacy or adoption to become mothers. Now a surgical womb transplant has become a reality since a revolutionary operation which has been completed in Gothenburg, Sweden. The womb of a woman in her 60s was transplanted into her 36-year-old daughter in the hope she would be able to conceive. It was reported in October 2014, in the British medical journal *The Lancet*, that this 36-year-old woman had given birth, prematurely, to an otherwise healthy baby boy who weighed in at 1.8kgs (3.9lbs). The identities of those involved are being kept secret. There are twice as many women who, potentially, could benefit from a womb transplant (if it becomes a viable operation) as need a new kidney.

Intercourse is both a psychological as well as physical process. When a female loses her virginity she must find a way for her mind to cope with the concept of a male invading her body, and in doing so she has to accept her position of vulnerability. This new experience of being dominated and penetrated by the male is a practical, mental and emotional process for her. In sexually penetrating his partner a male is getting as deep inside someone as it is possible to be (short of surgery), getting to her very core, making this a very significant and submissive act for the recipient; for him, the thrusting is a manifestation of his perceived dominance.

This continues to be a psychological as well as physical process for a woman each time she has intercourse. The context of her 'giving' herself and of being 'taken' will relate directly to the prevailing physical and emotional circumstances. Males and females, during lovemaking, share the same stages of sexual arousal and sexual climaxes they even have the same frequency of orgasmic spasms (0.8/sec) – however, women are capable of multiple orgasms. Ejaculation and orgasm are not the same; either in technical terms or as a physical sensation. They are equivalent bodily functions; they are reward systems. Men are like computers, if you can't get them to work properly turn them off, and then turn them on quickly; voila, you have a compliant male.

For a woman, as an act of love, intercourse can be an intensely positive physical and emotional experience. As a purely physical act of gratification an orgasm can also create untold pleasure for her. However, because a woman can be 'taken' against her will (raped) by a man (or by men) the result of unsolicited penetration can be, conversely, the subject of a grossly negative physical and emotional trauma. Even if the male concerned is her husband or a long-term partner, being entered against her will, can be both a physically and emotionally devastating experience. Not to be able to protect your body from assault; it is no different to being physically assaulted in any other way. A woman has a nurturing nature and to be violated in this way is counter to her very being. If a woman or child is raped, or harmed in any other way, and the male knows about it he is duty-bound to seek revenge; in some cultures this would include trying to kill the perpetrator even if it risked his own life. This can be a reason for some women not to reveal what has happened; the social shame is another. For the man, there is implied social pressure to behave in such a defensive way. 'Physically, a woman cannot rape a man because of how the offence is defined in law. Only men can commit the offence of rape as a principal. The definition of rape, in English law, requires a penis to be inserted into a woman's vagina, anus or mouth without her consent and knowing that she does not so consent... legally, a woman can commit the offence of rape if she acts as an accomplice to the rape (statutory rape) ...sexual intercourse with a minor (under 16) fulfils the definition of rape as someone of that age cannot be deemed to have lawfully given consent. When a woman has sexual intercourse with a minor she is committing a sexual assault, not rape'. (Bastion Lloyd Morris, solicitor advocates. 9th March 2014, Blog).

According to the BBC news on Friday 16th March 2001, an 18-year-old woman was convicted of statutory rape. In front of a group of peers, she helped to strip and pin the victim down before she was raped by a young man. By holding the victim down she was as guilty of the offence of rape as the actual perpetrator of the rape. In London alone, nearly 20 women have been charged with rape since 1997.

A man cannot, in practice, be easily 'taken' against his will by a woman (or group of women) unless he has an erection (legally, it is not covered by the definition of the offence of rape – see above); although he certainly can be penetrated anally against his will by another man (or men) – (Buggery, S12 Sexual Offences Act 1956, and others). The process of freely 'giving' yourself to another, of being vulnerable, allowing someone else inside your body, is a concept, process and emotional rite of passage that very few heterosexual males ever consider or even have the ability to be able to appreciate.

The whole concept of being coerced or forced to submit to being penetrated by another is totally alien to a male. Sadly, a woman walking home alone through the streets at night will consider a sexual assault as her potential 'nightmare' scenario. Meanwhile, for a man, the thought of being sexually assaulted or raped by another male(s) on the way home is frankly ridiculous in the extreme. Perhaps because of its unlikelihood, should he ever be in such a vulnerable situation he will find that it has the power to bring home the terror of such an encounter from a woman's point of view very vividly. Can I suggest that any woman try just watching the male rape scene from the film *Deliverance* in the company of her male partner; she will see that, however much he uses humour and bravado to divert attention from it, he will feel uncomfortably vulnerable.

The drive of testosterone pushes the male to copulate; to be dominant and passionate, in what can sometimes become an almost aggressive mating ritual. He needs to satisfy what can, in many young men, be a frequent and almost insatiable need to orgasm. The male need to 'come' is purely a physical urge that needs to be satisfied as opposed to lovemaking, the feeling of the consummation of an emotional bond. It is the difference between a shower and a bath; men prefer to take a shower, women prefer to take a bath. Some say that this male drive is just the manifestation of an inborn need to pass on his genes by fathering as many offspring as he can; but, that society's mores have taught him to temper his ardent desires for the overall benefit of peace within the community.

I realise that many men will try to deny this portrayal of these primitive urges as being relevant to them and the life of modern man; many women may deny that their father or husband or son could harbour such potent drives so near the surface of their being; they may say that their men are not like this and that it is a terrible travesty of a generalisation.

But, just look at what happens when men find themselves in an environment where they believe their actions will not betray them and where the situation stimulates rather than represses their testosterone fuelled actions. Men of all ages, races and creeds have been, and continue to be, perpetrators of acts of sexual conquest, of sexual excess, of sexual violence – as any war zone will graphically show. Although not always intentionally used in this way, the rape of a man, woman or child is an immensely powerful weapon; casting an enduring stigma, it is the ultimate physical, psychological and social humiliation. Because of the massive effect of rape on the individual, and their relationship with their own society and the dishonour it brings to their family, the victims feel so humiliated, dirty and ashamed that they frequently find they have no way to deal with it other than to commit suicide. Women, in general, given the anonymity of war do not behave like men.

Groups of women have always had the potential to protect one or more of their own; against males or whoever. The fact that, as mothers, women have been the authority figure for all of us since we were born has an often untapped potency; this is how primary school teachers keep control of their classes – by using the same authority in the same way as the children's mothers. Matriarchy rules.

If women do allege sexual harassment or assault it can be very difficult for a man to disprove; it has always been that way. But, historically, the public stigma of having been raped was powerful enough to stop most women pursuing justice. There seems to be a rash of people reporting sexual misdemeanours allegedly perpetrated many decades previously and usually by persons who have had a high profile in the victim's life, including the staff of care homes and the clergy. The potential damage caused by such claims, whether validated or not, is substantial. Their association with financial compensation or revenge cannot be ignored as a very potent motive. It will be difficult for the investigators and prosecutors to differentiate between bona fide evidence and malicious misrepresentations. There does not appear to be a rise in allegations against less high profile parties. The majority of all levels of assaults, and particularly sexual assaults, of girls and women are perpetrated by relatives or known associates. According to the Rape, Abuse and Incest National Network four out of five cases of rape were committed by someone known to the victim; 82 per cent of sexual assaults were perpetrated by a non-stranger; 50 per cent of rapes and sexual assaults were reported to have taken place in the victim's home or within one mile of the victim's home.

In many societies men still expect to control women and children as though they were some form of almost inanimate, low value and disposable possession; these men do not tolerate even the smallest of steps taken towards any level of equality. They realise that it is happening in the West and they see it as some form of pernicious disease capable of spreading into their society and destroying their current traditions and value systems; they feel vulnerable and believe that it should be either ignored or, better still, eradicated.

Apocryphal or not, it has been alleged that in an unidentified country which was once wracked by war, that the women and children who used to walk a respectful distance behind their men, now walk a distance ahead of them – because there are so many unexploded land-mines and bombs buried under the surface of the ground; they are being used as disposable human mine-detectors protecting the life of the dominant male. It's a matter of relative values.

The recent horrific acid attacks on Asian women by their menfolk, for not keeping to the traditional gender based norms, is barbaric and totally inexcusable; men feeling vulnerable at a potential loss of control, power and tradition is evolution, their reaction is totally and unforgivably evil.

Women have for a long time been brought up to deny their own sexuality. It is very sad and is probably the result of male invoked controls, preferences and constructs. Worse still, some cultures and religions have adopted female genital mutilation in any or all of its absolutely horrific guises. This 'rite of passage', illegal in Europe, has traditionally been performed by women on young girls. The rates of infection, sterility and death resulting from these procedures are mind-boggling. The ongoing psychological trauma is unimaginable. One cannot begin to understand this barbaric ritual. If you are interested in finding more about this subject, and feeling very brave, much information about it is available on the Internet.

An interesting extension of the FGM debate which is almost never raised – and certainly not in direct association with FGM – is male circumcision. Not that which is performed in a hospital for very specific medical reasons but that which is performed daily throughout the world as a ritual of religious belief. The procedure itself and the life-long effects of it are very less severe than FGM but, nonetheless, it would be interesting to hear an informed discussion on this matter too. Is the mutilation of a boy's genitals in some way of less concern, of less value?

When it comes to the etiquette of the toilet, it is a very different situation for girls and women when compared to that for males. Females are allocated one 'cubicle' each so as to ensure total privacy. But, considering that they sit down when urinating and therefore expose nothing but some of their underclothes it does seem rather biased when compared to the male who cannot hide his penis when standing shoulder to shoulder with other males and urinating. There are a very limited number of cubicles in male toilets compared to the availability of urinals; and, the social conditioning which makes standing at a urinal a more masculine, almost competitive, ritual also makes using a cubicle a statement that you are either 'strange' in some way or not just urinating. I'm sure that it would be feasible for women to enjoy the same community spirit as men by sitting next to each other on a long communal bench or a series of individual seats, to perform their task without losing any of the dignity not afforded to men; it would, doubtless, lessen the likelihood of long queues at ladies toilets. Or, perhaps, another option would be for men to also have individual facilities each enclosed in its own closet. Indeed if both sexes were to use closets would there even be a need for separate toilet facilities?

Would unisex comfort rooms be the ultimate in equality? In many French public toilets, and in some bars and cafés, it is not unusual for the facilities to be unisex. The men's urinal is usually to be found in an outer 'lobby' which must be passed through to get to the toilet cubicle. Thus, a woman wanting to go to the toilet cubicle would either have to pass closely behind a man peeing at the urinal or wait for him to finish, give it a shake, and move out of her way.

An interesting extension of the use of toilet facilities by women, and particularly young women, is the trend to go to the toilets with a friend – and not always just into the lobby of the unit but into the actual closet; for a chat, one presumes. So, perhaps a communal toilet would appeal to the convivial female spirit? Can you just imagine the outcome if one male were to say to another male 'I'm just going to the toilet, do you want to come too?' and then to go further and invite him to share the intimacy of the same closet.

Women tend to show compassion towards others – because they have been brought up to know its worth and to value it – thus, it is only natural for other women to show them compassion in return. Women can show compassion to each other, to children, to men, to strangers, to animals and even to some inanimate objects. From early in their lives, men are not exposed to giving or receiving compassion; they are taught to be emotionally self-contained – thus, they rarely show compassion in the same way that women do. It is an alien emotion to men; men are unidimensional beings. Many women's lives are perfumed by their caring and sharing; whilst men's lives can reek of their aggressive domination, their self-imposed isolation and of their loneliness.

The media always used to depict men as being the main bread-winner, the protector, the head of the household; the woman was the mother, home-maker and carer. Each knew their roles; they were unambiguous and mutually supportive. This is how an ideal life was portrayed.

The *Men Behaving Badly* TV programme showed young men submerged in a world of fantasy, often watching videos and computer games, and how they become obsessed by sex and ribald humour and are unable to communicate meaningfully with women – which had always been a difficult task for the male of the species. Many females saw it as a scenario too true to be funny. Young women in full-time employment generally earn more money than young men; and yet, often, they still expect the men to pay on the first dates (just look around at such behaviour in any of our bars and restaurants) and it is not until later in their relationship that they will split the cost of joint ventures. Females still expect the male to initiate a first date; it is not considered a very feminine attribute to instigate courtship; women should initially appear shy and unattainable – that makes them of higher value. Something which is easy to attain does not have the same kudos; traditionally, women who 'throw' themselves at men are likely to end up having a nasty fall. Perhaps Irving Berlin's song lyrics were right – 'a man chases a woman until she catches him'. But, nonetheless, is always expecting the male to instigate the initial steps of a first date and to pay for it a good way to establish a union of equals. But then how would the males react if the female took the dominant role, if they wanted to pay the bill too?

Nowadays, in certain quarters, the male is popularly characterised as an inept and almost superfluous adjunct to a woman or, worse still, as a dominant misogynist. Women don't necessarily need men but, they still want them; as long as it can be on their terms. It is not at all surprising that many men may have lost their way, lost a sense of self, a sense of purpose; but, have women found a new and potent identity. They may well have broken into erstwhile closed areas of the world of work but in most cases not in place of other domestic duties but as well as. In a survey of 3,500 people in 2013, commissioned by white goods manufacturer Beko, married women or those in relationships appear to have eight hours less free time than men each week. Some of the causes are put down to shopping, cooking and cleaning; more than a third of women would rather have a clean and tidy home than a holiday, a good night out or even sex. Whilst men may do some home maintenance, mowing the grass or maintaining the car, it is women's lives which are dominated by domestic chores. And women are not happy with the split of responsibilities!

For men, if you want to live longer, get married. Research from nearly a third of a million participants now shows that you will have a 20 per cent better chance of surviving a life-threatening illness if you are in a happy marriage or long-term relationship. It seems that being 'nagged' into visiting a medical practitioner sooner rather than later may be a large part of what helps men; single men just seem not to bother going to see a doctor until it is too late. For women, being more 'body-aware' helps discover problems early whilst having a supportive network of friends and family is a great positive factor in their recovery.

For women, Alzheimer's disease and dementia may be detrimentally affected by stress earlier in life says a *BMJ* article. A study of 800 Swedish women began, back in 1968, looking at women born in the early part of the 20th century and followed them at regular intervals for the next four decades. Their exposure to any of a list of 18 life stressing experiences, including divorce, close family illness or death, were noted. The more stresses encountered the greater the chances of being affected by harmful changes in the body in later life – between 15 and 20 per cent of those being surveyed were diagnosed with dementia or Alzheimer's. Stress is known to have a bad effect on blood pressure and heart disease and increases levels of all stress hormones at the time and this may well be 'stored-up' in the body. The Alzheimer's Society is calling for further investigation.

According to the Office for National Statistics, most women are happy with their life-work balance. Half believe the relationship between work and their social life is pretty good and well over 10 per cent believe it to be nigh on perfect (somehow, I don't think that I have met any of the type of women who completed this survey). Meanwhile, at the other end of the spectrum, 25 per cent were unhappy with their lot. Women seem to choose to spend more of their time with their children, families and friends rather than be at work longer. Childcare by a third party is not as high on their 'wish-list' as having the work-life balance to allow them to spend time looking after their children themselves. When women have problems they mainly use chocolate and talking to friends as therapy; whereas, when men have problems they use drink, solitude and aggression.

In the past few decades some women, and particularly young women, have been drinking alcohol to excess. Drinking alcohol causes an increase in the level of testosterone in women's bodies and, therefore, an increase in testosterone induced behaviour. According to the *Mail Online*, women rather than men are now more likely to be the perpetrators of crimes of violence. In 2009 there were 88,139 women arrested for crimes involving violence in 12 months; that's 250 each day. In the period from 2002 to 2010 the number of such offences doubled.

Lifestyles are changing; going to the pub for a drink or going to the cinema to see a film are now activities regularly pursued by only 50 per cent of the adult population. And, by a strange coincidence, the same sort of percentage are now regularly participating in activities such as jogging, cycling and visiting the gym. The smoking ban, drink-driving regulations and cheaper alcohol at supermarkets are blamed for the demise of 'drinking' pubs whilst in-home cinema equipment, downloads on-line and digital television services have left cinema seats empty.

In a recent survey, women nearing retirement age found more things to be optimistic about in their future than men did – perhaps not too surprising considering they are likely to live longer than their male peers. Two-thirds of them thought that they were less venerated by society in comparison to their own grandparents and felt misunderstood by the government.

Women are now setting the ground rules for marriage and they are finding men lacking. The statistics for England and Wales are recorded by the Office of National Statistics. The current population is around 62 million; the latest annual figures show the number of marriages being 234,464. Divorces are recorded as 'granted' to the person (or, occasionally, persons in a joint divorce where both agree) suing for divorce and thus the statistics are recorded in the same manner. In 2013 there were 114,720 divorces (thus, just under 50 per cent of the number of marriages in the same year) of which 65 per cent were granted to the wife and 35 per cent were granted to the husband; 0.01 per cent were joint divorces. Those figures represent a decrease of 2.9 per cent on the previous year. A decade earlier, in 2003, the total was 153,065 and it gradually fell between then and 2009 to a figure of 113,949; the number of divorces has remained fairly stable since then. In 2013 the majority of divorces were granted to persons between the ages of 30–50; the average duration of the marriages was 11.5 years. For 71 per cent it was the first marriage for both of them; for 29 per cent one or both had been divorced before (in 19 per cent of all marriages one or more people were divorcees). As an historic footnote, in 1911, over a century ago, the number of marriages was 274,943 (40,000 more than now) and the number of divorces was just 580 (114,140 fewer than now); the population then was 36 million which is around half of the current population.

Women's stress related illnesses rise and overworked women are tired, angry and frustrated; they are not feeling the glow of a victorious battle against men. When they shut the front door they are alone, lonely, exhausted. The men are, meanwhile, sitting alone in a bar or in front of a TV in a bedsit, with a drink in hand, unkempt and uncaring, unable to understand the root cause of their predicament. It is predicted that 25 per cent of all adults will be living as permanent singletons (albeit with children – in the case of many women) by the end of the decade. Since the 1960s women's suicide rates have fallen by well over 30 per cent; men's suicide rates have risen by almost 20 per cent; an irrefutable indicator of the true effects of gender-biased stress. All this has occurred over the same period of time that female inspired equality issues have gathered such a strong following.

Women like to gossip; gossip is just a casual conversation about another person – hopefully, one who is not present – and includes giving a wide-ranging appraisal of that person which is based on the speaker's personal opinion and is not necessarily true. From my perspective, men are not good at gossip; they tend to talk about things or about abstracts or, if talking about people, it is more commonly about those such as football or cricket personalities and based on their performance rather than on their personal qualities. In numerous modes of Internet search on the subject the system automatically defers to the negative dynamics of conversations between men and women. When it comes to examining everyday conversations between men it seems that men have got very little to say about it; how very out of character.

Many modern women have adopted another erstwhile male role by becoming the ones who run the home finances as well as the domestic arrangements because of their superior organisational abilities. Balancing books on the head for deportment has become an analogy for women to adopt the position of balancing the books in their private lives, often of the entire housekeeping budget. Women who become the 'breadwinners' can soon become disillusioned and uncomfortable with that lifestyle – just as some men have always been. Work for most people is boring, monotonous and uninspiring, even when initially motivated by the job. Younger women can escape by looking to an alternative, and socially acceptable, role for themselves as mothers and home-keepers; men do not have the same luxury. Women have easily been adopted into the world of work whilst continuing the roles of child-carer and home-maker; the few men who have tried have found any move in the opposite direction a painful and difficult, if not impossible, transition.

It is accepted that women can and do 'cross-dress' by wearing trousers, suits, shirts and ties; and, that it is legitimate for women to adopt a masculine demeanour when they feel drawn to do so. Men, on the other hand, cannot wear dresses or show feminine behavioural traits without being subjected to ridicule. Michelle Obama may sometimes wear a smart trouser-suit in public and, whilst wearing it she displays a more masculine deportment – but, if Barack were to appear in public wearing a skirt...

Women have all of the options normally open to women and now, at great pace, they are adding as many male advantages as they find appealing.

Women can have their hair dyed, wear a variety of colours, lengths and styles of wigs and hair extensions, they use coloured contact lenses and distort their true identity behind a mask of cosmetics. Their ballet and gymnastics lessons have taught them, from early childhood, about deportment, body language and how to stand prettily. Even those who did not attend such groups watch and learn from the behaviour of their peers. Their magazines are full of tips on how to look like someone else. With men, what you see is what you get; little wonder men are confused. And, who exactly are women strutting their stuff for, whose attention are they really dressing to attract? They say that it's just for their own pleasure but it's a bit of a coincidence that they tend to wear clothes which they know attract male attention when attending venues where there will be eligible men around yet when on their own or just 'chilling' with friends they don't make such an effort. And you expect men to be truthful with you?

Well, what did you expect, a reverential eulogy to women's eternally undervalued greatness? Scientists, historians, writers, social commentators, comedians; they have historically and almost exclusively been men; society's opinions are male, society's perspective is male, society's value system is male, society's hierarchy is male. Society's voice is a male voice and, it's basso profundo.

Not for long. The most her victims may ever be aware of is a light rustling in the long grass but, she has been following closely, watching their every move for a long time; she has been assessing their strengths and weaknesses. She is biding her time; when she is certain of overpowering her prey the Tigress will pounce. Struggle will be futile.

CHAPTER 8
DOGGED MEN

No-one doubts that ladies love a new puppy-dog. It is a magnetic attraction, not a learned behaviour. Instinct draws her to him; the anticipation initially causes the blood to rush through her body. Intuitively she knows the benefits of being close to him, of those tender cuddles together; she is now totally relaxed, deep inside she feels the same sort of glow that she gets when she eats chocolate, her blood pressure slows, she is at one with her world. On finding that special one, one needing a new owner, she immediately starts to imagine a life together and just how much fun it could be training him to become her 'pet'. She wants a companion, not a guard dog.

His puppy-dog nature made her smile. He appeared adorable, friendly, exuberant, uncomplicated, unquestioning, undemanding, his tail showed her that he was always ready to please her, and so much in need of her loving, her care; she saw in him the potential to be loyal and trustworthy, her very own special friend. She knew that she was infatuated, becoming immersed in 'puppy love' – and yet willingly accepting it as the potential beginning of her dog's life.

Puppies do, and indeed must, grow up. And he will need constant training, right from the start. It does not matter if you have a pedigree, a fine cross-breed or just a mongrel. You have to be cruel to be kind, they say – it pays in the long run. Not necessarily overt obedience training classes of course but, gentle day upon day of intensive behavioural management and conditioning. A deed well done deserves a fitting reward. Inappropriate conduct – if not the subject of actual physical chastisement, then, certainly an immediate reprimand; a very minor misdemeanour might just be treated as 'ignored behaviour'. Totally intolerable behaviour – absolute and immediate punishment; not to be pardoned until forgiveness has been earnestly sought. He must be trained.

For some, their only credible option is taking on an older dog and that is not such a carefree choice. It would be so good to have some company, the right company; knowing that there was always a tender welcome awaiting you. She might feel that she could give him a good home, be a caring new owner, to the right one – but, how to choose? Was he neglected, made homeless by the changing circumstances of an uncommitted previous owner, was he abandoned by someone who found him untrainable, is he a free-ranging drifter of unknown provenance, a stray who will stray? The stature of a strong breeding line is not necessarily a guarantee of potential impeccable behaviour; a cross-breed or mongrel may have picked up, by chance, the best of his forebears' behavioural traits or, equally, the worst. You cannot blame an old dog for the behaviour of his previous owner – can you? And all the time that still small voice keeps telling her that there is doubtless much truth in what they say about teaching an old dog new tricks!

So, what to do? If he becomes too problematic, untrainable, common sense dictates that the best course of action is that he should be rejected, so he might seek a more appropriate home; they often just run away if a door is left open – by mistake or intentionally – it happens all the time. Dogs released onto the streets tend to either join up with others of a similar nature and together form a predatory pack or, they become loners hiding in dark corners, slinking on the edge of the shadowlands. The advice of many of her peers would be to forget all about trying to find, let alone train, her own dog; get real, get a cat.

Men are endearingly uncomplicated when compared to women. They do not engage in the female arts of subterfuge and intrigue, especially in the courting game; they don't know how to and, if they did try their efforts would be embarrassingly gauche and they would be found out.

In the animal kingdom (although with a few notable exceptions) the male-female relationship is usually uncomplicated; it is based around the female coming into 'season', the males vying for her favour, she choosing one (or sometimes more), they mate and then go their separate ways until next time. Sometimes he stays around for her protection but often he is like an uninvited guest. It seems that the human ideal of being in a (fairly?) monogamous, mutually supportive, life-enduring relationship of equals has the potential to become the downfall of our species.

Sex is the guilty party in so many inter-gender conflicts and Mother Nature makes sure that the world is full of contradictions. For instance, most male birds do not have penises, they mate by just touching their genital opening against the female bird's genital opening; then there is the Argentine lake duck. It has a 17-inch (yes, 17-inch) spiral penis; it is proportionally, the largest of any vertebrate. The python has two penises each with a hook on to stop the female trying to get away, and the Argonaut octopus has a penis which detaches from his body and goes off on a mission of its own seeking a female to impregnate. And we complain about the complications of our sex lives.

The male human is frequently castigated for being the dominant partner in sex yet, the depictions of sex from Greek and Roman times show many more incidences of the woman being on top as opposed to the other way around; it may be that is a true representation of the trend in that period or it may just be that it makes a more aesthetically pleasing picture. In surveys of the most popular sexual positions, such as in *The Independent* on 11th February 2015, modern women say that they prefer the missionary position or spooning but not 'cowgirl' because they feel too exposed on top because they are very body conscious; heads you win, tails you lose. Men, generally, prefer it when the woman is on top; but, in truth, they are just pleased to be having sex, regardless of the position.

The length of time eye contact is held with another person is of great importance. Normally, we keep direct eye contact to a series of 'bursts' of a few seconds. As a sexual 'come-on' signal the length of each eye contact should be slightly longer; too long and it will be felt as being 'creepy'. However, two men challenging each other – especially where the likely outcome could be physical violence – will hold constant eye contact with each other. Diverting the eyes would be seen as a form of defeat.

At the end of a period of hunting our early male ancestors would have sat in front of a fire watching the flames, relaxing and contemplating. For them it recharged and refreshed the body and the soul; it was essential to their well-being. The same needs are there today; the male needs a time of quiet retreat and contemplation before being in a position to face the new challenges in his world; face to face interpersonal communication with a woman is a form of stress-inducing challenge for a male. When a woman is unhappy with her man she will often not speak to him – as a form of punishment. The reason that she does this is that for a woman to be denied verbal communication imposes unwelcome isolation. For a man, the silence is not a punishment but a release from the pressure to 'make small talk'. This type of stress relief is essential to the function of a male; it may involve watching the news or sport on TV (seeing other people's problems helps to take his mind off his own and can put them into perspective), a drink in the pub on the way home, going on the computer, jogging, mowing the grass or best of all (though least likely) having uncomplicated sex.

Male hunters often had to be able to find their way home in an unfamiliar environment, without aid, when returning from a long hunting trip; thus many more modern men than women retain the primeval ability to point towards the north (or in the direction of an intended destination) instinctively. Thus, men do not like to admit to a lack of these skills and will, only reluctantly, ask directions; an in-car sat nav is a welcome saviour from this predicament. Women rarely travelled far from the home area and therefore had no need for this ability as they could always rely on familiar landmarks. They navigate best by the recognition of 'things' – not by a set of directions or a map; to ask for directions is merely another opportunity for a personal interaction.

The morals and emotions required to successfully kill animals or the enemy have always been a part of the nature of a man; he cannot easily be soft and emotional (like a woman nowadays may often want him to be) he needs to be hard and dispassionate to be able to survive violence at an emotional level and this can make it difficult for him to be a compassionate and affectionate lover; often, as a result of this same testosterone driven behaviour, his sex act is also quite aggressive and unemotional too. This is an innate facet of being a male; trying to curb or deny this behaviour is counter to his essence and therefore does not come easily. And, the next time there is a war or some other situation requiring the benefits of testosterone induced behaviour he will be expected to revert to type. A man's identity is defined by his work; when he retires or loses his job he also loses that identity and thus the reason for his existence.

Traditionally, men dressed to intimidate and frighten their enemies; thus, they wore the skins of large animals with the ferocious head still intact and displayed above their own adding height and a certain grandeur. Frequently, animal bones and teeth were attached to various parts of their bodies too. Later headdresses, armour and even military uniforms performed a similar function. Women seem to have always dressed to look more beautiful both to their peers and to look attractive to a mate; in the absence of jewellery they may have worn flowers in their hair, a practice still popular in many areas of the world today.

Nowadays, with men, jeans, shirts, jumpers, suits and a few pairs of shoes are all that is needed for most occasions; and the same clothes, if kept well, can be worn for years without social stigma. If shopping alone they can be selected both quickly and easily and with a very restricted need for colour variation or co-ordination. The inherited tracking ability and decision making of the hunter allows men to home in on a limited 'prey' option and to make a speedy 'kill' and then return to home with his shopping immediately. In more modern times, many men have allowed (often with great relief) the prominent woman in their life to advise on if not actually purchase their clothes; men get no great pleasure from shopping and if left to their own devices tend to make choices which their partners feel are inappropriate. A man and a woman shopping for clothes together, be they for him or for her, has the potential for conflict.

Research, mainly in northern Europe, by Professor Daniel Kruger of the University of Michigan, as published in *The Journal of*

Social, Evolutionary and Cultural Psychology, has looked at our gender based shopping strategies and has come to these conclusions. The differences exist and are marked; there is a high probability that they originate from our diverse prehistoric roles as either a 'hunter' or as a 'gatherer'.

Men going clothes shopping with women are in unsafe territory and can be sure that whatever they say, whatever their opinion, they will be completely wrong. Men do not understand the importance of colour and style co-ordination, the subtle nuances between one detail and another, the need to look at so many different options and then to return and repeat the process in a slightly different order and on numerous occasions until the correct purchases are made, or not. Like picking berries you must find the right ones, wait for those to ripen and then to discard those no longer in their prime. For a woman to have spent the day clothes shopping (preferably with female company) and to return having hardly bought anything is not seen as a defeat but as an interesting exploratory trip giving the need for future forays.

In a food shopping scenario men tend to start at one end of the supermarket and then traipse up and down the aisles in order, picking up regularly purchased items and occasional 'spur of the moment' purchases. Unlike most women, they infrequently have meal plans in mind or think up menus 'on the go' dependent on what is on offer or what seems to be a bargain deal. Women will usually have a list, not a definitive list but a list of options, and sometimes appear to flit from aisle to aisle as though a bee collecting pollen from various flower-laden plants.

Sales of health foods, dietary supplements and grooming products, purchased by men in a bid to stave off the ageing process, have risen over the period from 2007–2012; in the UK they rose by 12 per cent, in the US by 20 per cent and globally by 70 per cent – according to researchers Mintel. There is no longer a stigma for males; it has now become more socially acceptable for men to buy grooming and health products. Sales of women's and children's products have grown too. Does a larger percentage of the population being older generate the market – or, does seeing large numbers of older people motivate younger people to try to stay young?

Few boys reach adulthood with many social or domestic skills because of their mothers. Mothers tend to do everything for their boys including cooking their favourite foods, keeping them, their clothes and rooms clean and tidy; they protect and nurture them. How can a young man leave home and live comfortably without soon having to find a woman who will continue this process and also provide him with sex as the adult 'bonus'. If he finds someone who treats him like his mother did then the chances are he will treat her just as he did his mother. This is fine if both parties are happy with their respective roles; and many are. Some men find that modern emancipated women are too threatening thus a market has evolved for men to find brides from cultures where traditionally dominant male roles are still acceptable Just remember that, as I have said before, men are uncomplicated and easily trained; being cross with them or nagging them will not get positive results. Accept the different learning and behavioural patterns between you and you could have a rewarding asset.

It is easy to understand why evolution has depressed the sense of empathy in males. Men needed to be as single minded when chasing and killing an animal as they were killing and mutilating in war. To feel empathy for your quarry, your victim, your foe – to think of them as another living being with a family – is not a good mindset to have when you are about to kill them or be killed by them. This way of thinking and behaving had always been a potent driver for survival which was not to be quashed by the more civilising influences of the post Industrial Revolution era; indeed, it is still evident today.

Looking at young boys and their duvet covers shows their male role models are mostly super beings, like Superman, Spider-man, kung fu fighters, special agents, etc. They are infallible righters of all things wrong, they instinctively know the answer to complex questions and always kill the baddie and get 'the girl'. They show no hint of emotion as, time and again, they save the virtue and life of their devastatingly beautiful female. They are never married or apparently in a meaningful long-term relationship. So, what a surprise that boys arrive at adulthood feeling that they have been and will continue to be unable to emulate their role models – but somehow they cannot expunge the implied pressure to be that person. Throughout his life a man will be reinforcing his sense of failure every time he does not fulfil a 'mission' – be that passing his exams, getting a job, mending his car, finding the 'right' girl or, later, putting up a shelf or keeping his woman happy.

Men internalise, they do not show or share their feelings easily even with loved ones and, most certainly, with their male peers. Small talk, with its bonding effects on relationships, is alien to them; a skill which men have never mastered. The difference starts early, research has shown that in the womb girl babies move their jaws much more frequently than boys do and that women use twice as many words in their daily life as men. Men's conversation tends to be focussed; they do not appreciate the social bonding that 'small-talk' can have for women.

Unlike women, men cannot talk and listen at the same time; in their conversations they need to be able take turns. Their conversations involve things and facts, not people and emotions. They may know about a friend's new car or golf handicap but not about the well-being of their family. Men were always naturally polygamous because of their sex drive and often they had rarity value; so many were killed either in hunting or in battle thus the surviving males were able to create a loosely formed 'harem' with the widows and their families. The younger daughters, not being directly related, were also viable mating partners. In our modern world it seems that women do not want young virile men to pursue their daughters; women want to look like their daughters and thus to have the young men pursue them.

Allegedly, Adam had to give up a rib to create Eve; she then took a forbidden apple from the Tree of Knowledge in the Garden of Eden so that she could have the power and wisdom of God and thereby impress Adam and hope that he would have his evil way with her. Thus men like to eat a rack of ribs when available whilst a woman would opt for a piece of fruit. Some might say that ever since, history has been repeating itself; men's primeval drives have had the potential to be exploited and used by women. Shouldn't equality have decreed a rather different scenario?

If men are having sex with numerous women whilst women prefer to 'keep themselves' and have far fewer male sexual partners – who are the men having sex with; is there a small minority of exceedingly 'oversubscribed' women or is it all just a male fantasy? If so, why do males need to create such untruths; is it for the benefit of other men, does it imply status?

Like almost the entire animal kingdom male humans are not naturally monogamous and when they do make such a commitment it is a matter of the frontal lobe of the brain imposing its will over the older and stronger natural instincts and drives; thus they frequently find it hard to stay monogamous in spirit if not in practice. The more self-reliant a man is in his own lifestyle the less easy it is for him to capitulate, to make the decision to commit to a monogamous relationship. For a man who has been brought up by his mother to be reliant on her, as an adult, he will still be in need of a woman's care and thus the motivation to commit is much stronger – albeit for all the wrong reasons.

A man's friends will joke that being in a committed relationship or getting married will end his freedoms and self-determination as well as his sex life, as can be seen in the treatment of most grooms by their peers on 'stag nights'. There have always been all-male pre-wedding celebrations called 'stag nights'; nowadays, sadly, they often descend into rowdy, drunken and antisocial public exhibitions of excess. When did the traditional, and much more discreet, female equivalent called 'hen parties' also turn into excuses for drunken excesses rivalling those of the worst 'stag party' and should anyone be surprised that, because of the behaviour of some of the participants, they will soon be known by some as 'slag parties'.

In an imaginary world, men can almost visualise a single's life with all the freedoms, social contacts, good looks and sexual exploits that would enable them to live the lifestyle of a James Bond type hero; the bleak reality for most, however, is rather more mundane. Therefore, the loss of his theoretical lifestyle is less significant than the everyday changes which will most certainly occur when he commits to a real-life relationship. An independent, self-reliant man who is just enjoying dating can be unaware of having triggered a woman's sense that their dating has now developed into a relation-ship which she feels is committed, monogamous and potentially permanent and thus of her expectation of equal commitment from him. His perspective may be that wedlock sounds more like an implement of torture rather than a blissful unity.

Men frequently slide into permanent relationships unknowingly; one minute he is having a physical relationship with a woman whom he gets on with and then he gradually becomes aware that she, her friends and family have decided that it is a permanent, long-term relationship; then, unwittingly, he is trapped. To try to extricate himself would be more difficult than to continue. Unlike a woman, he does not have the network of friends with whom to discuss the situation.

Men solve problems, practical problems (but, they cannot easily understand or solve emotional problems) – their jobs frequently revolve around solving practical problems; to their partners they can often appear to be good at mending things around the house too. They equate solving problems for their partner as caring, as an act of love. Many of them relate their own self-worth against such abilities and their spouses will often note the status of other males as being good at making or repairing, of being practical. Men like to amass tools for such jobs; these 'toys' are status symbols. Those who cannot or will not, perform such tasks (and cannot afford for someone else to do them on a regular basis) are made to feel of lesser worth than those who can. If he seeks advice it will be from some-one whom he believes is more proficient at such things and he will act on their advice; to ask advice is a sign of inadequacy, to be asked for advice is a valuable status enhancer. To be given advice when it is not sought, on any matter, is like someone inferring that you are not up to the job, that you are incompetent. If a woman offers advice she is trying to communicate and probably 'improve' her man in some way; he sees it as a statement of his inadequacy and the lack of her confidence in him.

His perspective is that 'if you tell me problems you will get solu-tions, if you don't want solutions then don't bother telling me your problems; sort them out yourself'. If a woman talks about a situation or a problem she is not necessarily seeking advice or a solution. The act of talking about things happening in her life is, for her, both cathartic and a way of bonding with others. She just wants to be able to talk and for him to just listen – without offering solutions for everything that is happening in her life. But, he thinks that he is hearing a request, an opportunity to resolve a set of problems which he believes that he is being asked to consider and cannot stop himself from fulfilling that perceived role and giving solutions. Conflict ensues. She does not want to hear the advice which he believes she has just sought from him; he will not just allow her to talk and for him to just listen, without proffering advice.

And, in my experience, because a woman's behaviour and logic is currently being affected by her hormones it is not a good time for her man to talk to her about hormone issues; when she is not hormonal there are no problems; her man is trapped in an infinite loop – wrong if he does, wrong if he doesn't.

Nag (nagging), is the male word for a woman who is, in truth, trying to get her man to do things which will make him better nourished, less susceptible to illness, better presented: and, to ask him to do (or not do) a few things around the home which will make her life better. He is usually very aware of the kind intention, the truth and the wisdom of her words (statistics show that happily married men have far fewer ailments than single men). However, he uses this derogatory word as a sign of annoyance, a defence mechanism, to appear to not need the advice, because he wishes to be seen to be in control of all situations and therefore not needing such instruction, especially from her.

Women sometimes taunt men by saying that all men are bastards. Well, maybe some men do occasionally behave badly and deserve to be told that but, at the same time, not all people who act like bastards are men. They do say that when you point an accusing finger at someone else, three of your own fingers are also pointing back at you.

All human interactions, regardless of gender, age, relationship or status are subject to an ongoing game of 'consequences'. If you do (or don't do) this or say that or behave in this way I will react in that way – therefore the consequence of your action will be my reaction.

263

Nagging is purely a symptom of a communication problem and, as such, is not a particularly surprising facet of some relationships. A reaction to an action (or words) or lack thereof. The logic behind both the male and female positions is apparent; the use of the derogatory word engenders hostility between them. Miscommunication is the problem; communication is the remedy.

Women who resort to constant and intense nagging often do so as a reaction to the feeling of being unloved and undervalued, of diminished self-worth and of personal powerlessness. She may feel that her man is not performing as she would wish or that he is immature; he will be accused of behaving childishly and will eventually, like a self-fulfilling prophesy, perform this exact role. Thus their relationship begins to morph into that of a mother and a child. These are both roles which, from their own childhoods, they are aware of and can easily replicate. Like a naughty child he will retreat to the solace of some substitute for his childhood (or teenage) bedroom, go silent, go inwards and sulk; if pushed he will become belligerent. This almost creates an Oedipus complex and is not a healthy position from which to approach any adult sexual relationship.

Women who have gained a position of power and control over their man have frequently acquired it covertly; they achieve this by providing an irresistible 'rewards' system to motivate the man (often with food, but most potently, through fulfilling all his sexual needs, desires and fantasies). These men are usually not aware of being controlled and look forward to their rewards so avidly that they willingly perform appropriate behaviour. Men cannot recognise or, perhaps, choose not to appear to recognise a woman's subtle cues and agendas; men are uncomplicated, they take words and actions at face value, can easily be satisfied and therefore readily trained. These are women who do not often have negative behavioural problems with their men.

At a practical level, research and experience shows that a woman has the ability to multi-task whilst a man does not; it should be clear that a man will frequently shut-off to repeated instructions or become aggressive; often he is already trying to process some previous information. Like a simple machine he can only process single units of information – he is not being difficult he just does not have the capacity to multi-task at a physical or mental level. Stood in front of a drinks machine you must do one process at a time (unless there is a special button for your particular request). You must first push the button for a coffee, then the button to add milk, then the button to add sugar; if you push any of the buttons before the previous process has been completed the machine will malfunction or break down due to information overload. Man is that machine.

Most comedians are men; from schooldays onwards, males remember and adapt jokes; it can make them popular and they act as a form of bonding and de-stressing. On the Internet there were hundreds of jokes posted within days of the New York 9/11 terrorist plane crashes – some of which have been examined in the book *September 11 in Popular Culture – A Guide* by Sara E. Quay and Amy M. Damico. Laughing and crying are, physiologically speaking, very closely linked to each other and provide the same sort of physical relief because they cause the release of endorphins thus protecting us from the harmful chemicals that would otherwise be produced by our bodies in stressful situations. Men in stressful situations, such as soldiers in the field of conflict, use swearing and, often politically incorrect, humour as a release valve. Under excessive stress, women tend to cry, men tend to joke; they are both serving the same purpose; don't be angry, don't be judgemental, of the means of stress reduction used by the opposite gender. Happy people make healthy people.

People respond differently to crying and laughing. Crying can be used in a manipulative way, usually by women and girls, to gain control of a situation, to gain attention or to gain things. The expression 'emotional blackmail' is often used to describe this latter type of behaviour. Laughing is never used in this way. Crying, as a learned behaviour, can be used by someone to try to exonerate themselves from blame or to lessen a potential punishment. A behaviour adopted in early childhood. Babies cry to cause an action, to alleviate hunger or discomfort which in turn creates a protective bond with their carers; women can also use tears when looking for comfort or when distressed, most particularly whilst in a 'safe' environment. Crying in reaction to unexpected grief is not controlled in the same way. Crying men are seen as vulnerable – not a good attribute in a protector.

Research has shown that in most cultures males, as opposed to females, are the ones who have an innate predilection for using strength (though not always physical strength), aggression and a competitive nature to determine and to improve status. Whilst some women can and do use similar strategies, in general, the female uses cooperation, social and interpersonal skills to achieve the same ends; they are also more risk-averse.

Most killing, most physical hurt – be it in fights, battles or even of animals – has been perpetrated by men and these were situations where there was one victor. Risk-taking in males seems to emerge just as puberty, and thus the hormone testosterone, begins to make its presence felt. Taking a risk, for a chance at the big prize, is a male trait – from gambling to mountaineering. Testosterone, which can enhance positive male traits associated with 'winning', can in extremis cause seriously antisocial behaviour. In tests, animals of both genders that were given extra testosterone showed more aggressive behaviour.

Most aggression is inflicted by males, most crimes are committed by males and most people convicted and punished for committing crimes are males; most psychopaths are males. Capital punishment has historically meant 'losing the head' – execution by beheading. It has been the ultimate penalty imposed by rulers on their peers, their subjects and their enemies and has been recorded since the 18th century BCE in Babylon. To show that this sentence had been carried out, and as a method of reinforcing the power of law, the executions were carried out in public. In reality, decapitation was only one of the methods used.

In the Middle Ages in England the authorities used 'drowning-pits' and the gallows as their preferred sanctions. For a short time in the 11th century execution was banned by William the Conqueror. He abhorred the taking of life, except in battle; however, he found mutilation an acceptable alternative punishment.

Ever since the medieval period (5–15th centuries) it has been the custom that children under 12 years of age were, in general, treated as below the age of criminal responsibility. From the age of 12 years they were seen to be subject to the Anglo-Saxon system of 'Frankpledge'. In this system there was a mutual responsibility between the members of a family group of adults, each for the other, for their actions and behaviour. They were responsible both to the judicial control of their 'hundred' and to their liege, to whom they would have pledged their service.

However, children were regularly convicted of crimes. Criminal responsibility once began at seven years old and there were numerous crimes with a mandatory death sentence for children aged 7–13 years old. However, the death sentence was usually commuted for these crimes – but not always. Records show that it was the girls who were seldom hanged or even severely punished for their crimes whereas the boys were frequently convicted and punished – and, for much less serious offences.

From the 14th century, a child of under 12 years of age could be convicted of a crime if a judge believed that they knew the difference between right and wrong. Trying to avoid the consequences of your actions was seen as proof of your culpability. There was no set minimum age for convictions. According to information recorded in the parish records by Sir Thomas Butler, a vicar and former abbot of Much Wenlock, in 1546 Alice Glaston of Little Wenlock, aged 11, was hanged with two others for an unspecified crime. Possibly the youngest boy to be hanged was eight-year-old John Dean; he was convicted of arson and hanged in 1629.

Since the 17th century, by law, a child could not be prosecuted under the age of seven, and from that age up to 14 years their ability to tell right from wrong had to be proven before they could be prosecuted. From the 18th century death sentences on pregnant women were always commuted. Up to the beginning of the 19th century there were a total of 220 crimes punishable by death including, 'strong evidence of malice in a child of 7–14 years of age'.

The Children's Act 1908 determined that a child under 16 years of age could no longer be executed. The age of criminal responsibility remained at seven years right up to the Children and Young Person's Act 1933 which determined the minimum age of criminal responsibility as just eight years old. In the Children and Young Person's Act 1963 this minimum age for criminal responsibility was increased to 10 years. That statute remains in force today.

Execution Statistics (children were not listed separately):

- 1735–1799: 6,069 men were executed; 375 women were executed

- 1800–1899: 3,365 men were executed; 172 women were executed

- 1900–1964: 748 men were executed; 15 women were executed

- Totals: 10,182 men were executed; 562 women were executed.

The last execution in the UK was in1964. Capital punishment for adults remained on the statute book until:

- 1965 for murder

- 1971 for setting fire to or causing an explosion in a naval dockyard

- 1981 for espionage

- 1998 for piracy with violence

- 1998 for treason

- Since 1998 capital punishment has been banned in the UK.

What might be the historic causes of almost 20 times more men than women being executed? It is a gender based difference, just as there is a gender based difference in prison populations in the UK, and other countries in Europe, in the 21st century. There are about 85,000 inmates in prisons in the UK of whom less than five per cent are women. Whilst there is no irrefutable and universally agreed explanation it has been generally accepted that the male's traditional roles within society have a part to play. Males are protectors and providers, they are more aggressive than women. When, through a combination of influences, they have not been socially educated well enough to ensure that they can get work to provide for their family's needs they become frustrated and feel degraded and inadequate. As a man, he feels that providing money is his responsibility and that women rightly expect to be cared for. This feeling of impotence can lead to a belligerent antisocial reaction, they have little to lose whatever they do; in situations of social confrontation they lose their tempers easily which in turn makes them less acceptable to society as a whole and often results in a low grade custodial sentence. They are now stigmatised as social outsiders, but they do have a place of honour in the greater family of criminals; so, they now accept that the only way for someone like them to get money is to take it from those who have, he believes, got a greater and undeserved level of wealth than him. Getting caught becomes an occupational risk factor, a potential consequence which he must accept.

When women commit a crime it is usually a less serious offence, one of lower quality in its execution, they commit such crimes less frequently and their criminal careers are usually quite short. The fact that there are fewer women in prison could equally be the result of women being more devious, better at perpetrating crime without being caught, of being more effective criminals. Most criminal gangs are male dominated and they seem to not want active female members; they see women in a support role. Women are more likely to receive a caution or a fine and in general judges are more lenient with them; except, it seems, when their crime is such that the judge believes their wrongdoing to be completely at odds with the nature of women in general (child abuse etc.).

Subsequent to their man's incarceration, supportive women and families can have a positive influence on criminals but often women find their partner's lifestyle too difficult to deal with. A prison sentence is a sentence for the prisoner's family too, it is a social stigma which affects the lives of their wife and their children; some women, understandably, give up on the situation, move away and try to start a new life somewhere else.

Only five per cent of the prison population is women. Over 50 per cent were abused as children, as opposed to 25 per cent of men; yet, they are twice as likely as men to have no previous convictions and over 25 per cent of women prisoners self-harm. Now, the Prison Reform Trust has been given a £1.2 million Lottery Grant to campaign against the number of women in prison. Proportionally, it would take a grant of £240 million to produce an equivalent situation with men; but, no-one seems interested in trying to follow that route. Less controversial to just leave the men in prison.

Because male-on-male competition, aggression and control is overt, it is easily identifiable; it always has been. For women to join the fray and compete openly with males is, on an evolutionary scale, a fairly recent phenomenon and carries lots of social potency. Female-on-female competition has always been 'played down'; as if women, being more social creatures, could settle any of their differences in a mutually supportive way. But, 'the cat is out of the bag'; women don't just compete with each other for men they compete against each other in many areas of life. It's just that they usually manage to do so less overtly than men.

It is interesting that the period of life at which testosterone is at its most powerful coincides with the same period when the more spontaneous people in society achieve their zenith – be they entertainers or robbers. For those who develop later in life it is their age which gives them their ability to use accumulated wisdom, wealth and experience to succeed in place of the ever diminishing drug-induced testosterone frenzy of youth.

Many times more men than women, in their late teens and twenties, drive recklessly, become involved in extreme violence – from street crime to award-winning bravery in the armed forces, the police and the fire brigade – and risk-taking promoted through the use of alcohol and drugs. So often these men do not consider that they are taking risks – because they feel invincible; boredom is erased by the lack of predictability of danger. In wartime it breeds heroes. In everyday life it fathers both criminals and creators. Strength and aggression, paired with their unspoken fragility, can cause young men to lead an exciting but brutally short life.

Attention Deficit Hyperactivity Disorder, ADHD, is alleged to be one of the most common types of disorders of its kind worldwide. It is not surprising that it should be so widespread because it is caused by a chemical imbalance in the body, generally the body of a male (at least five males have it for every one female who does) and it is a human condition which is not linked in any way to race or ethnicity. The apparent differences between countries, or even much smaller regions, can frequently be attributed to the level of acceptance or otherwise, of more extreme behaviour. For females, it is depression that is the most prominent symptom of the disorder; and that is more socially acceptable.

ADHD is evidenced by inattention, impulsiveness and hyperactivity – although the latter can diminish somewhat after adolescence. It is frequently found to be more common amongst close male relatives. The once traditionally charming caricature of an eccentric English aristocrat would, perhaps, nowadays be diagnosed as illnesses such as ADHD, dyslexia – or inbreeding. Medical studies have traced numerous differences in the structure and function of the brains and genes of people suffering with ADHD. The conjecture for some researchers is that any one such difference is not enough on its own to be the sole indicator of the disorder but that it is diagnosed by the interaction of various and varied factors.

The medical parameters for identifying ADHD have softened over time; no longer is someone expected to fulfil all of the criteria – just certain parts of it. The effect of this has been to raise the numbers of people diagnosed with the disorder but, most interestingly, girls who had low attention spans but no impulsive or aggressive behaviour have now been included in the numbers which has skewed the male-female bias. It is not that there are now more girls with the disorder it is that the definition and criteria have changed.

Specific Language Impairment is a communication difficulty which is separate from other similar problems. It manifests itself in an inability to easily perform oral language tasks. The child knows in their head what they want to say but cannot easily put it into words or, they hear someone talking but cannot translate it into 'brain speak' quickly enough thus, they may look and feel stupid; it is not a sign of hearing difficulties or brain damage or a lack of intelligence and does not deserve the stigma it often brings. It does not appear to be caused by any one particular problem in the body or mind but rather a complex of small dysfunctions which together can cause difficulties in developing these oral and aural skills. If one identical twin has SLI then the other will have it too, if one non-identical twin has it the other twin probably will not have it; thus it is a biological problem with hereditary potential not one related to the child's upbringing. It is said to affect seven per cent of five-year-old children but there is no indication that it is gender specific.

Males have, through evolutionary development, become larger, stronger and more dominant than females and because of the way humans have lived until now this has reinforced his advantage. However, a negative side effect of being a male is the weakness caused by their biological and genetic make-up. Men have always been great at achieving because of their aggressive and competitive spirit. As a result of this drive some men have become heroes, some have made significant advances in many fields from exploration to sport.

However, many men have died or been injured as a result of the pursuit of these goals; many have committed suicide because they feel that they have failed to achieve what they believe the world expects of them (although these are, in reality, often self-imposed values). It is the level of testosterone which is to blame for most male 'weaknesses' as can be proven by the fact that eunuchs (castrati) live 13 years longer than their 'intact' counterparts. Many men have struggled in an education system which did not benefit their needs. And, even though they visit doctors less frequently, men have more illness and more serious results to those illnesses. They leave seeking medical opinion for their ailments until they have progressed to a serious level – just because going to see the doctor with something that turns out to not be life threatening would damage their macho self-image. Men's average life expectancy is lower than women's, their life insurance rates and car insurance costs are higher because they are more likely to have accidents; their pension rates are lower because they are less likely to live as long as a woman. Men see illness as a character defect.

In westernised society, for thousands of years, the transition from being a working class boy-child to a nascent adult male happened long before the boy reached puberty. In much of the developing and third worlds this continues today. His work would have been arduous and his day long. As he reached puberty he would be treated as a man and consequently most of the potency of his testosterone was intentionally channelled into a demand for a higher work rate and for performing a role fighting for his liege. By these life demands his carnal desires were being partially suppressed and controlled until their legitimate outcome through marriage. For those few born into families with wealth and power they would be expected to become role-models for their vassals and thus to become leaders of men. Their power and influence, however, allowed them more liberty in sexual encounters and to be immune from the consequences thereof.

For the upper classes, education became a valued and necessary currency. Sending these boys away to boarding schools until they were young men allowed them to be educated, controlled and disciplined by older and wiser men – far away from the more gentle and relaxed influences of their mothers and other female relatives.

Ever since the creation of the first British boarding school, thought to have been The King's School at Canterbury, Kent which dates from 597, they have had an unstated, and initially unintentional, outcome. Putting large numbers of boys and young men in close company with each other, all with their testosterone rising, had potential for explosive outcomes. The boys, deprived of the company of girls and young women, spend all their time together. They work and play together, share their ablutions and their sleeping arrangements; it caused an obvious, if not necessarily intended, outcome. Many boys and young men have their first sexual encounters at their boarding school; their education in such matters is able to be further developed over their time at school. It has the benefit of saving many young girls from the unwanted attentions of young males and their sexual needs. It gives these same males a necessary sexual relief – and, it also gives them a better understanding of the role of a sexual recipient as well as that of a donor. This education system continues…

Studying has frequently been seen as 'sissy' amongst many males whereas for women it has an aura of empowerment. Males can find reading, writing and study too difficult, homework is uncompleted and study is against their natural bent and their self-image. Unable to organise their own studies many boys have benefited from their mother's organisational skills. Females seem to find reading and writing easier, are more organised and self-disciplined; they understand and value deferred gratification. Limited opportunities used to be available to educated women but their world has begun to open up. Has the disparity in the learning abilities and styles of boys and girls become a reason for once again segregating them in schools – for at least some of the lessons?

The kitchens of restaurants worldwide, and of particular note those of top international chefs who have become celebrities, have, seemingly inexplicably, had very many staff with poor academic histories. Commercial kitchens in hotels and restaurants are hot, the work is hard and the hours long and they work when everyone else is out enjoying themselves. But, it is an environment in which you can get paid good money, especially as one of the famous top chefs, without the need for academic excellence. The same level of achievement, in proportion to previous academic success, is achievable in other similar modes of employment. Few women can or will endure these kinds of working environment with their danger, shouting, swearing, abuse, aggression and the long and unsocial working hours. Just as many traditional trades used to be, it involves an apprenticeship to a 'master'. The tougher the environment the tougher the individual and the less likely it is to find women working. All of these types of jobs can involve antisocial hours and hostile environments such as those found on ships, oil rigs and building sites. They used to say that it was statistically more dangerous to be working on a building site in England than to be a soldier in Northern Ireland during the Troubles. When life is constrained by your academic achievements and doesn't offer too many choices, ones like these offer an interesting and potentially well paid alternative to working in a factory or an office.

Men who have had reading and writing difficulties at school find that they are able to use their superior motor skills to work as skilled tradesmen across a wide range of industries; they frequently have to work harder and longer than their better educated peers – but, in the end can earn good money. And, money gives status.

Men can become motivated to learn many of the things which had seemed so alien when they were at school, spurred on by their interest in their new jobs. They can develop their poor language skills via the jargon of their chosen interest and, although it may be a difficult and slow process at first, can learn to read related books and magazines and through their new skills engender a higher level of self-confidence. This then becomes a self-perpetuating learning environment. Even those previously constrained by their ADHD or dyslexia, now unrestricted by an irrelevant academic curriculum, have found success by picking out the pertinent details and omitting all the unwanted information.

Having behavioural or learning difficulties in one area of your life does not mean that you do not have talents in other areas. There is quite a long list of eminent persons, both present day and historical, who, whilst being apparently dyslexic, have been able to succeed in other areas of life. Thus it is possible to be at one end of the spectrum with one set of behaviours and at the other end of the spectrum with a different set of attributes. Einstein was apparently a very poor student with language and writing difficulties, as was found out by his publisher when attempting to edit his copy for a book. Nature abhors a vacuum; when it takes something off one side of the scales it puts something different on the other side. Thus dyslexics struggling to make sense of reading and writing can see pattern and symmetry in information which, to others, may seem random.

Carpenters, who once constructed roofs on site, have largely been devalued and replaced by factory produced trussed roofs; for brick-layers, brick walls have been replaced by those made with much larger blocks which can be erected with less skill or, by factory produced timber frames; plastered walls replaced by plasterboard with taped joints. All in the pursuit of corporate profit. Men, who as boys found it difficult to fit in and succeed in to school system took to a basic level of work with fewer academic qualifications; at a later age it became almost impossible, in their own minds, for them to retrain; in reality it is because of a negative self-image in relation to education. And then, a few well-educated, articulate politicians take an attitude of incomprehension at the vulnerability of such men and mistake their embarrassment at their own lack of basic literacy and numeracy skills for a reticence to retrain for a different type of work.

In complete contrast, and at the opposite end of the spectrum, well-educated men, and it is almost exclusively men, can become cosmology scientists. The will be paid handsome salaries to both research and to lecture on their personal perspective of how the universe might have come into being and how it will probably end. They learned how to do this from cosmology lecturers at the universities at which they were students. To be in a position to be able to philosophise about such matters elevates them into the realm of the 'all knowing'. The opinions of such august men are sometimes in consensus; otherwise, they are in a state of divergence. In other words, using the same data they frequently each come to totally different, conflicting conclusions. They are members of a self-perpetuating and elite club of thinkers; it is an exclusive and highly prestigious society and, well paid too. And it is exactly the same for many other similar status professions. Five hundred years ago just believing that the earth orbits the sun could put you in a prison or a mental asylum or even cost you your life; how things change.

Theirs is a fantasy world. These university trained professors of the unknowable do not have the learning or wisdom to foresee natural disasters, prophesy famine, prevent wars or predict human behaviour. That there are other dimensions which we do not have experience of, is a universal truth; it will always be so. Their paymasters, be they government sponsors or private benefactors, seem to believe that being associated with such fonts of wisdom and knowledge confers on them the air of being a sage themselves and that not to support such research by these illustrious few would be a sign of their own lack of intellect. But, surely, we do not need to expend the immense financial resources and the mental endeavours of some of our finest brains to play a game of 'what if'. Not whilst disease and famine and war are rife.

It is interesting that it is, in general, men who elevate themselves to these positions of arrogance from which they seem to believe that they are right and that they have the monopoly of truth and wisdom. They appear to feel that they have the exclusive authority to be the givers of answers to which few want to know the questions. They ask questions to which the answers are unknowable. They are best-guessing and extrapolating on improbable and unprovable theories. There are prizes for getting it right (or at least apparently getting it right for a while); there appear to be no penalties for getting it wrong. It is the acme of male folly. They are the purveyors of the 'Emperor's new clothes'.

Meanwhile, the average for working men's wages has hardly increased in real terms for decades, allowing for inflation; the average wage for women has risen considerably. According to the ONS in 1997, the first year that they began recording this data, the increase in median pay rose by 17.4 per cent. Their median pay, it must be noted, includes temporary and part-time jobs. During the decade from 2005–2014 the pay increase rose from three per cent in 2005 to 4.8 per cent in 2008 since when, taking account of inflation, it has dropped in stages to virtually nothing. The median gender difference is currently recorded at an all-time low of 9.4 per cent. But, the April 2014 statistics show that for women working full-time, for more than 30 hours a week, in the 22–29 age bracket they actually earn 1.1 per cent more than their male peers and in the 30–39 bracket there is parity. Wage equality is filtering through the system. Whilst young women take educational courses and succeed, young men frequently do not make the grade or drop out.

Historically, losses in the orders for the manufacturing industry, and thus losses in what are generally male jobs has occurred at the same time as increases in the health service, local and national government departments and communications services. Just think of the change between the traditional male doctor working on his own, and frequently from home, as opposed to the modern multi-skilled health centres. Health professionals now do work which, because of technological advances, once did not exist; and, the work is clean safe and socially respected. It is work which is mostly done by women. It is the same in many areas; more complex government imposed rules and regulations need qualified administrators and accountants, jobs women are good at. Jobs with socially convenient office hours and maternity leave. Both national and local government funded employment does not have to produce a profit for shareholders thus more flexible working practices can be adopted regardless of their financial implications. Women in the UK are 50 per cent of the workforce and, according to a report by the IPPR think-tank published in *The Guardian* on 20th October 2015, about one third of families now have a woman as the main breadwinner.

While women are in an elevator going up men are trudging down the fire escape stairs and heading for the basement. Now, due to government promotion, many more young people, and particularly women, have degrees; more than there are jobs for. Many of the degrees are not those required by industry and commerce; hence we have exceptionally well qualified people performing relatively menial work whilst at the same time we lack properly qualified tradesmen due to a lack of apprenticeships. Not the beginning of the end of men as such but an erosion of what men believe that they stand for, the traditional image of manhood.

Males often spend long hours at work; time which they think equates to commitment and hard work and includes a social, but work-biased, 'back-scratching' factor. Including the commuting time, 60 hours per week for 40 or more years, plus evenings weekends and holidays too – if necessary. The price that some men appear willing to pay for their social status. This scenario could relate as well to a storeman as it could to an MD; the storeman who knows every item, where it is stocked, and who the supplier is, can spend almost as many hours at work, and be just as committed, a 'Company Man' as any Managing Director. Is this a true reflection of an employer's demands of his male employees or is it, in truth, a caricature of a diverse group of males all hiding from their domestic life behind the 'sanctuary' of work?

In America and the UK it has become not only an accepted facet of the work culture but often, a non-negotiable sign of commitment to the company to work extra unpaid hours on a regular basis. Many workers believe that their failure to do so would either lessen their promotion prospects or, at worst, weaken the tenure of their employment. But, it doesn't have to be this way; from Scandinavia down to Germany this is not seen as an acceptable work practice, rather, an infringement on the employee; and, they believe it does not benefit the company. According to the *Science Alert* website,

Sweden has been introducing a six-hour working day with some success. The fact that a retirement home in Gothenburg has adopted the practice may not seem too newsworthy but, Toyota, in that same city, adopted the policy 13 years ago and they are very happy with the positive effect it has had on their company. They have reduced all unnecessary work and meetings and found that concentrating, being focused, on your work for a reasonable six hours produces better results than struggling through an eight hour plus working day. It is better for productivity and better for the workers and their families and, those factors beneficially reflect into the community.

The male genitalia and male bodily functions are subject to a barrage of ongoing negative comment and criticism by women and yet so very few, including the mothers of boys, have any real appreciation of the subject matter. Meanwhile, there is a permanent and progressive discussion both, socially and in the media, of just about every aspect of the female body and in particular its reproductive system; information which, at one level, is intended to engender sympathy from all males and to explain and excuse, beyond question, every aspect of female behaviour.

The penis, in its normal daily life, is subject to random changes of length and girth, softness and stiffness; and, numerous times each day, it is compressed, stretched and bent by external physical pressures. One moment it can be like a small, soft, shrivelled button mushroom; and then, in just a few instants, it is more like the rigid structure of an unripe banana and in the process it must go through all the stages in between. Almost all of these changes are autonomous and therefore beyond the control of its owner. These changes to its dimensions and rigidity means that the structure of the penis is subjected to all the associated internal and external stresses – potentially, hundreds of times a day each and every day; from its very creation in-utero until its owner's death. However much they may need airing, I am not even thinking about the life-cycle of the testes and the scrotum; that subject will have to hang in the balance. The penis is a miracle of engineering which it is impossible for modern technology to begin to emulate; we have neither the exotic and complex materials nor the manufacturing techniques.

The 'slip' style of men's underpants are meant to be supportive and for their soft fabric not to 'gather' and crease up in the groin of the wearer but, are frequently constrictive and can hold the penis (and the scrotum) in unnatural ways – or let any part thereof half-escape before painfully trapping it again. Boxer shorts by their design and by frequently having so much fabric in them can, in certain body positions, wrinkle up in each side of the groin, thereby cutting off the circulation of bodily functions, in exactly the place where a number of the most important body systems converge.

In that small region there is the penis, the testes and scrotum, two major arteries and the convergence of all the circulatory and nervous systems from the legs and feet to the body. Worn on the outside of the underpants are trousers which are made from tougher, less pliant and more restrictive fabric which, working against or in harmony with the underpants, continue the physical torture of the region around the groin. And women wonder why men try to sit with their legs apart or are frequently 'readjusting' their groin area. This region of the male body and its associated clothing are not exactly a triumph of design over function.

And then, when males are standing up, with their oft contorted member in their hand, and trying to direct it to urinate into a domestic style WC, is anyone even remotely surprised that the flow of urine is not arrow-straight from the penis and into the bowl. Sometimes the flow seemingly appears to exit the end of the penis at almost 90 degrees or, it exits like water from the rose on a watering-can; sometimes there is high pressure and sometimes there is little pressure at all; which all adds to the pressure on him. So, men feel under duress to perform without social disgrace and thus, in that process, put even more stress on themselves. Is it any wonder that most men enjoy taking any opportunity to pee, unrestricted, in the open air.

Yes, I am aware that a woman's body is subjected to immense distortions during pregnancy and the subsequent birth. This physical process though, is self-inflicted and occurs, at most, just a few times during the life cycle of a female and when her body is already mature and she is mentally prepared. The changes during pregnancy are gradual, spread over a period of months. The birth is of relatively short duration and nowadays, in much of the world, there are extreme pain relief interventions available. They are not problems exacerbated by the stricture of the clothing which society has imposed on them.

A female's genitalia are sleekly concealed by her body. Nothing is other than in the comfort, warmth and security of that area of the woman's body; that is how it was designed to be. And all of her undergarments and top garments have no detrimental influence on the function of these parts; the looseness, coolness and freedoms of her skirt is a clothing option unavailable to most western males.

A naked woman can stand right in front of a man and experience sexual desire, arousal and even a subtle orgasm and yet, at an overt physical level you would never know that it had happened. Men's sexual organs are always prominent and thus in their mind's – even when hidden under their clothes – and, they have a propensity to 'misbehave' at inappropriate moments; this, together with the male's unguarded reactions to some of his other bodily functions, have caused the lack of certain male social graces to become the subject of critical scrutiny and of humour. Men apparently have many habits which seem natural and uncontroversial to them but which are seen by their womenfolk as unattractive and antisocial. Farting (passing wind) is, apparently, one of a number of male dis-attributes, along with the frequent rearranging his 'crown jewels', high on the list of male habits which most annoy women. However, women readily ignore their own frequent readjustment of the shoulder straps of their bras and, contrary to what women would like men to believe, medical research shows that women fart almost as much as men do – in proportion to their body mass and food intake. It can't be easy being perfect.

Perhaps, many men would feel that the older rural French generation have one habit right. To see a French man taking a pee in a nominally public situation is quite normal and quite legal. He is usually peeing whilst facing a bush, wall or some other object (maybe he feels, unconsciously, that he is protected during this vulnerable moment from one direction); it is a natural function and he does not have to worry about his aim as he would in a modern domestic toilet and it re-enacts his primeval scent-marking instinct. Whilst not actively encouraged any more it remains, for many Frenchmen, and nowadays many drivers of cars and particularly trucks, a frequently used method of dealing with one bodily function.

Another, associated male thing which women are apparently uneasy about is swimwear. Women do not like to see men wearing Speedo style swimming trunks because they emphasise the male member of masculinity – yet, according to an episode of *Loose Women* women's eyes are inexorably drawn to look at, rather than to look away from, a man's 'power bulge'. Women say, according to a survey by holiday firm 'On the Beach' that they think them inappropriate and that men should don beachwear style swimming shorts instead. They do not see the irony of them, at the same level, defending a woman's right to wear a bikini or brief swimsuit and to go 'topless' whenever they choose; they then feel 'uncomfortable' with men 'ogling' their breasts. Meanwhile, they struggle to hold down their skirts when cycling – for fear of showing too much leg – and try to conceal themselves when breast-feeding. Mixed messages; little wonder that men are confused.

And, cliché or not, if men who are already in some form of long-term relationship, unexpectedly give flowers or offer compliments or other attention to their partner they are treated with suspicion – what have they been up to, what are they trying to hide. If those same men do not pay special attention to their partner or show affection they are in trouble for their lack of concern. They will lose both ways.

Men want good relationships just as much as women do; the trouble is that they think that a relationship is a natural right, something that will just 'happen'. They also figure that it will involve them getting sex on demand, having their laundry done and meals provided; they are, however, usually able to accept that they may, after some cajoling, have to mow the lawn or take the bin out.

For men, marriage is the healthy option. According to research published by the *Journal of Men's Health*, men whose marriages end in divorce are more likely to have higher rates of alcohol and substance abuse, depression, suicide (nearly 40 per cent higher than married men) and early death due to cardiovascular disease.

Ladies, it is not necessarily that your men are not listening to you, nor is it that men forget to do things intentionally, research now reveals that it is just that women are much better at these skills than men are and that women judge men's performance in comparison to their own abilities. It is thought that because females are programmed, genetically and by their life experiences, to both listen and absorb the content and meaning of a conversation and to be able to remember things or to develop and use memory-jogging techniques that they become used to performing these skills efficiently – and the more you repeat an exercise the better you get at it. It becomes a self-fulfilling strategy. Because women are involved in more conversations, have to do lots of things and have to remember to do lots of other things they become more adept at it; because they are becoming more adept at doing so, they get better at remembering. Men don't have to remember things because, traditionally, women have always done the remembering for them – since they were boys they have learned that their mother would always perform such tasks, and in adulthood they rely on their wife or partner. The way a male brain works and the way he is brought up are both detrimental to these processes. The male is a victim of his own nature and his nurture by his mother.

At the same time that many young women are becoming more competent and assertive, some young men appear to have been losing their traditional air of dominance, their erstwhile assumed social status, their unique maleness; these young men are, as a result, having a form of identity crisis. But, in fairness, it is not just certain males who are becoming confused about their social standing, their role in society and their personal worth, there can be a similar effect for some women too. Wearing tattoos can be more than just a fashion statement, they can create an overt and unique sense of self for a number of both men and women and, for a man, the current fashion of wearing a beard can appear to give an added sign of masculinity and virility. The tattoos have the ability to assign social status and reinforce personal identity. Short term there are the not inconsiderable financial implications, at a time when most people's personal finances are tight, in having them applied; in the longer term their permanence may become either a unique historical record or a liability. The practice of 'working-out' at gyms, in an attempt to show a more masculine and dominant physique, has also regained popularity and body mass is enhanced by the use of steroid drugs. Is this the male equivalent of females having botox or cosmetic surgery?

The relatively new feeling of vulnerability, in response to the burgeoning power of the women's equality movement, which is experienced by numerous men is, for some, reflected in a growing sense of paranoia. Subjugation runs counter to their life perspective, to the historical upbringing of all males. These men feel that their very essence is being undermined by women and that their very existence is at risk. Perhaps such men are, in truth, not being paranoid, perhaps they are very perceptive, perhaps their foresight is more accurate than even they fear. Meanwhile, the rest of the male 'herd' take-up the 'ostrich position'. The trouble is that when you bury your head in the sand you shut off your sensory organs and at the same time stick your bottom in the air; you are sending out an invitation to be attacked in the meatiest, tastiest and most vulnerable part of your anatomy and you can be sure that there is one particular feline predator ready and waiting to take advantage of your futile gesture. You are about to become dinner for the tigress.

CHAPTER 9
STEPS IN THE RIGHT DIRECTION

Now, let's begin to put the pieces of this jigsaw puzzle together. It all starts with your ideology. For some it will be belief in divine creation; for others it will be acceptance of the accumulated knowledge of the combined sciences. With the benefits of modern technologies we can now prove the genetic links from modern humans all the way back through hunter-gatherer societies to chimpanzees and bonobos. We have discovered cave paintings and we have unearthed fossilised remains, we have uncovered once hidden ruins of buildings and artefacts from earlier civilizations; and now, we have all the benefits both of DNA profiling and analysis and of carbon-dating. Our existence, before all that historical evidence, remains conjecture, theorising, best-guessing. Many religions suggest that we were formed from the earth so, the currently favoured scientific theory that we dragged ourselves out of some primeval quagmire, whilst not very romantic, is not a bad place to begin our speculations. But, you can join our journey at whichever juncture suits your personal preferences.

So, it is possible that our first steps were taken as we slithered and slipped around clambering up and out of some prehistoric mire. Ever since, we have been taking little steps. Each time, we stand on our current step trying to create the next step, trying to forge the way ahead. We have done so for millennia. We have chosen differing paths but, always the steps on our evolutionary path have lead onwards and upwards. We have often reached seemingly endless plateaus; we have got lost in the fogs of time, we have slipped

backwards, we have stumbled and fallen. Generation upon generation, like an unstoppable army of worker ants. As our technologies
have advanced it has become easier to create new steps; we have
been able to determine the rise of each individual step, the depth
of the tread and even how smooth it should be. We sped up as we
sensed our closeness to an interim crest, a significant pinnacle, but
we knew that it was not the true acme of our existence; our work was
not yet done. The perfection of that almost unattainable and final
summit beckons us. But, will we be reaching our nirvana through
consolidating and perfecting the status-quo or is there, lurking
deep within our communal psyche, the impetus for a revolutionary
social change.

We have already seen how, through the amazing advances in
scientific and medical technologies of the last five decades in particular, we can begin to understand something about what makes male
and female humans differ from each other, and how they are similar
to each other. The differences in our genitalia and our reproductive
systems have always been unambiguous; but, now we know that the
structure and the functions of our brains, our nervous systems and
our complex of bodily chemicals and electrical impulses – indeed
every facet of our being – are different in many ways.

Our reaction to this information can be to think 'well, I always
knew we were different inside – it's interesting that now we can prove it
beyond any doubt'. But, this appears to infer a restrictive, almost fatal-
istic limitation and finality about our very being; this is the way it is and
therefore this is the way it must forever be. However, if you look closely
at the results of this new body of medical research it becomes apparent
that whilst the brain transmits and receives information based on its
current status it is not a restricted and finite process. Science has proven
that the brain has a plasticity to it, an ability to be modified by new
inputs and that from this new modified status it can, as a result, operate
in a different way and change its resultant outputs. These differences
might have to be instigated by taking very small sequential steps up a
long and winding road but they are all incremental in their effect.

Over millennia, society changed little in relative terms and the
changes that there were happened slowly. Just look back through our

history; men and women performed very stereotypical roles not just for centuries but for thousands of years. For the long historical period before the Industrial Revolution a time traveller could, theoretically, slide in and out of vastly different centuries and still be able to easily adapt to both the social and technological situations. Yes, there were some uncharacteristic events, sometimes positive and sometimes negative in their nature; they were significant by their rarity. Overall, the way men and women were, as individuals and collectively, changed little; their environments and social mores hardly altered and so their complex of brain functions and the interconnected systems remained in relative stasis. Nothing much changed in these people's lives as individuals within a society, and thus their brain structure and function didn't change much either. There was little impetus to instigate significant changes.

As we moved out of the dark ages and towards the Industrial Revolution, the changes in technology and social mores reflected changes in the brain's functions; and, those changes in function permitted further changes in technology and social mores. Ad infinitum. The rate of change in society was a reflection of a stimulated brain and that was, of itself, changing society. And so, the rate of progress increased. There was always wool on sheep's backs and we knew how to weave, there was wood and stone and there had always been coal and iron ore underground, we knew that boiling water produced steam. Man invented steam-driven mills from those resources; it was a series of connections made in the minds of men which created change. There was no one bolt of lightning. Along the way there were instances of good luck; there were instances of bad luck. That's the nature of progress.

The printed word and quicker, cheaper and more comfortable methods of travel promoted the transfer of knowledge and information; practical ideas and social ideas. Thus, we advanced from being a mass of vulnerable peasants ruled by a tiny minority of well-armed overlords to a much more egalitarian society and eventually to being a true democracy. That's how we developed from women being the possessions of their menfolk, through the struggle for enfranchisement, and on to there being democratically elected female heads of state. It was called the Industrial Revolution because of the revolutionary effects these technological changes had on society. It was benign change. There was no revolution in the way that there had been in France or would be in Russia; our revolution was more discreet but much more potent, far reaching, and its effects longer lasting.

For the period from the Industrial Revolution until after the middle of the 20th century we were assimilating and fine-tuning technological and social changes and moving forward at a fairly steady incremental pace. Too fast a rate of change could not have been sustainable; we developed each strand of advancement to the full before moving on to the next. Like building a wall, one brick at a time. With the luxury of hindsight, from our position in the 21st century, it may seem that things were not moving fast enough but contemporary reports showed genuine fears amongst many people at the apparent headlong rush into a future of unknowns. Technological advances and social mores struggled to keep pace with a combination of the expectations of the public, the developments within the British Empire, our commitments in, and the effects of, various wars and conflicts and a global financial depression. Nonetheless, we managed to invent a plethora of technological and social advances including motor transport, aeroplanes, military weapons including nuclear bombs, telephones, radio and television, the Social Security system and the NHS.

So, that just brings us to the last 50 or so years. Our progression during this period, as you will now know, has been meteoric. It is the result of the accumulation and consolidation of all our historical, technological and social developments which has provided the secure foundation on which we have built all those subsequent technical advances which have, as a consequence, revealed the possibility of equally radical social changes. The tangible benefits of our technological advances can be easily categorised, their merits and demerits readily evaluated. The practical application of our new technologies just requires an extension of the theory of using any tool; choose the most appropriate one for the job in hand, as long as you can afford to buy it and are able to maintain it.

When it comes to social change there are, in general, just two alternative routes. Firstly, those changes which are based on a system of natural progression, created by incremental developments of existing social mores; which, in turn, are able to slowly improve and mature society as and when supported by both the pertinent technological advances and also the social will for such change to happen. That strategy, with a few notable exceptions, covers the vast majority of social changes throughout history. It is fired by the perpetual triumph of hope over experience. The second, and alternative method of change is through revolution; the dramatic, wide-reaching enforced overthrow of one social order in favour of some new, alternative system.

The radicals who promote and instigate revolutionary change do not have the patience to await evolutionary social change. They are excited by their own perspective, they see only the positive implications of their vision of a new and better society; it is too important to await the process of ideas 'filtering-down' through time. Their mission, empowered through their own evangelical zeal, is to impose their ideals right now and thereby to see change within their own lifetime. A common thread running through all such radical schemes is their proponent's absolute belief in the efficacy and benevolence of their ideals.

For these reasons, radicalism is the preferred route for many promoters of gender equality. They are individuals, and groups of individuals, who have been empowered by the benefits of existing developments in technology and social support systems set up by previous generations; now, from that position of privilege and strength, they seek to alter society's existing gender hierarchy. This, by implication, would demand extreme changes in every aspect of our existing society; legal, political and governmental systems, trade, business and commerce, child-care and education, familial norms and profiles and media perspectives. And, as a member country of a network of globally interconnected societies, it is difficult to see how such changes could be achieved in isolation. Mutual cooperation, at an international level, would be needed to facilitate, enhance and impel such changes.

Practical changes to technologies and systems are achievable goals. Governments and commerce control, and are controlled by, computers; computer systems can be re-programmed, the strictures of working environments can be reconfigured, contracts can be re-written, laws can be redefined. We have created, and live in, a culture where technology rules supreme, we have a 'can-do, will-do' attitude and the practical capabilities to match.

But, there is just one very minor snag. The personal autonomy of individual human beings; of real, every-day, people of both genders. You may have come up with the best idea in the world but, you cannot even begin to modify cross-gender thought processes and behaviour patterns, let alone generate an unprecedented demand for change, without first having some positive-biased means of raising the awareness of the validity and efficacy of your intentions. And, if your objective is to create a permanent reordering of social gender roles you will, at some point, need to ensure an overwhelming consensus across the whole of the populous to enable you to facilitate such changes as will be necessary. You may have a rather bumpy ride ahead of you.

Everyone has their own personal perspective of what gender equality means. It will be biased by numerous factors including one's own gender, age, social standing, wealth, education and the effects of external historical and ongoing influences. The validity of an individual's perception of the concept of gender equality is absolute but not immutable. It is based on that individual's life – experience, their personal narrative. For most women the perspective is likely to involve the negative effects of gender inequality on their life so far and then their perception of the potentially positive effects gender equality may have on their future life; for men, it could be a more pessimistic perspective, an absolutely reverse viewpoint. Perhaps men will take to heart the words of Shakespeare – 'The lady doth protest too much, methinks' (*Hamlet*). Whatever, there will be both positive and negative facets to each gender's perspective.

Currently, unconditional support from the majority of women for gender-based equal rights is not a foregone conclusion. Support for this cause from men seems even more tenuous; attempts at serious discussion are frequently met with evasion; therefore, the true level of support is difficult to gauge. In certain social circumstances a number of both men and women may 'pay lip service' to what they, in truth, treat as a transient fad and therefore inconsequential; to them there would appear to be few, if any practical benefits, ergo, they lack any commitment to the broader concept let alone show any signs of conviction. As selfish humans, we have an inbuilt cost-benefit calculator; if we see no direct gain for ourselves then why invest any effort into supporting, let alone trying to put into effect, any form of change.

Just look at the apathy there is when it comes to political elections. The UK population is around 65 million, of whom approximately 46 million are eligible to vote; in the general election of 2015 there was the highest turnout for almost 20 years – about 30 million voters. Which means, one out of every three people did not bother to vote. With something over 11 million votes, the Conservative Party won the election and were thereby empowered to form a government. Thus, less than a quarter of the total electorate or, about a sixth of the whole population, voted into government a group of individuals who will have the power to control our lives for the next five years. Put another way, more than three out of four people did not vote for the political party which was elected into office. Whilst this was the largest turnout for decades the inclination of the British public to involve themselves in determining their own futures is, at best, pathetic in the extreme; perhaps, it is because they see the system as not truly reflecting or representing public opinion and therefore believe it to be grossly flawed, even corrupt.

Results in general are, some say, more important than the process; but, results are usually only temporary and their relevance and fairness are relative. They say that people are not statistics, but they can be represented that way; although each one of us might be an individual our tendencies within groups of people can be represented and validated by statistics. As Disraeli is alleged to have said to Mark Twain: 'there are three types of lies; lies, damn lies and statistics'. Most things relating to people fall into a norm referenced curve (or bell shaped graph) – a few at the top, a few at the bottom but most of us scattered around the middle. That's how it is. It is a system that works for just about every aspect of the human condition – including things like height, weight, shoe size, health, wealth and politics.

Taking this example of politics as a template for the level of commitment required to be shown by the British public to enact a complex of permanent changes pertaining to the unequivocal enabling of absolute gender equality throughout our entire society – one has to ask what chance is there of any level of success. Sustained, high-profile media based campaigns and the lobbying of Members of Parliament might, in some small way, continue to succeed in bringing about some symbolic changes in legislation but, merely as a placatory gesture to quell the potential of overt civil disobedience by a group of radical activist campaigners. Why else would some politicians be willing to 'prostitute themselves' by publicly wearing T-shirts with the slogan 'Now you know what a feminist looks like' – T-shirts sold by The Fawcett Society for £45 each which were apparently made in a sweatshop in Mauritius by workers earning just 62p per hour. In truth, no conventional political party, whether in government or not, is going to even consider promoting radical feminist policies and risk alienating the vast majority of their voters in an attempt to placate a small, but vociferous campaign group who have been inflamed by the machinations of a few deluded women. But, government is being positively influenced by female equality pressures; the website of the Government Equalities Office – 'Responsible for policy and gender equality issues in government' – shows several pictures each depicting a content-looking middle-class woman and similarly biased wording. So, not much in the way of depicting equality then, rather more a female-positive discrimination department by another name.

Thus, it was no surprise, in the spring of 2015, that a new political party was formed; the Women's Equality Party (sexual discrimination in word and deed?). One of its most prominent early protagonists is the Danish media presenter, comedienne and writer Sandi Toksvig. From their inaugural meeting at the Royal Festival Hall on the 28th March 2015, their 'Mission Statement' seems to include just about every positive facet of the feminist dream including: equal gender representation in every sector and level of government and regarding every aspect of business and the world of work – including equal pay, the eradication of low-pay agreements and the initiation of a system of financial rewards for all facets of the lives of domestic carers; equality of opportunities for females in the workplace and in education; equally shared parenting rights and responsibilities; and an end to violence against women. It is not unlikely that, over time, a few more items will be added to this list.

Equal, by definition, means the same in quantity, size (including weight), value, degree or rank; being equal is, notionally, scientific by definition; it implies being quantifiable or measurable. Equality is defined as the state of being equal; of status, rights, opportunity; where status denotes relative social standing. Equality is a social construct, not an absolute; the definition is, of itself, social rather than scientific. No two humans, of either gender, can in any way be regarded as totally equal of themselves. The validity of their opinion or the value of their work may be equal to that of another human. To be equal things must be measurable. Nonetheless, the concept of equality is not that complex; most people have a fairly accurate sense of the meanings of both words as far as their everyday application is concerned. Equality issues currently implies an ongoing conflict of interests.

Equilibrium is a state by which balance is achieved through the influence of one side being cancelled out by the influence of the other side; where the resultant of opposing forces has been equalised. This in turn, should promote a harmonious state whereby each gender has their own strengths and weaknesses acknowledged and celebrated thus promoting accord, not conflict. Harmony should infer a pleasing and peaceful whole in a state of agreement, compatibility and concord. Is it a gender-related state that we could ever achieve, should we even aspire to such values; or, is the truth that we actually enjoy, perhaps even thrive on, being in an eternal state of gender based conflict?

What seems to worry many people when it comes to either being equal or how equality would affect them is not so much governed by their own perception but rather what practical changes, freedoms or strictures would be applied to their own personal lifestyles by externally imposed regulation. The public has learned not to trust the word of people in positions of power; they have a reputation of saying that they will do one thing, when seeking your support for their cause, and then, when they have achieved their ability to control the public, they change their agenda and revert to what the public can then see, with hindsight, was always their hidden agenda. Manipulation of the masses by an elite minority, for personal and political gain is, historically speaking, a not uncommon modus operandi.

As members of society we come in individual units, pre-packaged and pre-programmed; it's not that we have intentionally created ourselves this way, we are a network of our own physical structures and functions with the added complexity of the influences of our upbringing and environment. We can be grouped together in some circumstances but, as individuals, we can rebel against being cast into stereotypical groups. Thus, for any individual or group of individuals, attempting to influence us in such a way as to garner support for their new and unproven philosophy, there will need to be a flexibility of approach.

When it comes to equality and equality of opportunity it is not so much what the shared values of a group of proponents are but rather what the public perception of their intentions is; what their means of implementing change will be and what their goals are and, most importantly, if the public can trust them to deliver on their promises. Is this elite group of quasi-experts likely to be 'economical with the truth' in an intentional attempt to 'hoodwink' an under-educated proletariat? There would be motivation for them to act in this way; history shows it to have been a beneficial strategy.

Conditioning humans to accept change is an adaptation and extension of the same methodology as that used for training animals. Garner trust, use a reward system rather than coercion, and make one small, non-threatening change at a time. Repeat the exact same process as often as necessary until the change becomes an accepted norm. Now, you can move on to the next change. Progress is a series of slow incremental steps. Trying to force the pace of progress will be counter-productive; it is likely to obliterate all the trust already gained. Any individual or group intent on bringing about social change will be well aware of these principles, it will form part of their hidden agenda. They must be prepared for criticism and decide whether or not to be totally open and tell the truth about their long-term ambitions and their desired final destination.

These historically more recent initial and incremental stages of the development of female equality issues, and many more crusades like them, have not, as far as we can tell, come about through ongoing and cumulative actions instigated by just one complex cell of radical activists. There seem to have been a number of separate campaigns, fomented by like-minded but not necessarily interlinked groups, intent on righting existing and long-standing gender based inequalities and of promoting the conditions necessary for further positive changes. These smaller groups have then, through both an Internet and social networking process, come together to form a more homogeneous and thus more powerful umbrella group.

These activists seem to be both urban and urbane; a media-savvy web of London-centric well-educated and socially well-connected women; their sympathisers and supporters aspire to emulate them. They are splendidly adept at cultivating and exploiting their social and business connections in their pursuit of media exposure for the cause of women's equality issues. These are intelligent, well-educated women who, together with their peers, are in a position to take the greatest advantage of the potential benefits for high achievers. As a group, they include amongst their members individuals who already have, in their meteoric rise through business, shattered any notional concept of the glass ceiling. In and around such groups the vast majority of members enjoy the luxury of not having to live and work as part of a household reliant solely on a very restricted income and the State benefits system. The organisation has few poorly educated, low income working-class supporters and activists; yet, ironically, these are the types of women who, if not for themselves but for future generations of their family, would also benefit from the application of many of the ideals of female equality of opportunity. Perhaps they are seen by the activists as too socially maladroit; perhaps their support has either not been sought or has not been forthcoming. That is exactly what happened in the Suffragette movement a century ago. We will soon see the number and demographics of supporters for the political branch of the cause. Where would such underprivileged women find the time, motivational energy and money from to become effective activists? Meanwhile, the overwhelming majority of poorly paid and part-time workers, in areas of employment as diverse as production-line operatives and carers for the elderly and infirm, will remain working-class women.

Where does the campaign for equal opportunities go from here, will it just be a case of 'more of the same', a slowly incremental evolutionary style of progression? Will the cause, not having gained as much support and thus momentum as its proponents would like it to have received, just stumble along for a few years or perhaps a decade or two and, like its current band of supporters, grow old and in the process lose its sense of direction, its sense of self-worth? Will the eventual level of female autonomy be little improved on the way it is now and therefore that plateau will soon be reached?

Or, will the process gather support such that ongoing positive developments will take on an almost unbelievable exponential trajectory and if so, how will that increased momentum be generated and exactly which directions could a female based powerhouse develop? The only possible way for a meteoric rate of change to be brought about would have to be the result of some form of social revolution. By its very nature, revolution requires the few to inflame the majority into at least supporting, if not creating, the conditions for a transitional period during which there would be a burst of social upheaval and turmoil leading to a new, untried and untested social order. Who would be in power over whom; from where would they derive their authority and power and how would they keep order in the face of dissent. Who would be the winners and the losers; how would the losers be pacified or kept under control. Traditionally, in such radical social revolutions the only sure way to quell an uprising against the tide of progress is by exterminating the opposition; look at history, there seems to be no alternative.

This cameo of an explosion of support for the control of society by women is, hopefully, fanciful in the extreme. It implies a change in the very nature of women to impel them to become so dominant, to be the instigators, to be the aggressors; and, at the same time, for all males to become submissive and easily subjugated. Short term change of a radical nature is not going to happen and, even the most rebellious pro-feminist supporters – much as they may believe that this is the level of change their cause deserves – understand this. They will not see such radical change in their own lifetime; none of us will. That is not to say that true female equality, if not domination, is not a very real possible scenario for the direction in which society is likely to develop; it is more probability than possibility, perhaps, even a long-term necessity. Men have had control for millennia and, whilst they may have created many technological advances, too many of them have had aggressive and divisive outcomes when they should have been more positive, more socially constructive. Society has always been a patriarchy where male values are the dominant currency. That's what seems to happen when men are in control; whether nature or nurture, cause or effect, that is the truth. History, which was written by men, irrefutably proves that. Generation after generation, men have taken the short-term perspective; immediate gratification. It's a male thing.

If women are to continue to change society for the better, for the long-term, then it is going to have to be a slightly slower process than they might ideally envisage; it will require a sense of deferred gratification. Women are good at sacrificing their own immediate satisfaction for the benefit of future generations, accustomed to investing in the future; they are mothers, maternal by nature they understand that this is where one of their strengths lies, that this is where their true and enduring power is derived from.

Once this slightly longer term strategy is accepted, a plan of action can be developed. It will require a number of simultaneous, parallel, converging and diverging strategies; it must play to female strengths and, by implication be counter to male strengths, preferences or predilections. A well planned, long-term war of attrition. Men will not be easily moved from positions of power; they regenerate their hierarchy through the control of their own environments; their strategies abhor empathy and conciliation. Men will not readily accept being outnumbered and outmanoeuvred by women, they will not easily give up dominance and control. Forget all those 'new man' images; it is 'the nature of the beast'. Men cannot really be blamed for being the way they are; they are victims of their nature and their nurture in just the same way that women are; Mother Nature can be blamed for our design faults. We literally are very different animals; we have seen the evidence from various areas of research; through our historical roles programming our patterns of behaviour to the structure and functioning of our brain and other bodily control systems controlling our reactions to environmental influences.

So, something has to change; and we now know that the human brain can be reprogrammed and how that can change facets of our characteristics which will, in turn, permit further change. But how do we instigate such change; how do women change the nature and status of men, how do they wrest control from men's hands and take control of the direction of their own lives?

Firstly, self-belief. There is an appropriate sort of saying which I think can be attributed to Henry Ford: 'if you believe you can, you are right; if you believe you can't, you are right'. That is the effect of self-belief; if you believe you can achieve something then your mind empowers you to do so, if you lose faith in your ability to do something then your mind disempowers you. That's what positive thinking is all about; the brain, when correctly programmed to do or not do something, will try to obey. Don't believe me? Well, I once saw a very clever magician or hypnotist get a member of his audience up on stage and there, when she was in a 'hypnotic trance' and thus under his control, he convinced her that he was going to give her a really tasty apple to eat; he gave her a large raw onion, she consumed it like it was the best apple she had ever tasted. When she was out of the 'trance' she still had the onion in her hand and a mouth that shrieked out 'onion'. Mind over matter.

Here, I'm not suggesting that women should, could or would begin by hypnotising men and turning them into servants obedient to their every command. What I am saying is that by changing behaviour patterns the brain can be reprogrammed to react to various stimuli in a different way. It would be possible, in some small, incremental way to modify the behaviour and the mindset of men. As we have said it would have to be as the result of modifying the existing learned reward systems; where a particular positive action is rewarded, where negative behaviour is not rewarded. Some women have already realised the potential of this system; an unintended and positive outcome of women looking after every facet of their son's domestic needs is that women have created in these boys and young men a dependency which, whilst at one level has been seen as a liability, can also be most beneficially exploited in adulthood by the man's life-partner. Most men are reliant on women to facilitate their lifestyles; this lack of domestic self-reliance has, to use male parlance, scored an 'own goal'. Men, in general, need women to perform domestic roles for them to be able to flourish in their workplaces and in their social lives. Some women have suggested a subtle 'blackmail' – men don't get washing and ironing done or food prepared and cooked without the men showing overt behaviour which supports female issues of equality. Some women have indicated that their most potent weapon would be the rationing or withholding of their sexual favours.

From a longer-term perspective, women as mothers, carers and teachers are the ones who, almost exclusively, bring up and educate our children for at least the first 11 years of their lives; their influence is ongoing. In their relationships with children of both genders they could, through a complex of incentives and rewards, manipulate their children's behaviour and thought patterns. It already happens at a benign level. Historically and currently, the way that the relationship between mother and child develops has created behaviour patterns and thought processes. Women could make a concerted effort to inculcate in all boys a positive appreciation of female equality and a negative relationship to any unwanted male traits. We know that behaviour patterns influence appropriate brain development; it would be using this natural process to influence gender related attitudes and outcomes which, hopefully, would endure as the boy child becomes a man. In girls, women could develop a sense of self-worth not, subservience to male dominant behaviour.

Men and women each form around 50 per cent of the population. Another very efficient way of swaying the odds in favour of women would be if there were more women than men. Women could not, either morally or legally, reduce the current ratio of men to women but, perhaps, science could be used to ensure that more girls than boys were conceived. The history of the last century, according to the ONS report 'Focus on Fertility and Mortality' , shows us that the male and female birth rates for the period from 1915 to 2004 are an uncanny mirror of each other but it seems to average out at 105 boys born for every 100 girls born.

If half the boys currently born were to be girls it would mean that within just one generation there would be 75 per cent of the adult population who were females – women empowered by their mother's; there would be 25 per cent of the population who were males who had been brought up with a feminist bias. Multiply that by as many years as you like. So, no need to resort to the terrible antics of gender engineering by 'disposing of' unwanted children as has apparently been practised in certain countries in the Orient. Eugenics is improving the population (of whatever) by controlled breeding so as to produce desirable characteristics; as a concept, it was popular at the beginning of the 20th century and apparently supported by the likes of Winston Churchill. It got a bad press from the mid-20th century German model; that was an horrific, barbaric and murderous 'experiment' involving the brutal extermination of existing lives. But, as they say, you may kill the man but, in doing so you do not kill the idea; sometimes you give it extra impetus. Women could choose to change society by developing a more appropriate and benign form of eugenics, a controlled breeding program. Such programs, involving domestic animals and plants, are one of the reasons the world is now better able to feed itself.

Women are constantly complaining about the way men are, their mannerisms, their behaviour, their attitudes, their value system, their lack of empathy and compassion. Well, if women raise boy children they are responsible for laying down the foundations of the very children who will grow into these unsympathetic males. Women have had the excuse that all their good works were undone the moment a testosterone-fuelled male teenager began to be induced into a macho, patriarchal system. Well, if women have already influenced the system such that males are no longer dominant in number or behaviour then the outcome for their teenage boys will be very different. Result.

Women may even 'get a taste' for their new position of dominance such that they decide that there is little practical need for men at all.

Science has already begun developing the technology to create and recreate life; we already have cloned plants and animals and starving nations are now benefiting from a diet of genetically modified crops and livestock; and, a surgeon in the USA is pressing to be allowed to perform a head transplant. Apparently, a female Komodo dragon in Chester Zoo gave birth having never even seen another Komodo dragon; a natural occurrence of 'virgin birth' they have in common with the sea urchins. Some female African frogs can change gender when appropriate whilst seahorse males are in charge of bringing up their young. Nature is already extremely versatile and inventive. Soon, women will have the option of not just if and when but how they conceive, women will no longer have any need of males for them to reproduce, probably not even need of a sperm-bank; women could, theoretically, form a society solely composed of women. There is no way that men could do that; men, potentially, could become obsolete or, at best, little more than a curio. Not in some futuristic sci-fi world but within a generation or two; at a technical level it would appear that it is entirely feasible right now. Food for thought?

Mother Nature is a symbiotic mesh of interconnected creatures and systems which are in a constant state of evolution; she has a complex of ongoing research and development experiments including ones originating from the concept of a meritocracy based on female domination, a theme which has been under a process of continual refinement for millennia.

The social insect group known as Hymenoptera, which includes bees, wasps and ants, may merit particular investigation in this regard. Leafcutter ants are a social community of vegetarian female farmers who cultivate an underground garden of fungus which grows on the pieces of leaves which they bring into their food production facility; this fungal growth is their staple diet.

At the head of each community is the queen. In her early winged state, she flies from her natal nest and mates with a number of very much smaller winged male ants; immediately after copulation the males die. She carries some of the fungal culture from her home community in a special pouch in her mouth as she searches for the ideal location to establish a new colony. Once a potential new home is found, she begins her lifelong purpose of laying eggs; she builds a family around her from the eggs she produces. Soon she is attended by a retinue of females; sterile, wingless, worker ants who are her daughters.

The smallest in physical size in this emerging colony are the social sub-group of worker ants who tend the unending production of eggs and care for them as they develop from larvae into young ants; and, they also farm the fungus which grows on the leaves brought by the larger worker ants. This fungal food-bank will develop and grow, from the minuscule 'seed' fungus brought by the queen, into a production system large enough to sustain the entire colony of hundreds of thousands.

The next largest group of worker ants are those whose role is to go out and forage for suitable leaves for the fungal cultivation to thrive on; they then bring the leaves to the entrance to the colony for their farming sisters to process. The physical size and weight of the pieces of leaf which these worker ants are capable of carrying can be 50 times their own bodyweight, the equivalent of a human carrying a small family car.

The physically largest are the soldier ants. They protect the integrity of the colony and the workers foraging in the jungle for leaves.

The few tiny males are only produced when needed to mate with a queen; they have no other purpose. Males are created from non-fertile eggs and produce just one string of chromosomes. Their lives are short, orgasmic but tragic.

This is an example of a group of females thriving in a state of social harmony and cooperation whilst living on a vegetarian fungus-based diet and virtually without any need for males; a lifestyle aspired to by some groups of humans.

Numerous species have displayed the ability for the female to have young without any input from a male. Such creatures include rotifers – microscopic freshwater plankton, arthropods – insects and spiders, amphibians, reptiles and birds, including chickens. The latest headline-grabbing 'virgin birth' occurred at the Great Yarmouth Sea Life Centre, in February 2016, where a female Bamboo shark has produced two fertile eggs; we will have to wait around nine months for them to hatch. She has not been in the company of any male shark for nearly three years. Other types of sharks which have displayed this ability include the Black-tip shark, the Zebra shark, the Bonnet shark and the White-Spotted Bamboo shark. It had always been thought that these offspring would be infertile but already, in Munich, Germany, another Bamboo shark has given birth to young. As expected they were all female and they were complete, viable baby sharks. Somehow, the mother produced the full set of male chromosomes as well as her own female set – thus perfect female baby sharks. Scientists are trying to understand exactly how this process takes place inside the adult female shark. If, or perhaps when, they do find out the mechanism by which this has occurred they will try to replicate it and if they are successful it will, potentially, have benefits for the preservation of endangered species. And, the next question is, will it ever be possible to replicate the process in the human body. Picture this, female humans producing female young without the need for a male; now, that really is a recipe for a new style of human community.

There might have been, for some time, an ongoing war between the sexes in which women can be depicted as the dominatrices over an enemy of hapless and innocent men. But, it currently looks as though there is one seemingly intractable problem whichever side might win this conflict; that both sides have always enjoyed fraternising with the enemy just a little too much. Perhaps women will become more drawn to other women; that would solve another problem.

Feminism could be categorised as just one of many social campaigns; it could be seen by some as merely a controllable vent for a potentially destructive energy which builds up within society from time to time. The benefit of such movements is that they distract the population in general from the real predicament of their covertly controlled and manipulated lives. That is why it is tolerated by those who truly control the world's wealth and thus its peoples. Perhaps, that is the same reason why such movements will never be allowed to reach their potential.

We have been looking at this situation not only as if a tide of gender equality had swept over the country, but as if that same event rendered us economically pretty equal too. But, and it is a big but, the world does not operate in that way. In truth, the people who 'call the shots' on a national and international scale are in control of just about everything. It's something which those who are aware of it generally like to push to the back of their minds; those who are part of it keep quiet about it for fear of the public's reaction to the reality of the implications. We are talking about a small number of people who both own and control the vast majority of the wealth of the world.

On 21st to 24th January 2015 The World Economic Forum met in Davos, Switzerland. It is a conference with over 2,500 middle-aged delegates of whom just 17 per cent are women. They included 40 national leaders and represented, between all delegates, over 100 countries; most were from Western Europe and the US with the smallest number coming from Africa and South America. This giant networking group also included business leaders, politicians and diplomats. Their agenda revolved around the Global Economy, Global Instability, Climate Change and Inequality. Whilst pretty important and influential people, they are not the world's wealthy elite. What does make for really interesting reading are the statistics which they took with them and the subsequent tide of information released by charities like Oxfam, and other organisations, as a result of the international publicity this summit generated. I will list some of the most salient information but, not necessarily in any particular order:

Global wealth has risen by £15 trillion in the last year alone.

70 per cent of the world's population live in countries in which, over just the last 30 years, the rich have got richer whilst the poor have got poorer.

It was noted that there is more inequality within individual nations than ever before. The few rich are getting much richer whilst the many poor are getting poorer. The same increase in wealth is true for multinational corporations and for the mega rich. Meanwhile, the differentiation between individual nations is, on average, lessening (mainly thanks to the Chinese, the Asian and the Brazilian economies improving); ergo, the most wealthy individuals in those nations are getting richer but not the poor. China has more people in the top 10 per cent of global wealthy individuals than any other nation except the USA and Japan.

There are a total of 160,000 individuals, families and companies in the USA who own $20 million or more, each; that represents 22 per cent of the total wealth in the USA. The population of the USA is around 320 million. This sort of disparity has not existed since either just before the First World War in 1913 or in 1929, during the days prior to prohibition. Ninety per cent of the US has had income stagnation relative to the economy (taking account for inflation) since the 1980s.

In the USA four per cent of wealth is held offshore. In the UK 10 per cent of wealth is held offshore. That is one of the reasons the global rich want to invest in the UK. It is tax efficient. But, when it comes to being competitive, a European employee costs twice as much as his American equivalent for the same amount of work in the same job.

In the UK, the richest 20 per cent own 60 per cent of all national wealth, which is about twice as much as the rest of the population put together and 100 times more than the bottom 20 per cent. The richest one per cent have the same wealth as 60 per cent of all the wealth owned by the rest of the country; the poorest 20 per cent own around half of one per cent of the wealth. The UK is the only European country in which financial inequality is increasing.

The proponents of these imbalances say that it is the 'pie' that is getting larger – so everyone is getting a bigger amount in their slice. It's just that if you start off with a bigger slice the amount in your increase will be larger.

The 'managers' in big investment and manufacturing companies can create massive wealth (they can also lose massive amounts but, they keep quiet about it). It is their decisions which help to create the wealth; but, it is not their own funds that they are putting at risk. It is our funds, such as those from international pension funds (including from countries as diverse as Germany and China), which are invested through banks and stock markets. In the year 2000 these individuals earned about 47 times the average worker; in 2015 they earned 120 times the average worker. Being a bank clerk used to be a good job and for life; now, these jobs no longer exist.

In 1970, 63 per cent of the UK's wealth was paid to the workforce as opposed 37 per cent paid to the directors In 2014, 50 per cent of the country's wealth was paid to the workers and the other 50 per cent to the directors Since 1979 production has increased but the number of jobs has decreased by two-thirds. Those 'jobs' are now being done by technology.

In 1980 the average salary for a UK FTSE CEO was 40 times the average for one of their workers.

In 2014 the average salary for a UK FTSE CEO was 400 times the average for one of their workers.

Houses and flats in the centre of London are the preserve of the mega rich – often from far-flung countries – looking for a secure investment for their often suspect funds which they have extracted from their own countries. London is seen as a safe haven with tremendous potential for growth. The properties are usually not even bought to be lived in – by anyone; they are purely for investment. They increase more in value in a month than the average person can earn in a lifetime. Thus the price of everything in London has risen to extreme levels.

At one time, teachers and lecturers could afford a house some-where in London not far from where they worked. Now most cannot afford to buy; those who can are impelled to go out to the cheaper and unfashionable satellite towns and their suburbs, far outside the capital.

The average UK salary for traditional professionals of all grades is £40,000 (including teachers, solicitors, surveyors, etc.).

Independent schools now cost at least £30,000 per annum (and lots more for many of them). To be able to pay £30,000 fees you must earn at least £50,000 pre-tax. If just one child is at school from 7–18 that amounts to costs of not less than £550,000 out of taxed income. These schools are registered as charities for tax purposes. Ordinary middle-class people cannot afford it so these schools are filling up with the children of the wealthy from around the world whilst English children begin to return to state schools. Even the usually cheaper independent schools in the far-flung reaches of the UK are having to charge high fees just to cover costs. And, wealthy international businessmen are not so attracted to such schools.

Nowadays there are many more university educated people look-ing for fewer and fewer jobs. They believe that they are worthy of well paid, interesting careers – but, the jobs are just not there. Meanwhile apprenticeships, for so long shunned, are becoming more 'interesting' and the jobs more lucrative.

Statistics don't always indicate clearly what you might initially think they are saying. For example, the richest one per cent of the world population own £60 trillion, which is nearly half of all global wealth and the top 10 per cent own more than 85 per cent of the world's wealth; and, they all get richer every day. To be eligible to be a member of that top one per cent group you only need around £25,000 in capital, including the value of your home. To be in the top 10 per cent of that richest one per cent you need to have capital of around £50,000 and to be in the top one per cent of that elite one per cent group you need just £500,000 (or, to own a small terraced house on the outskirts of London). Meanwhile, the bottom 50 per cent of the global population owns less than one per cent of the world's wealth between all of them.

The five richest families in the world have more wealth between them than the poorest 20 per cent of the whole of the world's population. Eighty-five people could fit inside a double decker bus and, a trillion seconds is about 32,000 years; those figures give a sense of scale to these statistics. The richest 85 individuals in the world have a combined wealth of £1 trillion (£1,000,000,000,000) which equals just over £11.75 billion each (£11,750,000,000). So, if each of those 85 people had their share of the £1 trillion to spend – at the rate of £1 per second they would have over £600,000 per week to spend and they would have enough in the bank to last them for the next 376 years. That combined wealth of £1 trillion, shared by just 85 people, is the same amount of wealth that is shared between the poorest 3.5 billion people in the world. Global wealth has risen by £15 trillion in the last year. If you have wealth, interest ensures that it grows every second. If you have debts, interest ensures your debts grow every second. Now, that's what I call real financial inequality.

You may think that some film, pop and sports icons are 'super-rich'; but in this league, they are relative paupers. If wealth has gone up for a few then proportionally poverty will have gone up for the rest. It is the logic of the balancing of finite resources.

Wealth = power = control. What are the realistic chances of the wealthy elite compromising their financial position and thus relinquishing their power and control of the all the other humans in the rest of the world?

Wealth comes from people buying things. If a few rich people buy a few niche products from a few specialist producers it will create just a few jobs for an elite group. If the wealth was distributed to more people, to more ordinary people, they would buy more ordinary things made by other ordinary people. This would create more jobs and more wealth across the whole social spectrum.

A dissatisfied, educated middle-class is the spark which had traditionally ignited revolution. If this group feel that there is intolerable financial and social injustice in society, and that the ordinary people are not getting a fair share of the economic benefits, they are usually the ones who promote revolution. It has happened in France, Russia and the Far East. The aspirational classes, when disgruntled enough, are a potent force that should not be ignored. In the armed forces they are only too aware of the potential for such dissent and disharmony amongst the lower ranks which can be ignited by just one or two 'barrack-room lawyers'.

A small super-elite group of insanely wealthy individuals, backed by a rather larger group of mega-wealthy individuals covertly control, at some level, just about every aspect of each and every one of our lives. As individuals we are less than inconsequential pawns in their game, radical activists are merely a potential irritation. But, this vulnerable elite minority are unlikely to tolerate overt dissent. This state of affairs does not bode well for any form of equality movement. Except for two things; firstly because this elite group are, almost, not even the same species as us, they do not understand the subtleties of our culture nor are they able to comprehend our language; they must rely on their minions to keep them abreast of any hostile developments in the behaviour of the masses.

Secondly, they are still only humans, and mostly men; they have human frailties and vulnerabilities. As we have already discussed, women can be devious and manipulative by nature when impelled to act in defence of their own.

Between them, women do have all the skills and qualities necessary to manipulate the developments in both social reform and technology to allow them to become a self-perpetuating autonomous society.

Women in the 'first world' now benefit from a lifestyle which evolved from subjugation to untold freedoms at a cumulative pace in less than a century. It has been the result of a long but relatively uncomplicated journey; further developments along the same route will be far more complicated and more liable to meet much higher levels of resistance than ever before and thus will be more difficult to pursue. In light of this, perhaps, before expending all their energies and resources on promoting some systematic improvements in the lifestyle of women in the UK, it should be their primary responsibility as women of the 'First World' to use their skills, energies and finances to help the women of the rest of the world to attain the same rights, the same levels of freedom, that the women of the western world currently enjoy and then, from there, to move forward globally as one united homogeneous group. Poverty and racial equality are inextricably interlinked with female equality issues.

It would reflect women's more altruistic, cooperative virtues if our protagonists were to be more mutually inclusive of their global sisters; to prioritise, to work towards the more pressing need for equal rights and opportunities for the women of the rest of the world. For those women currently not in a position to bring positive influence to their own life chances – some who do not even have the right to freedom from male oppression or to be able to drink clean uninfected water or access to sanitation or access to a nutritious diet or any maternity care or other medical provision – it would be a life-enhancing process.

If you want to escape from captivity there's not much point in asking a fellow prisoner how to do it – if they knew how to get out they would be long gone. What the cause needs is women with creative minds, women who can think 'out of the box'. Whichever route women may choose to take, the future is pink, a, potentially, feminine world.

Be in no doubt, the Tigress will, one way or another, rule life's jungle.

CHAPTER 10
TAIL OF THE TIGRESS

I would like you, just for a few moments, to let me paint a picture in your mind's eye.

You are sat alone on your own bed, upright, but with your head and back nestled in plumped-up pillows, legs outstretched, hands by your sides; you are warm and comfortable. You allow your eyes to close slowly and you luxuriate, safe in the quiet and the darkness…

As you float at the edge of consciousness you feel your imagination drawing you into a different and exotic world. You become aware of an intensifying brightness, of a deep blue sky above you and of dry heat. The exotic smells and distant noises of a hot autumn afternoon on the high plains of India. Above and to your right, you notice the filigree of sunlit branches on an acacia tree. Your eyes follow the branches to the trunk, downwards to its base and closer, across that arid ground strewn with tiny clumps of dry grass.

You see the feet of a child, dusty feet; the child is sat on that sandy ground with legs outstretched. Your eyes are drawn closer, along the legs from the feet to the knees and then on either side you see chubby fingers playing with the dust…

Slowly, you come to realise that you are that child; that those are your own feet and hands that you are looking at; the sun feels hot on your skin.

You lie on your back, extend your arms above your head like a diver, you stretch your whole body from fingers to toes, and then relax again. You look up into the tree, then close your eyes, and allow the gentle slope of the ground to roll you sideways all the way down until you come to rest in the shade at the edge of the long grass.

Your outstretched hands part the grass and touch something pleasingly soft and velvety like a downy feather. Rolling onto your tummy and opening your eyes you see that what you have in your hands is, perhaps, the large fluffy flower-head of a grassy plant; coloured pale cream, tinged yellowy ginger, with streaks of black. It slowly moves from side to side as though nodding in the breeze; afraid of losing its beauty, you grasp it tightly.

A fearful crash of cream and ginger and black stripes. Head of the Tigress, yellow eyes flashing, white fangs in a blood-red cavernous mouth…

Right now you now have the 'Tail of the Tigress' in your hands. Do you drop it, afraid of what the future may hold and run away looking for cover; or, do you decide to hang on tightly and see where the ride takes you. When it comes to your encounter with the Tigress, will you be become 'the dinner' or 'the diner'?

BY WAY OF AN EXPLANATION...

My research for this book has been approached at two levels:

Firstly, I spoke to almost 100 women of various ages, from different classes and at various stages of their lives; I did this over a period of several years. They were teenagers, single women, married women without children, married women with young children, single mothers, lesbian women, women with older children, women with children who had left home, grandmothers and great-grandmothers. Some were apparently enjoying 'singledom', some happily married, some were not happy, some were divorced (and a number divorced several times), some were the instigators of their own divorces, some were victims of circumstances beyond their control. The depth, breadth and intimacy of our conversations, our discussions, varied considerably but most were amazingly frank. They included their own upbringing, their relationships with adults of both genders as a child, with authority, their own self-image, their relationship to sexuality, their value systems, their own gender perspectives, how these changed as their lives developed and how they affected not only their own lives but those of their partners and their children, the effects of their education and their encounters with the world of work. Most information was based on their experiences and feelings but, of course, they also included their own observations. I initially found some views and comments unexpected; I heard opinions varying from one end of the spectrum to the other. A number had life-questions they felt were unanswered, many had suggestions for a better world. A number of women I approached, of course, were not willing to share any of their information with me. I spoke to numerous men from diverse backgrounds – singletons, a man bringing up his family as a single-parent and most stages of adulthood including divorcees and retirees and I had a few notable successes but, overall, I was almost always unable to have really meaningful conversations with men. I learned more about men from the perspectives of their women. I feel honoured that all the people of both sexes that I spoke to choose to be so open and candid. The total anonymity of each and every individual, of every piece of information, is and will always be sacrosanct.

As a second strand, and often in parallel with the first, I researched the written word through books, documents, the media and the Internet.

Thus, the bulk of factual information originates from academic research of one form or another but most of the rest is a melange of information divulged by other people, mainly women. In effect, I have stitched together a patchwork quilt from the assortment of diverse, multicoloured snippets which I have collected together with a few remnants from my own cache. The material used has been outsourced but the finished article has been created by me. To paraphrase the 1950s American police series Dragnet – 'the stories are true, the names and places have been changed to protect the innocent'.

The heavy use of history, both in general and in its effects on the lives of men and women, is used to help to define what may be some of the root causes for both men and women being the way they are now – a result of their evolutionary roles as created throughout the development of society. This is not just a book about women; there should be no assumption of it being totally female-centric. It reflects aspects of the way society is and always has been; the definition of each gender is relative to the definition of the other gender. Thus, if one gender is going to change then, by association, the other gender must also change. It is important, whichever side of the argument one's sympathies lie on that, one has a comprehensive understanding of self but also – and perhaps more importantly, of the opposition. That's what battle strategies are all about; it's a boy thing. Well, it has been so far – but I think things could be about to change! And history, they say, is written by the victors.